Praise for
Valuable Content Marketing

"*Valuable Content Marketing* goes beyond words and lofty vision. It tells you what to do. In a landscape growing increasingly crowded by noise, this gets you to a higher ground."
Chris Brogan, CEO of Owner Media Group

"I have encountered no better book on this subject. It's comprehensive, practical, inspirational and accessible. I highly recommend it to anyone with any interest at all in this subject, but especially to those who are actively practising content marketing, and for those who are thinking about putting content marketing into their organization."
Tim Tucker, content marketing consultant and trainer

"What I love about this book is that it doesn't try to dress up content marketing as if it were akin to landing a probe on a comet and sending back data. Instead, it's a clear, honest and practical book that shows how powerful – and how simple – content marketing can be. It also puts content marketing in its proper context: as a means to revenue… If you care about marketing and want to do it properly, you're in the right place and in the best hands."
Doug Kessler, Creative Director and co-founder, Velocity Partners Ltd

"*Valuable Content Marketing* is a breath of fresh air in a world full of self-proclaimed gurus and experts. No snake oil here, just clear explanations of the how and the what and the why of engaging with prospects and clients. It is the first common-sense, practical book that helps people apply digital to their businesses in an honest and straightforward manner."
Robert Craven, MD and founder of the Director's Centre and author of *Grow Your Digital Agency*

"This book presents both the big picture and the nitty-gritty of content marketing for small businesses… If you're unsure where to start with marketing your business online or your current content doesn't generate enough interest in your business, then start with this book. You won't be disappointed."
Henneke Duistermaat, founder of Enchanting Marketing

"It's structured logically and clearly, and as you'd hope from a book with such a title, it contains both practical ideas and instructions in creating content that adds value. Definitely a book you'll pick up more than once!"
Jaya Chakrabati MBE, CEO of Nameless Media Group

"Full of commercial arguments about why content marketing is the backbone of revenue growth, and practical tips on how to create a sustainable and effective approach to building a great content strategy."
Paul Wilson, Chief Marketing Officer, Fortune 500 SunGard

"*Valuable Content Marketing* is just that... valuable! It is destined to be a modern marketing classic. Buy this book before your competitors do or you will be sorry!"
Lee Frederikson, Managing Partner at Hinge Marketing and author of *Spiralling Up*

"Valuable content is something interesting and valuable you can publish online; content that educates, helps or inspires; content appreciated by the reader. This book shows you how with vivid clarity."
Stephen King, author of *Finance on a Beermat*, www.f-works.co.uk

VALUABLE CONTENT
MARKETING

Don't ever try and sell me on anything.
Give me ALL the information and
I'll make my own decision.

RAPPER KANYE WEST IN A TWEET

SONJA JEFFERSON
SHARON TANTON

VALUABLE CONTENT
MARKETING

OW TO MAKE QUALITY CONTENT
OUR KEY TO SUCCESS

ND EDITION

KoganPage

LONDON PHILADELPHIA NEW DELHI

First published in Great Britain and the United States in 2013 by Kogan Page Limited
Second edition 2015

2nd Floor, 45 Gee Street	1518 Walnut Street, Suite 1100	4737/23 Ansari Road
London EC1V 3RS	Philadelphia PA 19102	Daryaganj
United Kingdom	USA	New Delhi 110002
www.koganpage.com		India

© Sonja Jefferson and Sharon Tanton, 2013, 2015
Illustrations © Lizzie Everard, 2012

The right of Sonja Jefferson and Sharon Tanton to be identified as the authors of this work has been asserted by them in accordance with the Copyright, Designs and Patents Act 1988.

ISBN   978 0 7494 7327 3
E-ISBN   978 0 7494 7328 0

British Library Cataloguing-in-Publication Data

A CIP record for this book is available from the British Library.

Library of Congress Cataloging-in-Publication Data

Jefferson, Sonja.
   Valuable content marketing : how to make quality content your key to success / Sonja Jefferson, Sharon Tanton. – Second edition.
      pages cm
   ISBN 978-0-7494-7327-3 (paperback) – ISBN 978-0-7494-7328-0 (ebk)   1. Marketing.
2. Internet marketing.   3. Customer relations.   I. Tanton, Sharon.   II. Title.
   HF5415.J42 2015
   658.8–dc23
                                                                          2015016196

Typeset by Graphicraft Limited, Hong Kong
Print production managed by Jellyfish
Printed and bound in Great Britain by CPI Group (UK) Ltd, Croydon CR0 4YY

CONTENTS

FOREWORD

In a few, head-spinning years, content marketing has gone from buzzword to bandwagon to full-scale juggernaut.

In that time, an awful lot has been written about the art and science of content marketing – mostly by people whose business cards (ink still wet) say things like 'Content Strategist' or 'Content Architect' or even 'Content Guru'.

Unfortunately but not unexpectedly, a lot of this advice has been... well, non-sense. Nonsense peddled by people who have a vested interest in making content marketing seem like a black art.

It's not.

Content marketing is very simple: use your expertise to help your prospects do their jobs. Work hard to add value in every piece you produce. Be generous. And earn attention by injecting passion, attitude and energy.

What I love about this book is that it doesn't try to dress up content marketing as if it were akin to landing a probe on a comet and sending back data.

Instead, it's a clear, honest and practical book that shows how powerful – and how *simple* – content marketing can be. It also puts content marketing in its proper context: as a means to revenue.

As a result, this is more than a super-useful workbook – it's also a *demonstration* of content marketing at its very best. In writing it, Sharon and Sonja have practised what they preach: working hard to serve their readers (us); delivering real, practical value without pushing a promotional agenda; and making the ride fun.

In a market packed with overnight experts and insta-ninjas, that's no small thing.

The kind of content marketing that Sharon and Sonja evangelize is what I call 'home run content': the ambitious, confident, smart and entertaining stuff that people actually want to consume. At a time when everyone is cranking out a steady stream of colourless commentary, it's never been more important to aim high, take a stand and create pieces that *resonate*.

To do that, it helps to have a guide. Or, better yet, two.

I first met Sonja and Sharon when they invited me to speak at a meeting of the Bristol Content Group – a group they started and continue to run.

I wasn't sure what to expect. What kind of marketing community could there be in a place like Bristol? Turns out, a lively, intelligent, fun group of like-minded marketers high on content. My kind of people. I've not seen a community like it in cities ten times its size.

Swinging by the Valuable Content offices, I was impressed by the breadth, depth and spirit of their work for a wide range of clients. These are the front-line experiences that power this book: real-world strategies and tactics that actually work.

The group, the company and this book are all testament to the intelligence, generosity, passion and professionalism of the VC duo.

If you care about marketing and want to do it properly, you're in the right place and in the best hands.

Enjoy.

Doug Kessler
Creative Director at Velocity Partners
www.velocitypartners.co.uk

ABOUT THE AUTHORS

Sonja and Sharon are on a mission to help good businesses flourish by creating and sharing valuable content. Together they run Valuable Content, a specialist content marketing consultancy and training business with a determined focus on helping independent businesses make the changes they need to win with this powerful and rewarding approach.

Sonja and Sharon have worked on hundreds of content marketing projects. Their experience of working with small ambitious businesses on the coalface of content marketing shapes their unique perspective of what works and what doesn't today. It's taken them to Lanzarote, training holiday companies to collaborate on content so the whole island benefits; they've worked with the University of Bristol's web team, helping create the institution's first content strategy; and it's led them to government-backed Tech City UK, where they are designing the social media course for the Digital Business Academy. They run the popular Bristol Content Group and are curators of the Valuable Content Awards, recognizing content excellence around the world.

Sonja Jefferson

Sonja is a content marketing consultant and trainer.

With a degree in Sociology from Bristol University, Sonja began her career in sales for professional services firms. It didn't take long for her to work out that cold calling and traditional sales tactics often led to dead ends, so looked for more natural ways to start conversations. She realized that the marketing material she was given to help her sell didn't do much to open doors either: prospective clients just chucked it in the bin. So Sonja started to send them copies of articles her MD had written for the trade press to open conversations. It worked! They appreciated the helpful, thought-provoking information. This realization coincided with the arrival of blogs, which cut out the middle man and allowed companies to tell their own stories. It ignited Sonja's interest in an approach that has become known as content marketing – engaging prospects and motivating sales with valuable content.

Sonja now enjoys helping unsung heroes in business create amazing content that helps their businesses fly. With a knack for going beyond the nitty-gritty to envision the big picture, she's the founder and strategic brain behind Valuable Content. One of life's enthusiasts, she gets a buzz from speaking about content marketing, and she'd love to make Bristol the content capital of the UK.

You'll find Sonja active on Twitter, where she enjoys exchanges with fellow content enthusiasts across the world.

She lives with her family in Bristol, UK, and dreams about a house in a cove on the rugged west coast. She's learning the intricacies of rowing a traditional Cornish Pilot Gig and occasionally braves the British weather and jellyfish for long outdoor swims (which is useful in the unlikely event that her boat capsizes!).

Say hi to Sonja on Twitter and Instagram: @sonjajefferson

Sharon Tanton

Sharon is a content writer and creative director.

In her early career, Sharon worked for the BBC and interviewed people for documentaries. This kindled her passion for telling stories in real human voices – whether it's a veteran talking about the Second World War, a mother sharing stories about her life in poverty, or an entrepreneur blogging about his lifework.

Sharon learned how to capture attention by teaching teens about grammar and literature. She's a wordsmith and ruthless editor, and understands how to tickle, touch and dazzle readers with words. Her most-read blog '5 ways to kill your book club' inspired features in the *Telegraph*, and on the *Today* programme and *The World at One*. With a special skill for turning drab information into engaging stories, she helps clients create compelling content to spread their ideas, engage readers and win business.

A self-confessed Instagram addict, Sharon sees the beauty in ordinary things. She's the wordsmith and creative spirit at Valuable Content. On a mission to stamp out factory-farmed marketing, Sharon would like more companies to be human and lovable.

Sharon lives in Bristol with her partner Bill and three of their eight children. She has written a novel, enjoys walking her dog, loves growing tomatoes and makes a mean chilli jam.

Connect with Sharon on Instagram and Twitter: @SJTanton

INTRODUCTION

Who this book is for and why you need it

These are exciting but contradictory times for anyone trying to build and market a business. There have never been so many ways to get your message across or so many ways to connect with your customers. Theoretically anyone can visit your website and buy from you.

Yet chances are you're not basking in the glow of brilliant sales figures; rather you're wondering how to attract customers and clients who love your products and services. How do you make sense of this new marketing world?

Content is the new connection between your customers and your company. This book will tell you why you need to focus on valuable content, what tools to focus on and, most importantly, how to get it right.

For if you continually create and share the type of content that people appreciate you have an unprecedented opportunity to win more of the business you really want. You'll find people that are happy to give you their time, their attention, and their support. Your customers will become your social sharing marketing tribe who will do the job of promoting your business for you.

What we're talking about here is an approach that's become widely known as 'content marketing' – a way of doing business that has really hit the mainstream since we wrote the first edition of the book in 2012.

Why read this book?

Thousands more businesses, both big and small, have diverted resources to content marketing. You'll find more content marketing books, resources, tips, articles, commentaries, guides and blogs than you'll ever have time to read.

So why are we adding to the pile? What does this book bring to the party?

In a world of content overload yours has to be valuable to stand out

We're swimming in content and not all of it is good. High-quality content that has your customers' best interests at its heart will help power your business marketing, and you'll learn how to do it in the way that's right for you here.

Help for small, independent businesses

There are many great books on content marketing for bigger businesses. This book is a direct route to tried and tested ways of making content marketing work in smaller firms.

We've found that small businesses often make the best content marketers of all. Independently minded, brave, resourceful and up for a challenge – the qualities that make a successful small business owner are all useful attributes for content marketers too.

If you're uncomfortable with the idea of marketing (and we know that lots of small business owners are) this book will teach you a way of marketing that feels natural. Marketing with valuable content is an extension of the way you help your clients and customers, not an artificial gloss you apply to sell stuff.

If your resources are limited, and you're mindful of how you spend your time and money, you'll learn how to build marketing with valuable content into your business effectively.

Help for the independently minded in bigger businesses too

There's much that bigger businesses can take from this book too. This is for you if you care deeply about your customers, and you're in a position to take action. Marketing with valuable content will mean some big changes in your business, but if you're up for the challenge then we welcome you aboard.

If you know your business is doing good things, and you've got a great story to tell, you'll learn how to turn ideas into useful and inspiring content that resonates with your ideal buyers and wins you more business.

Practical assistance with the hardest stuff

This book addresses the bits we know people struggle most with:

- I know I need to create content, but exactly what content should I be creating?
- How do I get my website right?
- What tone of voice should I use?'
- Content, social media, email marketing, SEO – how does it all fit together?
- I'm scared of writing.
- I'm too busy to do it.
- I get it, but I don't know where to start.
- How do I make it *work* for us?

An approach that feels right

If you feel jaded by a blanket bombardment of irrelevant advertising messages, irritated with cold callers, fed up with spam email and dismayed by new interruption techniques like remarketing that are spreading across the web, then you're not alone. We feel like that too, and so do your customers.

The approach laid out in this book makes a deliberate step away from techniques that give marketers a bad name. Play nice, people. This is marketing that people love.

What's changed for this second edition?

The conversation around content marketing has changed. When we wrote the first edition of this book we focused a lot about *why* you should be marketing with valuable content; this time we're focusing much more on *how* you can get it right.

Some things haven't shifted. Our mantra from the first book – 'Help don't sell, show don't tell, talk don't yell' – is as valid as it ever was. The conversation and tools may have changed, but the philosophy at the heart of the approach remains the same.

We've used valuable content to help many companies build and grow their businesses. We've used it to market our own business too, and seen it thrive. The content we've created and shared has taken us on some amazing journeys, and won us exactly the kind of work we want with some fantastic clients. We've still never made a cold call, paid for advertising space, or sent sales emails to a bought list of contacts (although people still try and sell them to us at least twice a week). Staying true to our principles has made us happier – and the right kind of clients keep finding us.

In this second edition we want to use our knowledge and experience to show you how to make this powerful approach work, for you.

How to read and use this book

Whether you're a business owner, leader, marketer, sales person, subject matter expert, a student of business or a one-person band there is help for you here. Digital native or not, we will guide you through the new landscape. If you're new to content marketing, or a seasoned content marketer who wants to do it better, we've structured the book so there's something here for you.

We've split the book into three sections:

- **In Part One we cover why valuable content marketing is so necessary and so powerful**. You'll learn the principles that underpin this powerful approach; with examples of companies getting great success by doing business the valuable way. If you're an advanced practitioner you have our permission to whizz through this section. The stories and summaries are handy if you need to put a business case together for content marketing in your organization.

- **In Part Two we look at the range of content options available to you today** – the mix of content creation and distribution tools that make up your valuable content universe, with insight and ideas on how to use each of them. This is your baseline – the fundamentals that every business needs in place to make marketing work today.

- **Part Three is for people who are ready to get serious about their content** – who want to use it to drive competitive advantage for their businesses. Read this section in detail if you are ready to do some hard thinking and really want to set your business apart.

There are case studies, stories and actionable tips throughout – from the 'how valuable is your content' exercise at the start to a wealth of checklists, templates and ideas starters in the resources section.

You'll find extra resources and courses on our website to draw from too – and an accompanying workbook to take you through the process of developing a valuable content marketing strategy.

Let's get to it!

www.valuablecontent.co.uk

Diagnostic: how valuable is your content now?

Take the valuable test – do you need this book?

Take the valuable content test to pinpoint how useful your marketing is today. This will help you to focus your efforts and improve your results and guide you to the parts of the book you'll find most helpful. So how are you doing?

1 **Our marketing activity generates good leads that drive profitable sales.**

   A Yes. It's all tickety boo, thanks.

   B Sometimes, but we'd like more leads.

   C No, it's a real struggle.

2 **We actively market our business online and get results.**

   A Yes. We have a website that works for us and we spread our content across the web. Fifty per cent of new business enquiries or more come via the web.

   B To an extent. We have a website but we don't do much else online. And we'd like better results.

   C No, we don't market our business online properly. Actually, it's embarrassing.

3 **Potential customers welcome our marketing.**

   A Yes. Our marketing is all about creating and sharing helpful, relevant and meaningful information and our customers tell us they appreciate it.

   B Some of it they appreciate. A lot they ignore.

   C No. The door gets slammed shut most of the time. Although it's hard to tell through the deafening silence.

4 **We publish fresh content regularly.**

   A *Yes – twice a month or more.*

   B *It's a bit spasmodic to be honest.*

   C *No, our content hardly ever changes.*

5 **We have a working business blog.**

   A Yup. We post a new article regularly and generate good leads from our blogging efforts.

B To an extent. We do have a blog. We post from time to time but don't really get much engagement or leads.

C No.

6 We engage in social media for business.

A Yes. We have a growing list of followers and lots of our stuff gets shared. It builds relationships and generates useful contacts, referrals and sales opportunities.

B A bit. We dabble. But it's not really getting us anywhere.

C No.

7 We make sure search engines can find our content.

A Yes. Search Engine Optimization (SEO) is an important part of our strategy – we're ranking well and getting found. We index our content carefully.

B A bit. We don't fully understand SEO yet.

C No. Our content is invisible.

8 We have built an engaged list of contacts and keep in touch with a useful newsletter.

A Yes. We send out regular, valuable content to our subscribers. We have an active and growing community, happy to receive our stuff.

B Kind of. We send out company news regularly.

C No.

9 We share deeper content on our website, eg useful guides, white papers, presentations, videos or e-books.

A Yes. We've invested in some really high-quality, heavy-hitting content that's easy to find on our website.

B We could do. We have some good resources lying around the office but we haven't yet put many of them up on our website.

C No.

10 Our marketing efforts are targeted at a specific niche (or niches).

A Yes. We know exactly what type of clients or customer we'd like to attract and we produce relevant information they connect with and value.

B To an extent, but it's a bit hit and hope.

C No. Our marketing is pretty generalist and scattergun. We think we might miss out on opportunities if we make it too specific.

11 We take a strategic approach to our content.

    A Yes. We have documented our content strategy and refer to it regularly.

    B We kind of know what we're aiming it but we've yet to think it through properly.

    C No.

12 The whole business is involved in content marketing.

    A Yes. From the sales team to the boss and the support staff, we're all in on the act.

    B There's a content team, but not everyone gets it.

    C Are you joking?

13 We are proud of our website and marketing.

    A Yes. The messages we put out reflect who we are as a business and tell our story well.

    B Hmmm, some bits but not all. Some of it's a bit cringey.

    C No. It just doesn't feel like us. To be honest, we feel let down by our website, and a bit embarrassed!

Your score

Mostly As. Congratulations! It sounds as if you are getting your marketing right with good results in terms of leads and sales. You evidently appreciate that regularly sharing valuable content is the kind of marketing customers seek. You'll find advanced tips in Part 3 of the book to make your content even more valuable. As a reward for your efforts please enter your website for a valuable content award: **www.valuablecontent.co.uk/valuablecontentaward**

Mostly Bs. You're on the right track but definitely room for improvement here. Get your content right and you'll see far better results from your online marketing in terms of leads and sales. Sections 2 and 3 and the additional resources will really help you here.

Mostly Cs. All is not lost but you are definitely missing a trick with your marketing. It's definitely not a source of happiness for your business. If you want to get found on the web and continually generate good leads from your marketing efforts, with prospects coming to you, you really need this book. Read it and act on it to transform your content and win more business.

PART ONE
WHY VALUABLE CONTENT?

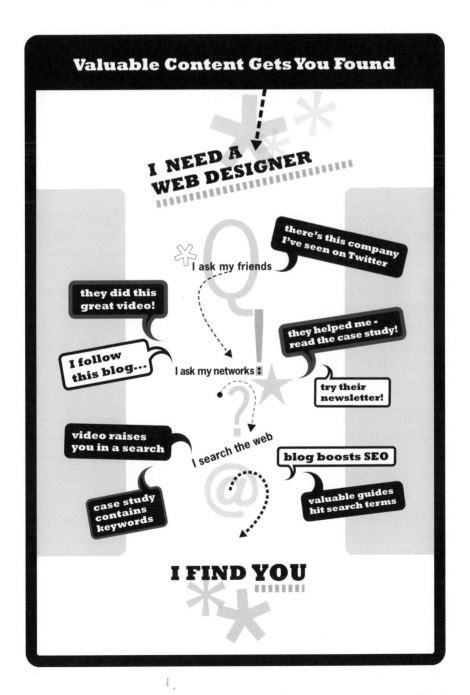

Why valuable content is the focus of all successful marketing today, and how to play in the new game

Marketing is no longer about stuff that you make, but about the stories that you tell.

Seth Godin[1]

Marketing has changed enormously over the past decade. People buy differently, so we need to sell differently. Marketing with valuable content has developed as a way to bridge the gap between the way people like to buy – researching online and via recommendations from social networks – and the way smart businesses like to sell – by demonstrating empathy, purpose and usefulness, not by shouting loudest.

This first section of the book explores this new marketing landscape in more detail. What is it about valuable content that is so right for the way we think and act today? And what principles underpin content marketing success?

If you're new to content marketing, this section will help you find your feet. If you have been marketing with content for years, you'll find new insights into the changes we see happening all around us. If you're already convinced that marketing with valuable content is the way forward, do feel free to whizz through this first part. If you need to convince others, there is a lot in this section that will help.

We'll show you what makes truly valuable content, and share examples of businesses that are winning with this approach. And with the groundwork in place, we'll get you thinking about what will make the most valuable content of all for you, your customers and your business.

CHAPTER 1

BUYING HAS CHANGED.

HAS YOUR MARKETING CAUGHT UP?

If you don't like change, you're going to like irrelevance even less.

General Eric Shinseki, retired Chief of Staff, US Army[1]

In this chapter:

- Business development is tough.
- Who's winning?
- What are they doing right?
- The factors transforming buyer behaviour.
- The new buyer mentality.

Think about a big purchase you've made in the last 12 months. What were the steps you went through that led up to you buying? What drove you to make a purchase in the first place? How did you do your research? What or who influenced your decisions and how did you feel along the way? What was it that finally tipped you over the edge to make that important purchase?

Chances are that your journey to buy has changed a lot over the last few years. Yet a lot of marketing acts like it is still 1985.

In this chapter we look at why some companies are winning the sales and marketing game, even in very competitive markets. We want to look at today's discerning and cynical buyers, and dissect the key trends influencing their behaviour. Don't be concerned – their discernment and cynicism are an opportunity for your business.

The business development challenge

Selling stuff has always been tough. Ask any business owner about the biggest challenge she or he faces and nine times out of ten 'business development' will come out on top. Seventy-two per cent of professional firms that responded to a worldwide survey by US firm Hinge Marketing put 'attracting and developing new business' as their number one challenge for 2015.[2]

How do we find new customers/clients? How can we differentiate and prove our value? How can we attract more referrals? How do we drive long-term profitable sales results?

Tried and tested activities for getting customer attention don't work like they once did.

- The response to mass cold calling campaigns has dropped off a cliff – you get voicemail 80 per cent of the time, and short shrift if you do get through.

- You used to email your way to leads but the blanket bomb approach results in emails unopened or junked.

- It's hard to justify the cost of press advertising (and like most people you screen out most adverts yourself, so this doesn't seem to be the right way to go).

- Trade shows cost a fortune, take a huge amount of time and for what return?

- In a tough market even the network of contacts you've relied on for so long fails to deliver all the leads you need.

We don't want to labour those points. If you're reading this book you'll know that something has to shift. Most likely you've already joined the digital revolution and started marketing your business online. But still the profitable sales results you desire seem frustratingly elusive.

- You may have invested in your website but where are all the promised leads?

- PPC and SEO drive some traffic to your site, but visitors rarely stick around.

- Twitter takes up your time and can feel like shouting in an empty room.

- You may well be blogging but it's a lonely old slog – does this content marketing thing work?

- The marketing automation system you bought with so much promise shows you exactly what's happening at the back end of your site (and it's clearly not enough).

If any of these statements ring true you're not alone. You are expert in what you do and know that there are people out there who would really benefit from your product or service. How on earth do you get their attention and build their trust?

It's enough to put some off marketing all together. Especially when you waste your time and money on 'techniques' that just don't work.

Surely there is a better way?

Who is winning with their marketing?

Some companies are winning the business development game, even in a tough market. They are consistently getting a stream of good leads – from their websites and from social media too. Their networks are expanding rapidly and delivering warm referrals that are quicker and easier to convert. They are doing all this without resorting to cold calling, expensive advertising or mass email blasts. In fact, clients and customers are calling THEM. To top it off, they say that they enjoy marketing too!

- **Information risk specialists Ascentor attract a stream of inbound leads: www.ascentor.co.uk**
  For the last three years Ascentor has published up to four blog posts a month, and offered a host of free e-books, guides and a monthly email newsletter covering the business risks associated with information security. Their content reaches board-level directors, government buyers and small- to medium-size business users via search, social media, email and events.
  'Our content has greatly increased our brand awareness. Now, people are coming to us instead of us always going to them,' says MD Dave James. Content marketing is attracting leads and helped boost the company website for niche online search terms.

- **IT services company Desynit builds a healthy sales pipeline: www.desynit.com**

  Desynit, a small IT services company, conducted customer research before launching its website in 2013. *'We learned what prospects needed from an IT firm and translated that into a strong brand identity that underpins all our content, including blogs, guides, infographics, slide sets, video and now podcasts,'* says Desynit marketing manager Amy Grenham. *'Our website traffic has more than tripled, and it's going up all the time. We now have a strong, consistent pipeline of sales opportunities that we never had before.'*

- **Product business Sugru: www.sugru.com**

  Sugru sells mouldable glue, lots of it, and it is content that makes their sales pitch deliciously sticky. They've built a community of fixers and doers through the content that they share. Sugru's founder Jane Ní Dhulchaointigh says: *'We needed a way to tell stories that makes people think that the world really will be a better place if we mend things. The way we find that easiest to do is through good video and content that brings the whole story alive.'*

- **Law firm Clutton Cox: www.cluttoncox.co.uk**

  This eight-person law firm is bigger online than legal firms with 50 partners. Early adopters of a valuable content approach, their online focus has helped them not just to survive but thrive in an era of great upheaval in law. Their blogs, guides, ever-creative SlideShare presentations and online guides have built their profile and people's trust so they become the local law firm of choice in their marketplace.

- **The Sands Beach Resort: www.sandsbeach.eu**

  The Sands Beach Resort in Lanzarote is thriving, and its success is down in no small measure to the content they create and share online. This fabulous beachfront resort has long been popular with families. But over the past three years, it has also built a reputation as a premier sports destination – and it's sharing relevant, high-quality content with each different audience via social media that has been critical to its success.

- **Create Health & Fitness Ltd: Createfit.com**

  Mark Durnford's fitness company offers personal training, swim coaching and sports massage. The Create team believes in empowering clients and others by sharing their coaching approach and knowledge via their blog, innovative e-books and video tutorials on YouTube. Marketing with valuable content has brought them international attention, opportunities and many grateful clients. *'New clients tell us they didn't hesitate to contact us. Before they've even picked up the phone or typed out their email, they are comfortable that Create will support their positive change.'* Mark Durnford

- **HSBC Bank – Expat Services division**: **www.expatexplorer.hsbc.com** Content that makes you love a bank? Sounds impossible but HSBC Expat's progressive approach to content marketing has cracked it. They provide a plethora of resources – guides, surveys, videos, crowdsourced hints and tips, a superb blog, interactive tools, social updates – all carefully designed and widely shared. This content helps to build the goodwill and awareness they need to attract new expat customers and better serve existing ones.

You'll find out more about these companies' strategies, and more like them, throughout the chapters of the book.

So what are these companies doing right?

All these businesses focus on making their marketing valuable to their particular customers and their generosity is getting results:

- **Marketing online.** They build relationships on social media and get their web strategies right.

- **With *valuable* content.** They create and share useful or entertaining content, rather than pushing out self-oriented sales messages. Online or offline they're using this valuable content to start conversations and build relationships.

- **Strong message for a niche audience.** They are clear on what they do and who their customers are, with a clear understanding of what makes their audience tick. Those that get the best results also have an inspiring purpose – a story of why they do what they do.

- **They are generous.** They freely give away information that is of value to their type of buyers and reap the return in terms of referrals, leads and sales.

- **Quality is their watchword.** They share genuinely useful, well-produced, creative content that sets them apart from the crowd.

- **Being valuable is the way they do business.** It's more than a marketing technique they apply. They are customer-focused through and through.

All of these companies turn their knowledge, expertise and ideas into information that is useful and meaningful to their niche customers. It is this information that they publish, promote and widely share. Potential customers get information that they can use, whether or not they buy from that company; this builds trust and goodwill and the result is more interest, more leads and more sales. Win, win.

It shouldn't need saying but it is worth pointing out – all these companies are *actively* marketing their firms. They are communicating consistently, taking action, doing stuff. Marketing has become part of their day-to-day activities, not an ad hoc campaign undertaken once or twice a year when leads run dry.

Companies that invest in online marketing grow four times faster

Research by US marketers Hinge Marketing in 2012[3] found that high-growth professional services firms place a higher degree of emphasis on a wide range of online tools, whereas average firms' efforts are more measured. In fact, the firms that generated at least 40 per cent of their leads online grow more than four times faster than firms with no online lead generation.

The three factors transforming buyer behaviour

Why is the valuable content approach so pertinent today and why are strong-arm marketing techniques heavy on self-promotion losing their impact? Let's take a closer look at three trends influencing the current buyer mentality:

1 the internet;
2 social media;
3 lack of trust in a sales message.

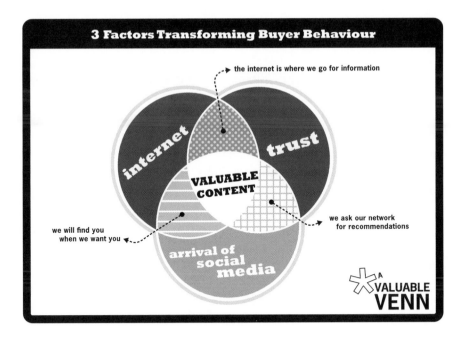

1. The internet has changed the game

Asking friends and contacts for a recommendation remains important but the internet plays a massive part in the sales journey, whatever you are selling.

Annual Google searches rose from less than 800 billion in 2009 to over 2.25 trillion in 2014.[4]

Your buyer will search for answers and options using Google. She'll ask her online social networks for recommendations and visit a few websites to assess the options. She is checking to see who she can best trust to solve her problem, and wants access to all the information she needs to do just that.

The internet has given buyers the reins and transformed the sales process in the process. As businesses it is time we caught up with the buyer's journey, and committed to providing the content they are looking for every step of the way.

Research from Google and CEB titled 'The Digital Evolution in B2B Marketing'[5] provides new insight into buyer behaviour, and challenges the conventional wisdom. According to the study, customers reported to being nearly 60 per cent through the sales process before engaging a sales rep, regardless of price point. More accurately, 57 per cent of the sales process just disappeared.

It's not just the accessibility of information via the internet that has changed the game. It's the sophistication and proliferation of the web tools available too. New channels mean that we have an opportunity to connect with more people in more ways than ever before. And better tools mean we can easily create and publish content ourselves – via blogs, easy content management systems for websites, sites such as YouTube, SlideShare, LinkedIn and other social networks.

We no longer have to pay for web developers to update our content or beg the paid media to publish our articles. We can wrest back control and tell our story directly, publishing our ideas and sharing our knowledge for free. This opens up huge opportunity for any business.

> *All you need is a good story, a digital platform and the social media network to spread the word. You don't need to – or shouldn't – rely on others to get and to share your story anymore. Instead, try telling your story your own way...*
>
> Ian Sanders[6]

2. The rise of the social web

The good news for good businesses is that there are now more ways to connect and demonstrate trustworthiness than ever before.

Social networks are the places where connected consumers spend the largest amount of their time online. They have transformed our ability to communicate and connect online. In 2014, over half (54 per cent) of all adults participated in social networking, up from 45 per cent in 2011. Almost all adults aged 16 to 24 (91 per cent) used social networks in 2014, but social networks are not just for the young. Around 37 per cent of adults aged 55 to 64 and 13 per cent of those aged 65 and over participated in social networking in 2014.[7]

You can no longer separate your company's message from 'technology' and social media.

From a buyer's perspective your online footprint has to live up to your brand promise. *What are they like on Twitter?* is something people would never have asked five years ago. But now it's a place buyers frequently go to check out a company. Does the story stack up? Are they who they say they are? How do they talk to their customers?

Impulse purchases aside, when we're looking to buy something, we ask around for recommendations before we do anything else. Word-of-mouth recommendations from friends and family continue to come out top as the most trusted form of advertising. Whether it's a holiday or someone to help with your web design, the first thing we are likely to do is to seek a referral from the people we know. Social media supercharges this referral process – and it's a huge opportunity for your business.

As we show in Chapter 5, social media is powered by great content. Share, Like, Tweet – posting and swapping links to valuable content fuels the social web.

3. We don't trust a sales message

The tweet from rapper Kanye West[8] that opens this book – *Don't ever try and sell me on anything. Just give me all the information and I'll make up my own mind* – shows he was having a bad day, but also sums up exactly how we feel as buyers today. The internet has given us choice and the tools to do our own research – and we hate being sold to, more than we ever did.

And in response to this dislike of sales messages, we've learned to block out most of the noise: we ignore most promotional advertising; chuck blanket direct mail in the recycling bin; slam the phone down on cold callers; turn away in the face of 'spin'. As buyers, we have been oversold to and we've had enough!

> *Trust is at an all-time low. Trust in governments, trust in corporations, trust in salespeople, trust in marketing messages – all are lower than a grasshopper's knee. This is precisely what happens when organizations and their messages become self-serving – a focus that leads them to twist the truth in their favour, even to lie. As a result, they are not to be trusted.*
>
> Charles H Green[9]

So who do we trust in a cynical world?

> *The more you focus on others the more you will be trusted.*
>
> Charles H Green[10]

Turn your back on self-promotion. Instead of saying how great you are, prove your expertise and your usefulness, your authenticity and your humanity. Build trust by helping your prospects and customers.

Strong-arm sales techniques hit the wrong note these days.

> *Uh oh, sales guy has just emailed with the words 'discount available if you sign up before the end of the month' – red rag to a bull.*
>
> Matthew Curry, Head of Ecommerce, Lovehoney[11]

Your audience won't accept the old-style hard sell. Cynicism is epidemic.

> *Really annoyed now – tempted to stop the whole sales process. I hate people trying to use sales tactics on me.*
>
> Matthew Curry, Head of Ecommerce, Lovehoney[12]

Just provide us with good information and we'll do what makes best sense to us, that's the new buyer reality. Don't try to manipulate us into buying.

Align your marketing with how people buy now

Public opinion researchers Roper Public Affairs conducted research cited by the Content Marketing Institute that backs this up:

- 80 per cent of business decision-makers prefer to get company information in a series of articles rather than an advertisement.

- 77 per cent of people understand that the purpose of an organization's content is to sell them something, but are OK with it as long as it provides value.

- 61 per cent say valuable content makes them feel closer to the company that delivers it and are more likely to buy from that company.

These are really exciting times for those who align their sales and marketing approach with the new expectations of customers and clients. In a world with little trust, where Google is the place we turn to for answers, where social networks are trusted more than traditional media, valuable content is what we seek.

Educate or entertain your buyers, show them best practice, tell them what to look out for, give them valuable tips on how to achieve success, demonstrate how you've helped others in their shoes. Answer their questions and solve their problems, open their eyes. Creating and distributing this kind of relevant, valuable and compelling information will help you turn prospects into buyers and buyers into long-term fans.

Take action

- Think about the last time you decided to buy a product or service. How did you research, find and select your chosen product or service?
- Did your trust in the process increase or decrease at any point? What swung it for you?
- Look at your own marketing. Does it tap in to the way buyers feel today?

CHAPTER 2

WHAT IS VALUABLE CONTENT AND WHY DOES IT WIN YOU BUSINESS?

*You can **buy** attention (advertising)*

*You can **beg** for attention from the media (traditional PR)*

*You can **bug** people one at a time to get attention (traditional sales)*

*Or you can **earn** attention by creating something interesting and valuable and then publishing it online.*

David Meerman Scott[1]

In this chapter:

- What we mean by valuable content marketing.
- Is this form of marketing new?
- Eight vital things every business needs, and valuable content delivers.

If you're not familiar with content marketing here's how it works. You create a website full of free information that is useful to potential customers, offering them the opportunity to engage your services or buy products which are closely linked to all that great information you're giving away.

You see content marketing in action every time you go online – think of the blogs, tips, articles and advice you've accessed when searching on the web. This approach can be used to market any sort of company and it's the best possible way to build awareness of what you do, attract new business and motivate sales.

This is a very human approach to doing business. Customers value it – it doesn't even feel like marketing, it feels like answers to their questions.

Content versus valuable content

Content marketing works really well, but only if the content is valuable, so we want you to make an important distinction:

- **'Content'** is the words on the page or the screen you are reading. It's the copy on your website, the blog you posted last night, the videos and images you share. When we're talking about content, we just mean words, knowledge and information.

- *Valuable* **content** is supercharged content. It's content with a bigger purpose; useful information created for a particular audience; content that hits the mark. By valuable content we mean the words, knowledge and information you choose to shape and share for your clients and customers: content that educates, helps or inspires them. Content they appreciate.

To be valuable, content must have uniqueness at the client level, and it must be meaningful.

Charles H Green[2]

Never forget that the purpose of sharing all this content is to drive profitable action. Valuable to your customer: valuable to you and your business – that's the balance you're looking to strike with your marketing.

Before embarking on marketing your business with content, you need to understand what makes certain types of content valuable, and why some types just don't hit the mark. Here is a quick quality control guide to help you create the right type of content.

Valuable content is...	Valuable content isn't...
Relevant to a niche audience	Vague – no sense of who this is aimed at
Written with a real person/people in mind	Written without a grasp of the person who will be reading it
Answering a genuine question – it's what people are looking for	Inward looking – doesn't answer a real question – the *'so what?'* factor
In line with your business goals	Not aligned with your business aims
Well designed	Looks shabby, hard to read/watch/listen to
Findable	No one can find it
Shareable	Hard to share
Created in a spirit of generosity	Created with a cynical mindset
Unputdownable – *this is fantastic*!	Unpickupable – *I can't be bothered to look at this*!

Let's dig a bit deeper into how you can create the kind of content in the first list. What makes content unputdownable?

The content that works best for businesses is:

- **Helpful** – it answers people's questions.
- **Entertaining** – it evokes emotion or inspires.
- **Authentic** – it feels real, genuine and sincere.
- **Relevant** – it is focused and meaningful to its intended niche audience.
- **Timely** – it hits the spot at just the right moment.

In any combination, these attributes form just the kind of content that gets read, shared and acted upon. Businesses that really win exhibit all these qualities across the variety of content they put out there.

> *The content I regard as valuable is: useful and functional – gives me answers; beautiful and entertaining – gives me pleasure. It has to do at least one of those things. If it does both, I consider subscribing.*
>
> Jane Northcote

Like beauty, the value of a piece of content is in the eye of the beholder. What's valuable to me isn't necessarily valuable to you. This is how Sonja sees it:

The content that is valuable to Sonja

It's Monday morning. I sit at my desk with a packed week ahead. I open up Outlook and face the usual deluge of emails. I delete about 30 of them straight off (starting with the spammy ones I don't know and didn't ask for), but there are a few emails I always look out for:

- The newsletter from Chris Brogan for business owners like me that always makes me think and consistently gives me good ideas on how to run my business better.
- Finisterre – their celebration of cold water surfing and mixture of beautiful videos, articles and occasional offers feels like the right balance.
- Do Lectures – life and business inspiration with a big dose of the great outdoors. What's not to love?

I valued the content on these companies' websites enough to sign up for their email updates in the first place and it feels like a fair exchange. I read them, even look forward to them despite the pressures on my time. Now, don't get me wrong, I'm fully aware that all these companies are trying to sell me something:

- Chris Brogan wants me to sign up for one of his courses (we have done) and buy his books (they're all on our book shelf).
- Finisterre want me to buy surf gear (yup – I do too).
- The Do Lectures people want me pay to listen to great speakers and sleep under canvas in deepest darkest Wales (I'm going to do that someday).

But the content these companies share on their websites, in their emails and across social media doesn't major on the hard sell. Their marketing all starts from the premise of delivering valuable information to me, their kind of customer. They understand me well enough to know exactly what type of information I appreciate, and they focus their marketing communications on generously sharing this with me. Their marketing majors on delivering high-quality educational, informative and entertaining content – just the kind that customers like me really appreciate.

This is valuable content – content that is generously shared and willingly received. This rest of this book will show you how to create it for your customers and your business.

Hang on a minute. Is this form of marketing new?

The terms 'content' and 'content marketing' are relatively recent additions to the language of business, but the notion of giving a bit of valuable knowledge away for free in return for attention is nothing new. Think of Michelin Guides, Lego magazines, and white papers from professional firms. These were generating interest and sales long before the internet. Here's a UK example.

Be-Ro recipe books: 1920s content marketing, still valuable today

In the early 1920s, self-raising flour was a novelty. In a bid to make it more popular, Newcastle grocery company Be-Ro staged a series of exhibitions where freshly baked scones, pastries and cakes were sold for a shilling to visitors. These were so popular that people demanded that they had copies of the recipes so that they could bake the dishes at home.

As a result a free recipe book was produced and handed out at the exhibitions as well as door to door. The Be-Ro cookbook contained recipes to feed hungry families on a very low budget. They soon became an essential part of a young woman's education in running a home and feeding a family. Consequently, the cookbooks achieved their objective of making Be-Ro the best-known flour in the North.

The first Be-Ro cookbook was produced in 1923 and contained a total of 19 pages. Forty editions later, the book has grown to 86 pages, and is arguably one of the best-selling cookery books ever with more than 38 million copies having been sold.

See: **www.be-ro.co.uk/f_about.htm**

Advances in the web have given the valuable content approach wings. In essence, everything has changed, yet nothing has changed. New web tools and the arrival of social media mean it has become far easier and cheaper to publish and spread our ideas. Good marketing has always been about putting your customer first but the difference today is that buyers will no longer tolerate or respond to marketing that is less than good.

Marketing the valuable way is an approach that's come of age; one that is starting to explode in popularity in all sectors of business around the world because of the results it brings. Old school values, new tools.

Eight reasons to love valuable content marketing

If your business is to succeed in our internet-dominated, low-trust, social media age it needs to be found, known, liked, trusted and remembered when the time comes to buy.

Let's have a look at these benefits in more detail, with stories from those who have put valuable content at the centre of their marketing and are getting great results.

1. You get found

You want your business to be found in a direct search by a buyer searching on the web for your niche products and services.

> *I want to find someone to help me with G-Cloud accreditation – information risk management advisers Ascentor came out on top in a Google search.*

And you want to be the company that gets stumbled upon in a general web search:

> *I was looking for ideas on how to transform my IT department when I found a very informative slideshow from a management consultancy on the subject. I called them in for a meeting.*

Inksters get found through their content

Forward-thinking Scottish law firm Inksters Solicitors attracts new clients from the web. They have turned their website into a valuable resource for people looking for their services, putting their years of legal knowledge online. Their marketing focuses on creating and sharing valuable content in each of their niche areas and it's an approach that is getting them found.

One of their specialties is crofting law. Go to their website and you'll see pages of useful information, articles, videos, case studies, even lectures given on the subject. They also have a separate crofting law blog. Search engines love all this niche content and reward Inksters with high page rankings, so if someone with a legal issue types in 'crofting law' Inksters website and/or blog appears right at the top.

Even in a traditional profession such as law, valuable content works. It gets Inksters found on the web, turns visitors into new clients (20 per cent of new business came from direct web search last year) and motivates even more referrals too.

> If you don't tell the world about your professional expertise and achievements it is likely that only your existing clients and people they refer to you will know about them. Cast your net wider by publishing your knowledge, expertise and achievements online – you never know who might be searching for the specific assistance that you can provide.

Brian Inkster, Inksters Solicitors

inksters.com

2. You build your reputation

Reputation is everything in business, and referrals are gold dust. Valuable content is an easy referral tool, and it gives people something to talk about and share. People are far happier to pass on something useful or compelling they've read or seen (it makes them look and feel good), than hand over the spare business card you gave them (in fact, they've probably lost that already). Valuable content builds your reputation and will prove the rightness of their referral.

Balsamiq grows on the strength of their referrals

Balsamiq is a software company with a simple and hugely popular website mock-up tool used by designers all over the world. From day one founder Giacomo 'Peldi' Guilizzoni blogged openly about his experiences, even giving away details of his revenue figures from the start. Written from the heart, his blog quickly built an active community of followers who cheered him on and spread the word. All this goodwill and exposure helped his software go from zero to leader in just 18 months.

Today at Balsamiq everyone blogs. Peldi encourages each member of his team to become a leader of their chosen niche and share valuable content with their community. The Balsamiq website is rich with useful, authentic, inspiring content that helps their reputation grow and spread. Type Balsamiq into Google or search on Twitter and the buzz is clear for all to see. The results are remarkable: started as a one-man operation in 2008, by 2011 Balsamiq had cleared $5 million.

balsamiq.com

3. *You become more likeable*

Content marketing is as much about personality as persuasion.
People trust people they understand. But they also trust people they like.
And it's a lot easier to like someone who entertains us than someone who merely informs us.

Andy Maslen, MD Sunfish

Just as you can instantly warm to or take against someone in real life, because of something they say, or the way they act, so it is with your business in the online world. Being likeable might sound a rather woolly objective, but likeability will get you a long way in many lines of work. Of course there are exceptions. If you're researching heart surgeons you're looking for the world expert over the nice guy with a good line in Twitter banter. But for most small businesses where forging good relationships with clients is key, and larger ones where customer service really matters, likeability is a real bonus.

Lovable and sticky – how Sugru's marketing makes people smile

Giving glue a personality isn't the easiest things to do, but Sugru have done just that. *Sugru is mouldable glue. Stick it, shape it and it will turn into rubber. We invented it to make fixing and making easy and fun. And now it comes in 10 handy colours! Doers of the world, it's time to get excited.* Their celebration of the doers of the world is what drives their content, and it's what gives a practical product a very human face.

The 'our story' page sets the tone. *'While studying for my MA in Product Design (read "playing and experimenting with materials") at the RCA in London, I had a bit of an idea. "I don't want to buy new stuff all the time. I want to hack the stuff I already have so it works better for me." (I didn't really say it out loud. I just thought it.)'*

And this tone is carried over to the rest of the site. There's a gallery of fascinating stories and pictures showing how people use the product (to fix skis to get to the North Pole, to fix a camera to a plane for aeronautical stunt filming, to make a camera drop-proof in the hands of a three-year-old). The combination of brilliant mini-stories and smiling faces means you can't help but like the product and the people behind it.

People love when they can get to know us as real people. From the beginning I starred in the videos and I used to write all the blog posts. Now, usually once a week I'll write something on Instagram or on the blog. I think people's attention is so small, that a way Sugru has been successful is that people believe who we say we are, they believe that we care and that we're real people, working hard like them, trying to make a go of it and that Sugru is a product we believe in so it's worth trying.

Jane Ní Dhulchaointigh, Sugru Founder and CEO

Like Sugru, remember that people do business with people so create content with real personality.

sugru.com

4. You become trustworthy

The Trusted Advisor approach made famous by Charles H Green (trusted-advisor.com) sets out the four underlying principles that govern all trustworthy behaviour:

1 A focus on the other for the other's sake, not just as a means to your own ends.

2 A collaborative approach to relationships.

3 A medium- to long-term relationship perspective, not a short-term transactional focus.

4 A habit of being transparent in all your dealings.

Those who are trustworthy act consistently from those four principles. With our trust in many institutions at an all-time low, and our intolerance for pushy sales techniques at an all-time high, gaining trust is not something that happens lightly today. Sharing genuinely useful content that helps your customers without asking for anything in return is a good way to prove you are worthy of their trust and business.

Trust begins to emerge when we have a sense that another person or organization is driven by things other than their own self-gain.

Simon Sinek[3]

Clutton Cox build trust in house-buying process

Paul Hajek runs Clutton Cox – a small but far from traditional high street legal practice in Chipping Sodbury, Bristol. Digitally – they get it. They were early adopters of content marketing: the first firm of solicitors in 2008 to blog about conveyancing (the legal process involved in buying and selling a house).

Sharing helpful content helps build confidence in their firm.

> **36 Things You Won't Get From Another Conveyancing Law Firm When You Move House** was our first SlideShare presentation way back in April 2014. To date it has reached over 7,830 views. We certainly got the flavour and created a Conveyancing Jargon Buster to demystify the conveyancing process entitled What's the Name of that Legal Thingy? 11,011 views (that's viral I reckon in the legal world).

Their business strategy relies on bricks with a lot of clicks. Valuable content draws 7,000–8,000 visitors a month to their website, and builds valuable trust in the services they offer.

cluttoncox.com

5. You become memorable

Apart from impulse purchases, most people take their time when deciding to buy something. And the bigger the purchase, the longer they take. Something that makes you easy to remember when the time comes to buy is invaluable for a business whose products or services fall into the considered purchase category.

Being in the right place at the right time is useful, and valuable content lets you do that. We will show you how to keep your business on that radar in a way your clients like.

> **Swimming coach Mark Durnford's content kept him on Sonja's radar.** 'Mark was referred to me by a friend, so I checked out his website. The swimming tip video clips were incredibly useful, and I downloaded his e-book that gave me lots of tips. I didn't actually get in contact with Mark for about a year after the initial referral, but I kept going back to the e-book and videos, and when I finally realized I needed some one-to-one coaching to fine-tune my technique, Mark was the natural choice. It was his consistent, high-quality content that had built my trust and kept him at the front of my mind until I was ready.'
>
> createfit.com

6. Your business clearly differentiates

None of the examples we've talked about in this chapter are selling anything unique, and none of them stands in a field all of its own. Other law firms, swimming coaches and fixing products are most certainly available. What marketing with valuable content does is give them a way to demonstrate the unique way they help their customers. The content you create, and the way you share is the living, breathing embodiment of your brand. It's the way you show, not tell, the difference your business makes to the world.

Newfangled stands head and shoulders above the rest

Web development is another overcrowded marketplace but US firm New-fangled most certainly sets its business apart. The quality and focus of their content gives them stellar status in their field. They differentiate themselves by focusing on a niche market (website development for advertising agencies and marketing firms). Unlike many design firms their website is far more than a flat, online brochure. Their home page leads with valuable tips and articles for their audience, not flashy graphics or just an online portfolio. Their active blog, superb monthly newsletters, Twitter feeds, webinars and books help them attract, inform and engage the right audience. All this valuable content guides and educates their clients and wins them more work. It's turned their website into a lead-generating machine.

President of Newfangled Mark O'Brien explains:

> Our content-rich website is the cradle of our marketing universe. It differentiates us and validates our expertise. The website is independently responsible for 20 per cent of our new business but its benefit to us is wider still. Because it does such a thorough job of documenting and sharing our expertise on a continual basis, it attracts the attention of many prospects, but also other key influencers in our field whom we are then able to foster relationships with. These relationships open doors which enable us to start engaging in a wide array of off-site marketing activities such as speaking at key industry events, publishing in industry journals, and publishing books through the right industry publishers. Valuable content is the foundation for all our marketing efforts.
>
> newfangled.com

7. Your marketing investment stands the test of time

Post something useful online and it is there forever, generating interest for your firm – long after the advert or sales email have died.

> Posts on my blog that I posted more than three years ago are still generating me hot leads today. What's more, if you're smart about using it, and re-using it, one piece of content can be used in various contexts – from a talk to many from a conference platform to a one-to-one sales chat over coffee.
>
> Bryony Thomas, author and founder of Watertight Marketing

Content lives on long after the ads and emails have died.

> *Content is an evergreen asset. Ads and emails are like yodels without the echo. Our content was the tortoise, the crass ads were the hare. The content will keep generating search traffic for years.*
>
> Doug Kessler[4]

8. You feel good!

Many of our clients start their journey with us as reluctant marketers. A sizeable number don't really enjoy marketing, some actively hate it. Yet once the focus switches from pushing slippery self-oriented sales copy to creating content that helps real customers they find it's actually enjoyable.

Getting the wider team creating content will always uncover content stars. Sometimes it's the unlikeliest candidates who turn out to have the best ideas, or to have a flair for blogging. Giving people a voice, and trusting them to be a part of the face that you show to the world makes them feel valued.

Marketing that people love. That's got to be worth aiming for!

Take action

- Think: what content do you value personally? What is it about this content that you appreciate – is it helpful, entertaining, timely?

- Note down the types of content you could create that your customers would appreciate in this way.

- What is that you really want valuable content marketing to do for your business? Are you looking to get found, differentiate, or just enjoy your marketing more? Write down your goal.

CHAPTER 3
GUIDING PRINCIPLES FOR YOUR VALUABLE CONTENT

In a busy world, our competition is this: people are just busy. To grab their attention, we have to remember a simple rule: be interesting.

David Hieatt, founder of Hiut Denim[1]

In this chapter:

- Eight actionable principles for your valuable content marketing.
- An insight into a very different marketing mindset.

We've looked at what's involved, with examples from businesses getting incredible results by giving value through their marketing. We hope you're feeling inspired to make some real changes to the way you promote what you do.

Before jumping ahead and trying any new tactic it is important to establish some solid foundations. The valuable content approach is a very different way of communicating so let's look at the principles that underpin success when working this way.

In the course of our work and training we've looked at how hundreds of businesses are using content to communicate around the world. Time and time again we see the same patterns. There are a few fundamental truths that underpin the content marketing efforts of those that succeed. We've narrowed these truths down to eight actionable principles. These principles blend both hard and soft attributes; they are both business focused, and very human.

Studying these underlying principles will help you prepare the ground for success the valuable content way. Hold onto your hats! This is a complete turnaround from much of the marketing you see (and ignore) today.

Eight guiding principles for valuable content marketing

Rethink what you know about sales and marketing communication. The valuable attitude is not 'Look how great we are' (as in a traditional brochure) but 'See how useful and interesting we are – we have the answers to your questions'.

Here are eight fundamental principles to hold in your mind as you embark on creating valuable content.

1 Put your customers first.

2 Help don't sell.

3 Give ideas away generously, for free.

4 Always know why.

5 Think niche.

6 Tell a bigger story.

7 Commit to quality.

8 Write from the heart.

1. Put your customers first

Nobody cares about your products and services (except you). What people care about are themselves and solving their problems.

David Meerman Scott, The New Rules of Marketing and PR[2]

As proud as you may be of your company/product/service, you should know that your customers or clients are not as interested as you are. No way near. Their only concern is how well you can help them to meet *their* challenges and needs. If you want more of them to buy from you, your focus needs to be on them, not on you.

Many businesses are convinced that the purpose of their marketing is to continuously talk about how fantastic their company is; that the louder they shout, the more sales they will get.

Yes, of course the purpose of marketing is to help you to win more business, but if you want your marketing to be welcomed rather than seen as an irritation then shift your focus. Make every marketing communication primarily of benefit to the people who receive it and secondarily of benefit to you and your business. This is not rocket science; it's a simple awareness of human nature. And it will make all the difference to your marketing.

In some ways, content marketing is a cover, a front for *customer-focused business*. It's changing businesses by stealth to do right by their customers – that's its hidden agenda. People have been waxing lyrical about customer-focused business for decades but we haven't seen much evidence of this until now. Marketing is leading the revolution. Content marketing is forcing businesses to turn themselves inside out – from thinking of themselves first, to thinking about providing true value to their customers.

Action: Put your customer first

Take this quick test: How self-oriented is your website? Look at your current website or marketing material and try this test. How much of the wording is devoted to promoting the company? How much focuses on your potential clients and customers? How often do you say 'we' compared to how often you say 'you'?

Play by the 80:20 rule of content. As a quick rule of thumb, that's the ratio for useful content to sales pages to aim for. That's 80 per cent customer-centred valuable stuff; 20 per cent information about your business, what and how to buy from you.

So, to make your content valuable, talk more about your customers and their needs than you do about yourself and your business.

2. Help don't sell

The most valuable coin of the business realm will be the ability to collaborate, trust and play together nicely in the sandbox with other human beings.

Charles H Green[3]

The businesses that get success from the content marketing approach act like good citizens. All those things your parents told you when you were growing up – think of others, be helpful, stop being annoying, don't interrupt, be generous, smile, work together, say 'thank you' – are the values and attributes of good content marketers. Good behaviour is good behaviour wherever you are. They were right, damn it.

Yet for some reason, when we're marketing or communicating, particularly on the web, it's easy to overlook this. And it's very easy to get it wrong online. Because the web is so unimaginably large it's easy to forget that we're dealing with real people.

But the online world is not so different from real life. How do you feel when you go to a party and get stuck with the person who keeps talking about themselves, and their marvellous career and their fabulous children? A bit bored, we'd guess. And how do you feel when you meet someone at the party who is interested in you, who asks you questions, and is obviously listening to what you say? You're far less likely to slink off to the kitchen at the earliest opportunity if you're talking to someone who shows a genuine interest.

The purpose of marketing is to build good relationships – to get people to know, like and trust you, and think of you when the time comes to buy. Once you've gained your audience's trust and they grow to see you as a helpful resource, they will *choose* to take the next step in your sales cycle. Build relationships first with valuable content and you earn the right to sell, when the time is right.

With these human values in mind we have a new marketing mantra to guide you and help you strike the right tone with your marketing.

Help don't sell, talk don't yell, show don't tell.

This is the essence of all good marketing today. Let us explain.

Help don't sell: Make this your approach if you want to make an impact online (and off). Remember the web is where we go for answers, and we're all sick and tired of being sold to. If you help, people will like you more, that's the long and short of it.

It takes discipline and focus *not* to 'sell' with your content. But the more you help and the less you try to sell the more you will sell. The better a business understands its customers, and the harder it tries to help *them* with their challenges, the more successful that business becomes.

Talk don't yell: The web is a social place. We try and avoid people who scream self-promotion and never listen, but we all like people who demonstrate empathy and connect with us.

Show don't tell: And there's no point in creating a website that says 'We are great.' Far better, and far more effective, to demonstrate your greatness through your actions. Do great stuff, and be judged by that.

> Harness your resources on behalf of your customers to create something genuinely useful for them. You have to trust that if you get this right, then your business needs will also be met. Certainly, that has been our experience at HSBC Expat.
>
> Richard Fray, Digital Marketing and Social Media Manager, HSBC Expat

Action: Help don't sell

Keep the valuable mantra in mind, whether you are writing content for your blog, your newsletter or even a tweet. Provide value at every contact.

3. Give your ideas away generously, for free

> Think about 'commercial karma' – give your ideas, tips and advice freely and without expectation, it will come back to you in terms of referrals and reputation that will more than pay for itself.
>
> Bryony Thomas, Watertight Marketing

The valuable content marketing approach means producing content that provides independent value to those who receive it, whether or not they choose to buy from you. This means giving away some of your hard-earned knowledge and ideas for free, in the spirit of generosity. Now business and generosity might not seem natural partners, but when it comes to creating content, the more you give, the more you will receive.

You might disagree. Selling goods and services to make a profit is surely at odds with giving valuable stuff away for free. Stealing a march on your competitors is miles apart from working with others towards a joint goal. And besides, generosity is such a fluffy notion. You don't want to be Gordon Gekko, you know greed isn't good, but there are limits.

The notion of reciprocity is rooted in human nature. In her excellent book *Webs of Influence* psychologist Nathali Nahai explains that if someone gives us something we are hard-wired to feel like we want to give something back in return.

> *We have evolved to value reciprocal exchanges at a very deep level. If you want your customers to 'like' you, give them something to like you for.*

From *Webs of Influence* by Nathali Nahai[4]

So it works in business. If you give away useful content that helps a customer to think differently, that customer is more likely to give you their time and attention.

In the course of researching great businesses for this book we see a strong link between success and sharing. Millions of businesses *say* they care about their customers, but it's only the ones that put those words into actions by being genuinely generous and helpful that *show* it. And when you show it, you reap the benefits. More referrals, deeper loyalty, more sales.

> *Give content freely, with generosity. If you're concerned about giving away too much or you're otherwise holding back in any way, worry less and give more.*

Andrea P Howe, Founder, The Get Real Project and co-author,
The Trusted Advisor Fieldbook

Action: Be generous

Three things you can do today:

- Give away something so valuable for your customers it hurts!
- Share some content you wish you'd created, but that was created by somebody else.
- Write a detailed blog post that helps one client who you know is struggling with a tough challenge. Don't just scratch the surface, write it as if you had time to tell them all the things you know would help them.

Human values and successful business – that's not a contradiction. Despite what you see on TV shows like *The Apprentice*, back stabbing, trying to steal a march on your colleagues, shouting loudest and giving everything 110 per cent (at least) isn't the way to get ahead in business. Treat people as you would like to be treated and you will see greater success.

There is of course a time to 'sell' – and that is when the customer is ready to buy. Even then the hard sell, close 'em down approach has had its day (if it ever had a day at all). The best sales people are helpful sellers (see Chapter 14).

4. Always know why

If these rules are starting to feel a bit goody-goody for you, this one is more hard-nosed.

Valuable to your customers and valuable to you – that's the balance you want to strike with your content marketing. So focus on fantastically useful or entertaining content, but make sure it also ties in with your business goals.

Be clear on why you're creating each and every piece of content. What's the purpose you want it to fulfil for the reader, and for your business too?

Action: Know why

The more clearly you can define your business aims upfront, the clearer your content strategy will be. Complete the exercise on getting clear on your goals in Chapter 11. And ask yourself why you're planning each piece of content.

5. Think niche

The better we are at knowing our audience, the better we'll be at writing content they're likely to read and respond to.

Christopher Butler, Newfangled

The businesses that win in the digital age are the ones that absolutely understand their market, their service and their customers.

To succeed you'll need a laser focus on your customers or clients and their specialist needs. The way to get results is to specialize – stick your stake in the ground and target your content efforts at a particular niche.

Customers buy when they find that you are in their bull's eye – i.e. exactly what they are looking for. But the more bland and boring your marketing message, the more you become one of many in the outer rings of the target.

When you have a niche – either by who you serve or by what you do – then you stand out as a specialist.

Paul Simister, Differentiate Your Business[5]

If you truly specialize you'll know more about your customers and area of focus than most firms and you'll have something more relevant, unique and interesting to say. Your expertise becomes so much deeper.

For a larger firm serving many different markets this means creating specialist targeted content for each niche community you serve. HSBC Bank has recognized this. Take a look at their niche site for the expat community: **www.expatexplorer.hsbc.com**

With its specialist websites, social media feeds, blog, guides, videos and tools, HSBC Expat meets the specific needs of expat clients and customers and shows it understands them better than its competitors through the different strands of niche content that it shares.

For a small firm with limited resources the niche question can mean some hard decisions – which market will you choose to serve? If you focus too narrowly will you miss out on opportunities? Seeking general appeal in large markets is seen as the safer option, but you run the risk of trying to be everything to everybody and failing to be remembered. The more precisely you can identify your customers, address their issues and deepen your knowledge the more relevant and valuable your content will be and the more success you will have.

Also having a niche makes your story so much easier to tell, and much easier for people to understand and retell.

Action: Think niche

Answer these questions: Who are your dream clients and customers? Go as niche as you dare. What do they need? What issues and challenges do you solve for each group? When should they pick up the phone to you?

6. Tell a bigger story

Good content marketing is alive. It is your story. It is conscious. It is about emotion.

Robert Rose and Joe Pulizzi, in *Managing Content Marketing*[7]

Good marketing has always been about telling great stories (think *Mad Men* and the age of advertising) and marketing in the digital age is no different: good stories, great ideas – that's what gets spread.

The most successful marketers anchor their content around a strong story. Being able to define your theme will unite your content and galvanize support for your ideas.

Here are a few companies with a clear central message, an idea that spreads – they've got their positioning and their content just right:

- High-end jeans manufacturer Hiut Denim – *do one thing well.*
- IBM – *smarter planet.*
- Surf clothing company Finisterre – *cold water surfing.*
- Software developers Desynit – *good systems change your life.*
- Mouldable glue product Sugru – *for the joy of fix.*

All these companies know what they stand for. Their various forms of content are anchored around a strong idea that connects with their customers and spreads.

Remember: valuable content is meaningful content. Don't just produce content; say something so good the reader forwards it on!

Action: Tell a bigger story

Think about the businesses you really rate. What story do they tell? Start thinking about your own business story. You'll find much more on this in Step 2 of our valuable content strategy framework in Chapter 11.

7. Commit to quality

How do you create content so valuable it can't be ignored? If you really want to win, it has to be high quality. To stand out in a sea of content make yours *'inherently valuable, surprisingly human or unexpectedly useful,'* says Joe Chernov, Talking Content, **theidgroup.co.uk**[8]

Quality over quantity any day. More content is good but not if it's at the expense of quality. Lack of quality will definitely hurt you long term. As Doug

Kessler says: *'The ideal is both. You must make sure your content passes the quality test. But once you do that, you might as well do as much as your resources can afford. Most budgets don't allow for great quality at scale. So I'd choose a few pieces of the very best content you can produce, then promote them hard.'*

Sands Beach Resort ups the quality of its content

Next year my focus is on improving the quality of our content even further. Sometimes that's about slowing down. I now post one beautiful photo a day, choosing the best picture I have. In a world where everyone is publishing, only quality content will stand out. Even better cameras, high-quality video production teams – I can see the benefit in investing in quality next year.

John Beckley, Online Community Manager, Sands Beach Resort

Content excellence relies on inspiration, creativity and also on good design. It's not enough to simply publish a very well-written article. How your content looks is as important as the content itself.

Action: Commit to quality

Design your content carefully. Style it to attract and focus the attention of the time-pressed reader. Make your words easy to read, on a webpage that is effortless to navigate, and a pleasure to look at. Great content needs great design and quality production to help it connect with its audience and make an impact.

How your content looks on the page is as important as the content itself. Take time to properly style your content. Use good-quality photos and illustrations, clear text styling and design elements that compliment the look and feel of your website.

Justin Kerr, Creative Director of Newfangled

8. Write from the heart – and have fun!

Authentic, genuine, sincere – that's what works when it comes to your content. You cannot fake this, although a lot of people try. It's a tricky line to follow; saying that you 'care about your customers' has become so much part of the corporate furniture we don't even notice it, let alone really believe it.

Motives matter. Having the right motivation behind the content you create will make a difference to how it is received. People can tell the difference between lip service and stuff that really means it.

The best marketing strategy ever? Care.

Gary Vaynerchuk, founder of WineLibrary.com[9]

It's also about not being afraid to show your personality. Writing from the heart means being honest, sharing your feelings as well as your ideas. In a web full of homogenized, safe, formulaic content it's the stuff that bursts with real personality that gets noticed. Small business owners can really make their mark here. You don't have to toe the party line; being the best version of yourself is good business.

Action: Write from the heart

If you really don't care about your job or your customers – leave and do something else. Life's too short!

Take action

- Keep your eyes open for content that feels authentic and packed with personality. How has the writer made you feel connected?
- Write down the eight guiding principles for valuable content marketing and stick them on the wall by your desk. These are words you don't want to forget. (You'll find a lovely poster of these on our website.)

PART TWO
WHAT VALUABLE CONTENT?

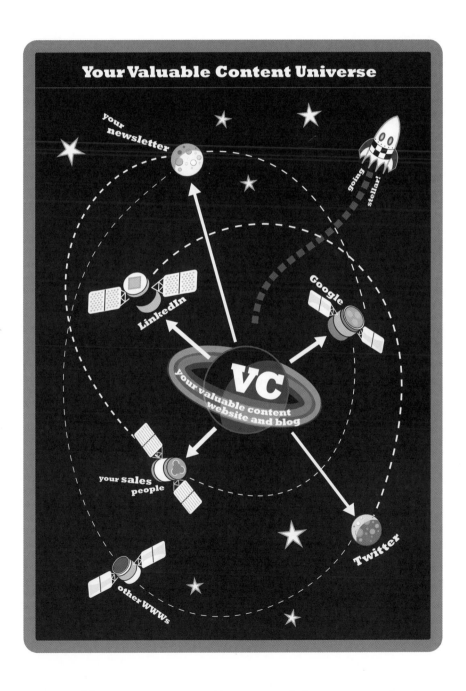

Your valuable content universe

The internet has changed the world. It has levelled the playing field for the small guy. There are many tools to tell the world we are here now. They are very powerful. And very free. But, also, available to everyone else. So we have to learn how to use these tools well. Or die.

David Hieatt, founder of Hiut Denim[1]

With a good website, blog, email newsletter and social media presence you have the basic building blocks in place if you want content marketing to work for you. They're all part of what we call the 'valuable content universe'. The purpose of this chapter is to give you an overview of the main content creation and distribution tools that make up this universe, and some advice on how best to configure them to build a community that supports your business.

Over the past few years these platforms and ways of communicating have become ingrained in the fabric of everyday life, and you are probably familiar with many of them already. Although the tools in this section are commonplace now, it's how you use them, the ideas you share, and the way they all fit together that will make the difference to your content marketing success.

A handy analogy to keep in mind throughout is to think of your website as your home base, your planet earth. It's the centre of your content marketing universe, and it's the place you want to pull people back to – with lots of valuable content you can share to draw them in and build their trust. The other tools we write about in this section – your social media, search engine results pages, PR, events and content placed on other websites – these are your outposts.

A good content marketer knows to engage people with valuable content at the outposts, and to pull them into the website when the time is right. And why do we want them there? Because your website is the only place where you can set out your stall and sell. Selling in the outposts is the main mistake people make with the content marketing tools we're going to outline here. Writing selly blog posts, self-promoting tweets, and self-interested newsletters will fall flat. Be helpful, interested and valuable and people will be happy to keep talking to you. Relationships will develop, and you'll start to build a community around what you do. Building a community will serve your business well. Potential clients in the community will be happy to buy from you, and the word will spread. The number of people who know about you will rise, and you'll create an army of advocates, who will happily refer you and share their networks.

The web might seem a techie and distant entity, but the businesses that do best online treat it as a very human place. Use these tools to engage, connect, entertain, help – be a good citizen here and you'll go far.

If you are new to content marketing read this section and refer to it as you set up each tool. If you are an experienced content marketer you'll find stories of businesses that are really making the most out of these new tools, and some inspiration for new ways of looking at what you do.

CHAPTER 4
BLOGGING

No single thing in the last 15 years has been more important to me professionally than blogging. It's changed my thinking, it's changed my outlook, it's the best damn marketing tool and it's free.

Tom Peters[1]

In this chapter:

- Why blog?
- How to create a successful blog.
- How to write a good blog article.
- How to promote your blog.

If you are committed to creating and sharing valuable content then a blog is an essential part of your toolkit. Your blog will become the hub of your valuable content marketing activity. It is your instant content creation tool; a cost-effective and rewarding way to start creating information that your customers will appreciate.

Writing and sharing articles has always been a powerful way to lay your claim to your territory, to show what you know, demonstrate your authority, and build up a following for your ideas and your business.

> *Blogging isn't an SEO strategy. It isn't just a way of getting a bunch of stuff on your site and links to it to impress Google. The primary purpose of blogging for business is to provide a quick and easy way to build credibility and trust with your potential clients.*
>
> Ian Brodie[2]

Blogs may have been left field once, but now they're part of the establishment. With the surge in video and other visual medium you might think blogging has fallen out of favour, but we disagree. There's a place for blogging, and it's still at the heart of your content marketing efforts. A good blog continues to separate the winners from the also-rans.

The thinking that you do around creating a good blog will help you with all the other stages of your valuable content strategy. The only real cost is your time, and this chapter will show you how to use that time effectively for maximum blogging returns.

Some blogging back to basics

What is a blog?

'Blog' might not be the most elegant of words, and for some people blogging has an unfortunate reputation of being the home of the web's worst excesses of self-indulgent journal-style writing, but we urge you to take blogging seriously. Blogs come in all shapes and sizes but when it comes to your business on the web, blog has become the default term for 'a place to house and publish your thinking'. For the purposes of generating business, what we mean by a valuable content blog is a place where you write about your subject for the benefit of the people you do business with – your personal spin on your area of expertise. A valuable blog is where you regularly share your ideas in a form that is interesting and helpful to your customers.

What's not a blog?

A stream of promotional sales messages isn't a blog. A company news page isn't a blog either. 'We're happy to welcome Jane to the board' isn't really blog material, nor is 'We were thrilled to receive a mention in the local paper.' Yes, it's writing about your business, but a good blog article is helpful, takes a personal view and demonstrates thought. Straight reporting of facts isn't a blog, nor is PR puffery.

Why blog?

Companies with an active blog generate 67 per cent more leads per month.[3]

A blog helps you build relationships, and can stoke up a lovely warm feel-good factor around your business. Continually answering questions, giving your thoughts on the subjects your customers care about builds trust and shows you as expert in what you do. A good blog will get you leads. You'll demonstrate your authority over your subject in a way that makes connections rather than one which puts you on a pedestal.

Seven reasons to blog

1 To spread the word about your business more widely and draw people to your site.

2 To give people a reason to keep returning to your website.

3 To build your reputation and lay claim to your territory.

4 To show your human, approachable side.

5 To help your clients and customers and make their lives easier.

6 To improve your website's search engine ranking.

7 To get even better at what you do.

A company's blog is one of the very first places many people look at when checking out new people and companies. It's a shortcut to getting a gut feel for how a business thinks and feels. A website without a blog implies a business with a lack of ideas and empathy, whereas a well-written blog shows you care. Its benefits reach deeper too. Your blog will generate sign-ups for your email newsletter. And blogs are a big hit with search engines. The more genuinely useful content your business blog contains around the terms your customers are searching for, the higher you'll rank and the more traffic you will get.

The more you blog, the more you increase your reach to customers who stumble upon these blog articles while they're searching for answers to their problems. A blog demonstrates that you're a doer, as well as a thinker. You are working in the areas your customers are interested in, and have hands-on, up-to-date experience. It's an easy way of showing, not telling, what you're up to – you're a busy professional who absolutely knows your stuff.

There are big benefits in honing your writing skills too. Good blog writers have great communication skills, and it's hard to think of an area of life, let alone business life, where that isn't a great skill to have. Whether it's writing headlines for social media, giving a presentation, or talking to a crowd – being able to structure your thinking and make a direct connection with an audience is a useful skill.

When you learn to write a good blog post you can use that to help you write anything.

Henneke Duistermaat

CONTENT STORY   Consultant and trainer Vaughan Merlyn's blog wins new clients

---

Vaughan is a business relationship management consultant and trainer. Blogging is helping to fuel the success of his business. Here's some insight into his blogging strategy:

The content I share varies. It is mostly things I've learned from my consulting – insights into the way the IT and business relationship management world works, sometimes musings on the future; occasionally lessons learned from my hobbies (musician, scuba diver) that can be applied to my area of work. I try to post weekly.

It took time to see tangible results. I hung in there because blogging helped me process what happened to me in my consulting work, and I was getting a strong and growing readership, so I sort of believed that good things would happen/were happening, even if I could not see direct results straight away.

Then I started getting new consulting clients who told me they came to me because of my blog. One in particular made an astounding comment. She said, 'Vaughan, we selected you as a partner not just because your blog demonstrated deep knowledge and a passion for your work, but also for the way you handled reader comments. You responded to every comment, no matter how inane, with grace and humility. You convinced us that you were the kind of consultant we could work with!

Traffic to my blog has built week over week, and now a good percentage of the inquiries and bookings I get for BRM training and consulting mention my blog as the reason they contacted me.

I use Evernote to keep track of ideas for posts (generating ideas is the hardest part!) Then I try to set aside a couple of hours on a weekend to write a post to publish the following Tuesday – which is a good day for readership. Also key is reading blogs – I spend quite a bit of time tracking the blogosphere in the domains I operate in. I learn a lot through that.

Vaughan's tips for other businesses:

- Don't blog because you want to attract business. Blog because you want to engage in a global conversation about topics you are passionate about.

- Be prepared to give a lot of content away – the more you give away, the more the client base is going to pay you to help them apply it.

- Be in it for the long haul.

Lots to learn from Vaughan's fantastic blog – IT Organization Circa 2017 at **vaughanmerlyn.com**

How to create a successful business blog

OK, we've convinced you. You're going to commit to blogging. So what should your blog be like? What are you going to write about?

Great business blogs come in all shapes and varieties – from expert blogs to CEO blogs, and technical blogs to inspirational blogs. Each has a very different style and tone and different objectives to achieve. What writes them all is the passion of the people who write them. The best blogs are not necessarily written by those who know the most, but by people who care deeply about their subject and want to communicate with their audience.

Your level of enthusiasm matters. You'll be writing on the subject consistently, constantly mining it, looking for new angles, listening out for things your customers say that contain kernels of potential blog articles. If you're bored writing it, you can guarantee your audience will be bored reading it. Pick something that genuinely motivates you, and you'll make your blogging journey far more fun and fulfilling.

Seven things to prepare for once you're blogging

1 Not everyone will like what you say, but that's okay.

2 It takes time to build up a following and drive traffic to your website.

3 Blogging means listening as well as writing.

4 Good visuals are important for a blog – even more so than they used to be.

5 You'll hit times when you'll struggle to know what to write. Work through them.

6 Promoting the blog and sharing it via social media is part of the process. Make time for that too.

7 Having a content plan, and a blogging schedule improves your chances of keeping up the pace.

CONTENT STORY   Jim O'Connor: confessions of a blogging convert

Jim O'Connor wasn't keen on blogging originally, but now...

As I began to experiment with creating and sharing valuable content it became apparent that it's not just valuable for the reader – it's also immensely valuable to the company providing it. Not just because it creates traffic and loyal readers who either spread the word or become customers (often it's both). But because it gives that company a way to share its knowledge and experience in a manner that just doesn't work in sales copy. They become a trusted go-to expert in their field and build long-term relationships with people they would otherwise never have been able to reach through traditional media. How valuable is that? It's priceless.

So, I'm a convert. Writing content that has value for people is something I find immensely satisfying – not least because it's attracting a string of new clients who now appreciate just how I can help them. It's easy to be sceptical (I know, I was). But try it for a few months and you'll be amazed at the results.

Twenty blog topics to inspire you:

1 Lists of tips or ideas, like this one. Numbered lists work well.

2 Reviews of books that you recommend.

3 'How to' articles.

4 Your comment on news that's relevant to your clients.

5 'Why?' articles.

6 Articles stating the benefits of your recommended approach.

7 Your response to a question you have been asked by a prospect or client.

8 Articles that state what your clients should avoid like the plague.

9 Add a seasonal twist – refer to a recent celebration or seasonal event.

10 An interview with one of your clients or customers.

11 A critique of someone else's article or opinion, with your view on what works or what does not.

12 Like a journalist, review what you learned from a recent talk, industry conference or event.

13 Ask other experts a question and share their response.

14 A case study on a company you have worked with or who can demonstrate success in your field.

15 Conduct a survey and share the response.

16 A round-up of topical news for your community.

17 Share slides from a recent presentation you have given.

18 Feature guest posts/articles from experts in your field.

19 Information on products or services that will benefit your audience.

20 Share or create a cartoon or graphic that sums up your argument nicely.

Over time you are aiming to build up a body of work that demonstrates a deeply layered understanding of your field and the way you can help navigate clients through it. Varying your blog approach and style adds value and will widen your reach – some people love quick 'how to' guides, others appreciate deeper analysis of key questions – but you have to start with one, so pick the one that sparked the most ideas, and that you feel most comfortable with, and begin.

How to write a valuable blog article

So, your business can benefit from a blog, and you've got some ideas for your first article. Now you need to give yourself some time – say two to three hours for your first article (you will get quicker) – and a bit of peace and quiet (shut the door, turn off distractions).

A simple template for your blog articles

There's no set length for a blog article – anything between 500 and 1,500 words hits the blog zone. If you're not sure how that might break down word count and structure wise, here's a very basic template to help you structure a 700-word blog article:

- 100 words for an introduction setting out the question you are answering.
- 3×100-word paragraphs answering your question.
- 50 words to introduce a list.
- 200 words in list form.
- 50 words conclusion and question.

Here's that template with some more detail.

Headline

The role of the headline is to grab attention and make the reader want to know more. It also needs to summarize the article in a way that leads the reader in. You'll find detailed help on writing good headlines in Chapter 13.

First sentence

You need a hook here. Ask a question; throw up something interesting or unusual. Make the first sentence short. A rambling opening line can switch people straight off.

Next paragraph

Get quickly to the point of your blog. Web readers skim rather than dig deeply, so no long preamble or sideways digressions. You've set out the question; start answering it straight away. Still keep your sentences short.

Main body of the blog

Your paragraphs don't need to be uniformly 100 words long, and there's no perfect number of paragraphs to aim for in this middle section. Blogs are a very flexible format, but as a general rule, short paragraphs are better than long. A blog should feel like a conversation between you and your reader, rather than a lecture. Adding a few questions, and creating plenty of white space helps keep your blog conversational.

Bulleted list

Numbered or bulleted lists are great for blogs:

- they add structure;
- they allow you to pack in lots of valuable content without a lot of extra word padding;
- they feed web readers' hunger for answers now.

How many points on the list? Up to 10 works best. We are all busy. A shorter list reassures readers that this is going to be a quick win read, not *War and Peace*.

Conclusion

Sum up your argument. Writing a blog is a bit like giving a talk – tell people what you're going to say, say it, and then tell them what you've said.

Question

Ask a question that encourages people to get in touch with you. Blogs are unashamedly opinionated, so ask to share other people's views. Remember this is a conversation, and you want the right people to get in touch with you.

Making your blog look good and read well

However persuasive your argument and however pithy your writing, if the article is a struggle to read and a horror to look at people just won't give you the time. Sad, maybe, but it's true. Luckily there are some simple things that you can do to make your blog comfortable for your reader.

Invest in some design love. There are lots of fantastic free blogging templates out there, but customizing one to fit your brand will be well worth it. A good designer can make your blog look more professional and welcoming, and should be able to give you some helpful advice on the kind of images that will work well for your blog.

Easy to read

If you've followed the writing template above you'll have created some text that's already fairly well broken up. Make it even easier to read by adding some meaningful subheadings.

Subheadings

Subheads act like bannisters, leading your readers down some steep stairs. As readers we scan pages rather than reading straight from start to finish. They'll tell people at a glance what they'll learn from your blog, so well-written subheadings can act as secondary headlines, pulling people in and keeping them reading. Subheadings are important from an SEO perspective too, reinforcing your keywords and helping your blog get indexed and found.

Other formatting tips

Paying attention to typography will vastly improve the look and readability of your articles. Consider the text size (not too small), line length (not too long), line spacing and font – they all determine how the body text looks. This may sound trivial and unimportant but we can assure you it's not if you want your blogs to be read to the end.

We rate Butterick's rules on typography. Here is a summary:

- Text size. Don't make it too small – especially if your readers are over 40! That means 10–12pt in printed documents, 15–25 pixels on the web.
- Line spacing should be 120–145 per cent of the point size.
- The average line length should be 45–90 characters (including spaces).
- Put one space between sentences.

- Text colour. It's much easier to read black on white, than white on black. (And grey is very hard to read.)

- Don't justify the text.

- Choose heading, subheading, and quote formats that you're happy with and use them consistently in every blog you write.

- Choose a professional looking font.

You can check out the full list of rules at **practicaltypography.com**.

If you buy an off-the-shelf blogging theme then the formatting style will probably be pre-set. If not, make sure your designer pays close attention to this when setting up your blog (any good designer will know to do this but it's worth checking).

Image

Find a picture to illustrate your point: professional or quirky, stylish or funny, whatever fits your brand. You want readers to stick around, and a well-designed page with a strong visual appeal is more likely to keep them than a wall of unbroken text. Stock photo sites on the web are a source of reasonably priced images, although you'll find yourself wading through a lot of dated visual cliches in your search for something that fits. (Fingers pointing at whiteboards, goldfish and jigsaw puzzle pieces are a few of the worst offenders.) Create some rules for yourself about the kinds of images that will work well and stick to them. Be consistent when using images in blogs, keeping them the same size, for example, or in a similar style.

Quick checklist for your blog articles

- Will my target readers find this subject interesting and useful?

- Is the post in line with our field of expertise/what we want to be known for?

- Does the headline have impact?

- Does it include keywords people would search for to find us?

- Does it have a clear beginning, middle and end?

- Have I stripped out any jargon?

- Have I broken up the text with useful subheadings and bulleted lists?

- Have I asked a question at the end?

You'll find a full blog template and structure to follow in the Resources section at the back of the book.

And that's it! You've done the hard bit. You'll find more on writing in Chapter 13. Now it's on to getting your blog found, loved and shared.

Promoting your blog articles

Okay, I'm there. Now what? How do I get people to read my blog?

The key purpose of your blog is to pull people back to your website and get them to sign up to your email list, so you can continue the conversation. You want your blog to inspire trust in you, and give you the permission to start useful conversations with potential clients and referrers. For that to happen, people need to know that you and your blog are really there, and that you will respond.

We write about how to get your content read in Chapter 15. But for now, let's look at some of the elements you can incorporate into your blog to help you get it read, and shared.

Share button

Make your 'share this article' buttons unmissable. Strike while the iron is hot, and make sharing on social networks super easy.

Encouraging sign-up

Adding a call to action to subscribe to your email list (along the lines of 'Liked this? Sign up for more') at the end of the blog is a good way of getting your blog quickly and efficiently to interested parties. If people like what they read, they might like to join your email list so that the next blog you write gets delivered straight to their inbox.

Read more like this

Guide the reader towards other blogs you've written on similar themes. Highlighting other relevant articles will pull them deeper into your website, showing them other ways that you can help.

For example, if they'd found you via '10 things you need to know about e-commerce' they might well be interested in 'E-commerce platforms compared', or 'E-commerce case studies' or 'E-commerce snarl-ups and how to avoid them'. By offering your readers more layers of help, you're demonstrating an easy control over your subject matter, and a generosity that will make them well disposed towards you. Embed the links to the other articles through the relevant catchy headlines, so that more help is just a click away.

Promoting your blog via social networks

Blogs are perfect material for sharing on social networks. In fact it's hard to take part on social networks without a blog – it's like turning up to a networking events with absolutely nothing to say.

Currently Twitter, LinkedIn, Google+ and Facebook are the key places where you can post links to your blog. We promote our blogs to all four places like this on the day of posting.

- once to our Facebook page;
- twice to LinkedIn and Google+ (on each of our personal profiles); and
- 10 or more times on Twitter (that's a mix of our own personal feeds and the Valuable Content feed).

Valuable Tip

A time-saving tip is to write a batch of different promotional headlines as soon as you've finished writing the blog – while the ideas are still fresh in your mind. You can then use Tweetdeck to schedule the tweets to go out at different times of the day.

When to promote your blog

It's good to consider where people are and what they'll being doing. So on a wide scale – where in the world are they? And on a small scale – is this a good time? (For example, people often check social media feeds when they're commuting so 5.30 pm is a good time to tweet in the United Kingdom.)

Comments

When people comment on your blog, respond! Build engagement through your blog, and it's more likely to get shared. And it goes without saying, you should respond generously, thanking people for taking the time to comment in a brief reply. If you have lots to say, you can always continue the conversation with the reader via email.

(Clearly, you don't have to respond nicely to the spammers, or the obvious loons – and good spam catcher software will block most of these anyway. It's your blog, do moderate it and feel free to delete comments that are way off the professional mark.)

Blog content can be visual

If you've read this chapter and thought 'I'll never be able to do this', don't despair. You can still enjoy many of the benefits of writing a blog without clocking up a huge word count.

Remember that a blog is really just a place for sharing information. That information can be text, but it could just as easily be visual or audio. Visual content in particular is hugely sharable. Whether that's photographs, infographics, illustration, SlideShares – a picture can sometimes save you writing a thousand words. Embedding podcasts or videos into a blog is an excellent idea (you'll find more detail on these in Chapters 8 and 9).

Photographs are valuable visual content. They portray a message and story instantly.

Amanda Thomas, photographer

And even if you are looking forward to getting stuck into the writing, don't overlook other forms of content. Mix up the formats and you'll keep your readership interested, and increase your chances of your blog spreading further.

CONTENT STORY The sky's the limit for designer Iain Claridge's visual blog

Freelance web designer Iain Claridge's visual blog has won him work all over the world, and even landed a design project for NASA.

As a designer, with limited skills or experience in writing engaging copy, it's no surprise really that the vast majority of my blog posts are visual rather than pithy words of wisdom. But I would hope that my digital scrapbook of ocular delights is more than simply eye candy and can serve as an example of how as a designer you can build an audience and even gain work through being a curator of engaging content.

I started my blog as a means of organizing material that I found inspirational to my work as a creative working on web projects. Web design is a curious mix of disciplines that can draw inspiration from many aspects of design including product design and architecture as well as print. Most of my blog posts reflect my approach to design and form a rich seam of material upon which to draw while seeking inspiration in my work as a digital creative.

My blog started out purely as a personal repository but soon became a destination for many who share my aesthetic, seeking inspiration for their own projects, and has helped to start several working relationships with likeminded individuals. It has actually been more effective than my online portfolio in attracting the type of people and organizations I really like to work with.

A blog is a great way of communicating to potential clients your depth of understanding of your field, how you tick as a person, and transmitting both your personal and professional manifesto in a non-sales-pitchy way.

Have a look at Iain's stunning design blog at **www.iainclaridge.co.uk/blog**

Blogging Q&A

Q: Who should blog in our business?

A: If you're a lone ranger that's an easy question to answer – *you* should blog! If you're working in a larger business then ideally you'd have a range of people sharing the writing reins.

Subject matter experts, especially those on the coalface of customer interaction, make great bloggers. They know the questions people are asking, and know what help or advice hits the mark. (So, if you're working for a law firm, the lawyers should blog. If you're a part of a tech firm there might be an admin person who's on the frontline answering customers' queries who would have great insights, as well as technical experts.) And if the CEO gets blogging then your content marketing efforts have a much greater chance of success. CEOs who get this stuff are able to inspire staff and give the support that teams need to keep up the blogging momentum. The size of their network will really help to spread the word wider too.

Q: How often do I have to blog?

A: Just one blog a month will bring you benefit. Two a month is an ideal start for better results. Up the frequency as your confidence grows. One blog a week will make a huge difference to your business.

Blogs need content, but you don't have to break your back creating it. In most niches, updating a blog with 1–3 highly valuable content pieces each month is enough.

Derek Halpern[4]

When you're truly up and running, Lauren McGaha of Newfangled suggests you should aim to add 3,000 unique and indexable words to your website each month.

The reason that we recommend 3,000 words is that Google has a number of factors that fit into the SEO algorithm that they're using to rank sites on search engine results pages. One of the things that they're really looking for is frequency of new content posted to your site. If Google comes and crawls the site and realizes when they come back to crawl it again that there's been new content posted, that's a clue. That's a cue to Google that they need to come back. They need to be coming back and frequently crawling the site to index any new content that you post.[4]

Q: What do I write about?

A: People use the web to search for information, to research problems, or to be entertained, so you need to fit your blogs into one of those categories. Your best bet is to write articles that give the information people are looking for and provide the answers to their problems (see Chapter 11).

Q: I don't think I have anything to say.

A: This is a common fear. Look again at the list of 20 suggested topics. Write down the single most common question people ask you about your product or service. Then write down the answer you give them in 10 sentences. Voila – you have just created the draft of your first blog!

Q: But I really hate writing – do I have to do it?

A: Read our writing tips in Chapter 13, use our blogging template and give it a go. It's a skill, like anything else, and you will quickly get better with practice. Think of your blog as a friendly conversation with a potential customer, rather than a tough sales presentation in front of hundreds, and the words should flow more easily.

Q: Is there no other way? What about ghostwriters?

A: Of course, an alternative to blogging would be to find a freelance writer to help you. Find someone whose writing style you like, and who understands your industry. If you find talking much easier than writing, ask the writer to interview you and shape your words into a blog article that reads with your voice, but it's your ideas that should shine through. It's your business.

Q: I'm way too busy, what can I do?

A: If you have a high level of expertise, and you want to build your business, then blogging is a very effective use of your time. Make time, and the effort will be repaid. No business can ignore online marketing, and your blog is the best way of showing potential clients what you can do.

Work it into your week – create a system and a time that works for you – see CEO Richard Edelman's 6am Blog (**www.edelman.com/ conversations/6-a-m**) for example. Richard, like many executive bloggers, fits it in by writing outside the 9–5 working day.

Consider getting freelance help from a writer. If dictating some blog ideas, and answers to customer questions, will fit more easily into your day, then start your blogging route with some external support.

Share out the responsibility with the team. Make a plan and lighten the load.

Q: Can blogging damage my business?

A: Not if you do it well. It will build your business. Blogging is only damaging if you are:

- Inconsistent – saying one thing in one article and contradicting it in others.

- Lacking a clear direction – if your blogs are rambling, people won't be convinced of your authority.

- Jargon-filled/confusing – if people can't understand what you're saying, you won't feel like the right person to help them.

- Continually selling in your blog articles – this is not the place for overt sales messages.

- Slow to update your blog. If last Christmas's blog is still up at Easter it looks like you've gone out of business.

Take action

- Find three good blog posts. Print them out, then look at the way they're constructed – circle the headline, opener, main body, conclusion, and call to action.

- If you're new to the blogging game, comment first on a few blog posts you like. This will help get you comfortable with publishing your ideas. You can post one on the Valuable Content blog if you like – go on, try it – we promise to respond!

- Write the blog post you choose from our list, using the template in the resources section.

- Show the blog to a colleague for feedback – getting used to sharing your words is part of becoming a good blogger.

CHAPTER 5
SOCIAL MEDIA

Social media didn't create content marketing, but it's an unsurpassed tool for getting it distributed.
Sonia Simone[1]

In this chapter:

- Social networks – the main arenas for businesses.
- Tips on using the big platforms: Twitter, Facebook, YouTube, LinkedIn, Google+, Instagram, SlideShare, Pinterest.
- Which platform is best for sharing content?
- How do you choose the right channel for your business?
- Valuable content guidelines for all social networks.

Great content doesn't spread itself. Without help it can sit on your website or blog, untroubled by visitors, and not reach the desks and minds of the people it was written to engage. Something is needed to get your ideas from A to B, and a big one of those somethings is social media.

Valuable content creates a ripple effect on social media, spreading your ideas across your network and around the world. But just joining social networks won't automatically start the ripple effect. Having a Twitter account won't get your blogs read, or your sales registers pinging. You need to do and say the right things consistently over time in the right places if social media is going to help you build your business.

How you *behave* on social media is enormously important. Platforms come and go, but many of the same rules apply to all of the ones you're likely to want to use for your business – now and in the future. In a nutshell, you need to be as human and helpful on social media as you are in every other area of your business. There are tweaks in tone, and nuances to negotiate, but if you stay rooted to human and helpful you won't go far wrong.

> Social media allows us to get as close to our clients as our grandfathers and great grandfathers did with their businesses: first name terms; knowing their likes and dislikes and demonstrably showing we care. Social media makes caring more scalable.

Paul Hajek, founder of Clutton Cox Solicitors

Social media and content are inextricably linked. You cannot succeed with one without the other. This chapter will explain how to make social media part of your valuable content approach. It will give you the lowdown on the various social networking options open to you, and the best ways to navigate them for your business. But first, here's a snapshot of a business that's thriving because of the way it uses social media.

CONTENT STORY   Winning with social media – Sands Beach Resort

Sands Beach Resort realized early on that social media is a powerful business tool. While some other businesses have been slow on the uptake, avoiding Twitter etc because they believe it's too trivial, *just people sharing what they ate for lunch*, Sands Beach have grasped it with both hands. Digital marketing manager John Beckley believes that social media is just like having a telephone on every desk. It's the way people like to communicate these days. It makes sense to be there.

> A couple of years ago we knew the theory and we did a lot of experimenting. Now we're fully committed. This IS our marketing. Advertising, exhibitions etc. have all taken a back seat. It's really driving business for the resort. Our digital footprint has grown phenomenally in the last couple of years. Our back catalogue of content from 2012 is still driving business today.

> Our day-to-day actions all revolve around social – taking photos of what's going on in the resort, working with groups who come to visit, particularly on the Active side producing video. The tools of my trade are still my iPhone and Nilox camera. And now there are more people involved. We even have our lifeguard taking photos and video with our guests.

We prioritize video so our YouTube channel is big for us. When we select our interns we look for experience and knowledge in video production. It's a key marketing skill these days. Blogging will always be important. We cover all our events, take photos, video and write up reports. The Lanzarote Marathon was huge for us and we covered it widely. Flickr remains a vital channel. We have over 9,000 photos and over 1.5 million views. It's a massive community but it takes work.

It's more than a full-time job. We have an intern programme – they get great experience and help us to research, share stories, follow up.

Our CEO is right behind the approach. He understands the urgency, the real-time nature of the content we must share. He has a strong presence on social media himself and pushes us to publish quality content, fast.

For us it's all about engagement. The days of obsessing over numbers of followers are over. We're working out ways to measure engagement across all channels and we use these reports to learn how to do it even better.

Real time is a challenge. We're still working 9-5 but social media and the web are always on. We need to work out a way to respond live. Our customers increasingly expect it in the online world.

The biggest challenge and opportunity is motivating people to come along with us on this journey. Our partners, our staff, everyone. There are 20 people in our management team. They're all on LinkedIn now and getting involved in Twitter too. We're talking change here and change is scary for people. Time is always a factor so you've got to really inspire people so they find the time.

Social media is not a separate entity – it's just an extension of who we are.

The picture John paints of using multiple channels, getting whole company involvement, teaching people best practice, pulling in the wider community, devoting 24/7 attention and complete commitment to the social media cause is a textbook example of how to get results.

John has experimented and tested the various channels, so he knows how to use each one to connect with his different audiences.

Why your business needs a presence on social media

Many readers of this book will already be social media converts but if you're still struggling to understand why on earth fiddling around on Twitter has any relevance to hard business, here's a quick overview:

- People like to do business with people – social media is a place to show who you are, behind the corporate façade.
- It's the way many people communicate now – join the conversation and make your voice known.
- It'll help your ideas and content to spread – from social media to your website to a sale.

Finding the best arena for your business is going to be key to your success too, so here's some information on each of them to help you plan your own social media empire.

Social networks: the main arenas for businesses

Social networking sites such as Twitter and LinkedIn enable busy professionals to manage large networks of contacts – many times larger than is possible face-to-face. They generate consistent opportunities for those prepared to invest time in them.

Heather Townsend[2]

We are conscious that the social media landscape changes fast. Things have changed since we wrote the first edition of this book in 2012; the tools and platforms are ever-evolving. The tools we mention today in 2015 will date, but one thing we're confident of is that embracing social media is crucial to the success of marketing your business with valuable content.

At the time of writing there are four main social networking platforms for the business owner – Twitter, Facebook, LinkedIn and Google+. YouTube, Pinterest and Instagram have very strong followings too, and offer different ways to connect. Here's a brief rundown of these platforms.

Twitter

Twitter is a serious business tool. It builds important relationships and will help you market your business. It's an unrivalled platform for sharing your valuable content, building relationships and engaging with potential clients. Because tweets are limited to 140 characters, there's no room for waffle. Add links from your Tweets back to your blogs, and you will generate more traffic to your site. It's possible to build really powerful connections on Twitter, fantastic both as a way of attracting people to your content, and expanding your network and motivating referrals.

> *Before we started our company we were worried we might have to cold call to get business. We weren't looking forward to this I can tell you! Then we noticed that many of our potential customers were on Twitter. What has really surprised us is that just by connecting with them on Twitter and swapping ideas and useful articles was enough to pique their interest. The 'Twitter handshake' is amazingly powerful – you get a totally different response to a cold email or call. You can really build relationships via Twitter and for us those relationships have led to profitable projects.*
>
> Jay Bigford, **www.thisisyoke.com** @thisisyoke

Should your business be on Twitter?

Yes, probably. Any business in any sector will benefit from being on Twitter.

If you're in a business where personal rapport with clients is key, then Twitter is a particularly useful tool. Sharon interviewed a law firm's clients for a new website project and the interviewee told her that she had been very nervous about approaching a lawyer, so had followed the ones who had been recommended to her on Twitter to see what they were like. One Saturday evening, she read a tweet from one of them, who was watching Doctor Who with her family. That was what the interviewee was doing too, and that instantly made her seem more approachable. So that's the lawyer she chose.

Facebook

With 1.44 billion users worldwide in 2015 (it was 800 million when we wrote the first edition), Facebook has become the world's biggest meeting place and social networking site. You'll find big brands there, as well as pages for businesses. Facebook works by sharing your content with your friends, who in turn share it with theirs and so it spreads. 'Like' something on Facebook, and potentially it will be seen by thousands. Your customers and clients probably have personal accounts; setting up a page is free, and very easy.

What kind of content works on Facebook?

People don't really go onto Facebook to learn, but to be entertained, to keep up with people they like, to connect and socialize. This is your most human of human faces – it's not your professional face (LinkedIn), and it's not the same as Twitter. Because it's geared towards entertainment, you need to share things that are funny, beautiful, or inspiring.

Should your business be on Facebook?

Possibly. If you're a B2C company then being on Facebook is an easy decision. Why wouldn't you want to connect with potential customers and build a Facebook fan base? B2B companies need to find different things to share, but having a clear story about why you're in business should give you plenty of scope and an idea of where to start. Both B2B and B2C types can make themselves at home on Facebook. But it's not right for everyone.

Copyblogger left Facebook in October 2014, saying that the Copyblogger community just didn't engage there. Copyblogger's founder Brian Clark commented:

> It's not our job to tell our audience where we live. It's to grow communities where they live. That's the real message here, folks. It's not that 'Facebook sucks for marketing.' That's just patently untrue. There are loads of brands who do quite well with Facebook. The real message is never be so married to any platform that doesn't perform for you that you can't bring yourself to a quick divorce.[3]

We think that's fair. Getting the most out of social media is a matter of finding the places that help you interact best with your community. Test the various platforms. Give them a proper go. (That means at least six to twelve months of effort, not three weeks of tinkering.) If one platform just isn't performing – eg if you're getting very few comments on posts and not much sharing or conversation – then ditch it and focus your efforts in the places that are working for you.

Facebook quiz

Should your business be on Facebook? Take the quick quiz below to find out.

TABLE 5.1   Should your business be on Facebook?

Your Business	Yes/No
Are you in the travel, food, hospitality or leisure industry?	
Do you have lots of good pictures and video content to share?	
Does your business interest people beyond their working lives?	
Does your business inspire people?	
When you talk about your business at dinner parties do people's faces light up?	
Is your business a source of great anecdotes?	
Do you help your clients achieve personal ambitions, not just work goals?	
Does your business create loyal fans who love to share what you do?	

If the answers are mostly no, then you might want to divert most of your social networking energies elsewhere.

LinkedIn

The professional networking site LinkedIn is a much more serious place than Facebook, with a bit more space to say more than on Twitter. It's a business networking tool, and it doesn't mix business with much frivolity. That's not to say you should be boring here (don't be boring anywhere) but you wouldn't share photos of your weekend walk in the Lake District on LinkedIn, whereas you might well on Facebook or Google+.

On LinkedIn you can share your valuable content with your network in the status updates, via groups and the more recent LinkedIn Publisher. Commenting on other people's discussions, and starting your own threads is great for raising your profile, although the valuable 'help, don't sell' mantra still holds. With over 313 million users worldwide at the time of writing (up from a 100 million in 2012) and highly ranked by Google, LinkedIn will help you get found, make and maintain connections, build relationships and keep you front of mind.

Five important elements from a content perspective:

- Personal profiles – valuable for referrals.
- Status updates – to start conversations and distribute your valuable content.
- Publisher – allows you to write and share articles.
- Company pages – useful for building the credibility of your company.
- LinkedIn groups – worthwhile forums for connecting with others in your field.

Should you be on LinkedIn?

Yes! Every business professional should have a personal profile at the very least.

Eight ways to write a better LinkedIn profile

1 Make it clear about the kind of projects you're looking for. There's no harm in being upfront, and it makes it easier for potential clients to find you. Using the keywords your clients will be searching for gives you more chance of being found.

2 Tailor your experience to fit the kind of work you want to be doing. LinkedIn works best when you treat it as more than an online CV, so pull out the details that are relevant to projects you'd like to have and add them to strengthen your case. But...

3 Be succinct. Think in headlines rather than essays.

4 Think about clients' needs first. A section on 'How I can help' makes your profile stand out.

5 Keep it up to date. LinkedIn profiles are easy to edit.

6 Share your mission – although this is the most conservative of the main social media channels a bit of business passion goes a long way

7 Include links to your valuable content – SlideShares, publications, etc.

8 Get recommended.

LinkedIn FAQs

What kind of content works best on Linkedin?

If you've invested in some deeper content – white papers, industry guides or SlideShares for example – then LinkedIn would be an excellent place to promote them. Join LinkedIn groups that share your interests, and you may well find an eager audience for your deeper content.

How often do I need to update LinkedIn?

A couple of times a week is enough. There are some really valuable discussions happening all over LinkedIn, so make time to keep up and join in.

Should I join LinkedIn groups?

Quite possibly, but it depends on your customers. LinkedIn groups are extremely useful if you're in the professional services or B2B line. They build new connections and engage and if you share the right content in the right groups, can lead to new business.

You can start your own group in your space, and host the conversation too.

Join the LinkedIn groups most relevant to your line of business and share your ideas and content. We're sure you know this, but this doesn't mean name-dropping your blog at every opportunity. Remember the valuable social media rules – be valuable, not self-promoting. Leave a comment if you think it will add value to the group. A sales message in a group discussion will hit all the wrong notes. This is not the place to sell.

Google+

Launched in 2011, this platform was just finding its feet in the United Kingdom at the time of writing the first edition, but it's become one of the main arenas for content sharing over the last couple of years. It doesn't rival Facebook in terms of numbers, but if you're looking for a place to distribute your content and have interesting conversations then it makes sense to have a presence here too.

Posting directly onto Google+ lets you make the most of Google's enhanced search function. Google rates its own content highly. Social sharing is starting to dominate search engine rankings – Google will deliver search results based on what people are saying and recommending to each other, over and above simple keyword searches. Engaging with Google, still the number one search engine, makes sense.

Google+ gives room for longer form content than Twitter – you have space to present and share more information in a variety of formats. We like the way it allows you to choose who you share information with, and it's very intuitive to use – easy to update, easy to upload pictures and videos. The fact it's ad free is very appealing too.

Should you be on Google+?

Yes, especially if you're a B2B business.

YouTube

This is the world's biggest video sharing site and it's growing all the time. YouTube's Head of Content and Business Partnerships, Robert Kyncl, predicts that soon 90 per cent of all internet traffic is going to be video, with YouTube being far and away the biggest channel.

Setting up your own YouTube channel is an easy way to share your business video content with the world. YouTube is not just a video content streaming site. It's also a social networking site, because of the way it allows you to connect with others and create a community. Set up a YouTube account and you can comment, rate, favourite and share videos that are relevant, interesting and helpful to your type of customers. All of this helps to send traffic back to your website. You don't even need to load up your own videos to do this, although evidently it will bolster your authority if you do. There are a lot of ways to use the platform to inform people, get them to participate, and grow awareness of your organization.

Seven ways to get the best out of YouTube

1 **Make your channel look like home.** Add your branding, customize the colours to complement your company's look, and add relevant information and links.

2 **Add subtitles.** Auto captioning is available to all YouTube users. You'll need to edit for accuracy as the process uses voice recognition. Adding captions makes your content more accessible.

3 **Don't be a loner.** YouTube is a social platform, so be sure to check out other content on the site, favourite appropriate videos and make suitable YouTube 'friends'.

4 **Make it easy for people to find what they're looking for.** Organize your content to be viewer-friendly rather than just offering a linear stream of video uploads. Create playlists to group relevant videos together, or lump older content into time-related (October 2014, Summer 2015 etc) folders.

5 **Don't overlook tags.** Take the time to add the correct tags to your videos, and think laterally.

6 **Be a promoter.** Don't assume viewers will come to you, or automatically think to look you up on YouTube. Every time you post a video that's relevant for general sharing, blog about it, tweet it or add it to your Facebook page.

7 **Use YouTube's free analytics tools.** YouTube offers every user free analytics data via the 'Insight' button on every uploaded video. This free-to-view info should not be overlooked as it can offer you some valuable info on not only views stats, but demographics, community, and the most useful – 'discovery' data – info on how users came across the video, including the popular links they followed to get there. The tools are there – be sure to use them.

You'll find more on creating and sharing video in Chapter 10.

Should your business have a YouTube channel?

If you're not here already, you should be heading that way. Even if you don't have your own videos to share yet, sharing other people's content is a fine place to start.

Pinterest

Pinterest has made big strides in popularity since we wrote the first edition. The latest figures show 70 million users worldwide, 80 per cent of whom are women. Pinterest's online bulletin board format makes it really popular for businesses that have visual content to share: retailers, travel companies, fashion businesses, anything to do with food and drink, home and gardening, photographers, wedding planners.

Should you be on Pinterest?

Yes if you're a visual business or in the categories mentioned above. Not essential for professional services firms, tech companies etc. (Unless you love it, in which case, dive in.)

SlideShare

SlideShare is the world's largest community for sharing presentations. With 60 million monthly visitors and 130 million page views, it is the 200th most visited website in the world. Besides presentations, SlideShare also supports documents, PDFs, videos and webinars. Excellent for sharing your content, getting inspiration for new ways of looking at your material, and for helping your content find a wider audience. (See page 121 for more on SlideShare.)

Should you be using SlideShare?

It's certainly worth a look. Growing in popularity and influence, it is excellent for thought leadership-type content.

Instagram

Instagram is a smartphone app that lets users add different filters to their own photographs, and share the images with the online community. Jamie Oliver (beautiful food photography, lots of engagement) and Red Bull (sharing photos of events worldwide with 2.2 million followers) were early adopters of Instagram along with many small businesses around the world. Brilliant for visual businesses – designers, illustrators, photographers, artists, holiday companies, architects – its potential is impressive for many other sectors too.

> *The power of Instagram for Sands Beach has really surprised me. We have separate Instagram feeds for the families and one for our sports visitors too – with over 5,000 clicks on the Active feed last month. It started as a hobby for me really – I love taking photos – but it's become so much more. Twitter still performs well but Instagram has been outstanding.*
>
> John Beckley, Digital Marketing Manager, Sands Beach Resort, Lanzarote

At the moment Instagram feels very authentic and spontaneous. People are sharing because they can't stop themselves. There's a joy and sincerity to Instagram you may not feel on any of the other social platforms, but while we both have personal accounts we don't use it directly as valuable content. Maybe that will change. At the moment we're huge fans of it, even choosing holiday destinations on the basis of Instagram pictures shared by people in our online networks. (If we had a holiday company we would be focusing a lot of our attention here!)

Instagram was acquired by Facebook in 2012. The jury's out on whether the introduction of sponsored advertising will dent its popularity.

Should you be on Instagram?

Yes, if your business makes beautiful things, or takes people to beautiful or interesting places.

Which social platform is best for sharing content?

The Content Marketing Institute's 2014 B2B Content Marketing report gives a helpful snapshot of the percentage of marketers using each platform to distribute content, and it's interesting to compare the way the figures have changed from two years ago. Twitter is still top, but all channels are being used more. The biggest leap is in the use of Google+, Instagram and Pinterest.

The percentage of UK marketers who use various social media platforms to distribute content is as follows:

- Twitter 89% (74%).
- LinkedIn 85% (71%).
- Facebook 75% (70%).
- YouTube 65% (60%).
- SlideShare 33% (20%).
- Google 55% (13%).
- Pinterest 42%.
- Instagram 20%.

Figures in brackets show the 2012 figure where available.[4]

Twitter, LinkedIn and Facebook are responsible for the most sharing. Which you choose to focus on depends on what type of business you are in and what is right for your customers.

Looking at our analytics, Twitter works best. For us it's an unsurpassed tool for spreading valuable content around the web. Through Twitter we have connected with some fantastic people and won new work. It has genuinely helped us to build our business. So Twitter's best for our business, but it's Instagram that we enjoy most. It will be different for you. You need to find your mix.

How do you decide where to be? It's important not to make assumptions. One large organization we worked with previously devoted a lot of time to Twitter, convinced that this was where their young audience hung out, only to find with some research that they weren't engaging there at all.

So go where your customers are but also choose what you love – where it feels natural to you.

That's the strategy that's working for Fforest Camp in Wales. Campsite owner Sian Tucker shares beautiful pictures on Instagram (See instagram.com/coldatnight). But she didn't choose Instagram to promote the campsite. She says: *'I take pictures and share them because I can't not.'* Her enthusiasm and love of the medium shines through, and makes her one of our all-time favourite Instagrammers (check her pictures out @coldatnight). Her pictures of the Welsh landscape are stunning. The steely greys and blues of the Ceredigion coastline are like little drops of calm meditation in our too-frantic days. You can smell the sea air and hear the waves. You can't see her images and not want to be there. So it's love that inspires the images, but sharing them online via Instagram drives business her way. With a tribe of over 3,400 followers, the pictures inspire people to visit Fforest, to buy the beautiful products they sell, and to spread the word on the camp's behalf.

Like Sian, you might fall in love with one channel over the others, but it's good to have a mix and cross-fertilize your content sharing. (Post Instagram pictures on Twitter, share YouTube videos on Google +, start conversations around your latest SlideShare presentation on LinkedIn.) Here's how the mix works for an ambitious start-up.

CONTENT STORY   How Wriggle has got its social media marketing mix right

Wriggle is a mobile app that offers immediate dining and event discounts at independent eateries around Bristol and London. Daniel Waller explains how social media has helped them launch and develop.

Wriggle wouldn't be here now without social media. As a startup, it would be out of the question to invest a large sum of money for a marketing campaign to even get close to the number of people who have downloaded our app.

Twitter has been the best platform for us and it's certainly helped us get thousands of downloads. Pinterest and Instagram have also been extremely useful.

Our mission is 'Love local'. There's more to life than high street chains, so we try to promote local and independent places that we think are interesting and unique. We don't use Twitter to tout our offers – we want to show we've got a voice in the city and show people that we care about the places we're promoting on the app. We want to show people what's on and be taste-leaders.

Our social channels don't just promote Wriggle places – since we want to create additional value with our feeds by making them engaging and insightful. On Twitter we tweet about three of our own offers a day, and 18 or so tweets that share different things. These can be anything from coffee shops or bars we're visiting, to promoting food bloggers that we like, or other content we know our audience will enjoy – music or exhibitions for instance.

You can have great conversations on Twitter and it's much easier to have a human presence than Facebook. We find we can speak directly to people which is a brilliant way of hitting the people in Bristol and London who really appreciate the places we work with and the causes we support.

For us, Facebook has never really been the best tool to communicate. We tried to use it various ways but found it didn't achieve the best results, especially in terms of social reach. We still drive high-quality posts through Facebook such as articles and blogs we write, but these receive greater engagement on Twitter. Often we use Facebook for paid advertising because it's great for targeting people for specific Wriggle deals.

Pinterest is a great way for Wriggle to engage with a visual audience. We connect with people who have a love of food and drink as well as individuals from Bristol by creating folders and repinning images from different boards. Lately we've been finding Instagram an incredibly positive experience, utilizing hashtags such as #fireworks150 or #igersbristol to interact specifically with likeminded individuals and trending events.

There's been an element of trial and error across our social media. Finding a tone of voice that works for Wriggle took a few months. Now the whole team can talk 'Wriggle' so when we tweet it sounds authentic, especially from the much newer London Twitter account. You have to work at that, try things out, experiment. The tone evolves, but it has to be practised and polished. Soon, this becomes very natural.

The key thing to remember on Twitter, or on any other social network, is to be human. People don't want to feel like they're just communicating with a business – they want a unique, interactive and engaging social experience. Be a good person and you won't go far wrong.

Valuable content guidelines for all social networks

The key in social media is to share things of value.

Charles H Green[5]

There are many different social media options and there will be others to come, but if you want to get the best results across any social media platform there are some enduring rules to apply.

Guidelines for valuable social networking, whichever platform you select:

1 **Be there.** Join the conversation – be sociable, communicate – show up regularly.

2 **Be valuable.** Be helpful, entertaining, educate your clients – become a valuable source of information for others.

3 **Be generous.** Be generous in the content you share and generous to others too. Share other people's content. If it is valuable to your kind of customers then help them find it. Become known as someone who offers things up to others, and people will come to you.

4 **Be interesting.** Mix it up – all sorts of different types of content. Have something to say.

5 **Be on message.** Talk around your area of expertise. Let the golden thread shine through your message so it's clear to those that follow you what you stand for and where you play.

6 **Be polite.** Say thanks to those that follow and share your stuff. And 'remember your ABC – always be crediting.' (Hat tip to Charles H Green for this one.)

7 **Be yourself.** Let your personality shine through. The personal touch wins over corporate party line.

8 **Don't be a content bore.** Promoting nothing but your own content over and over again doesn't go down well.

Chris Brogan, President of Human Business Works and a social media expert, advises you to post 10 Tweets about others for every one Tweet you post about yourself. That sounds good to us, although if ten to one feels unachievable, aim for five to one.

The people who are best at social media follow valuable content principles. They aren't constantly pushing sales messages; they are the ones that are engaging with their audience and peers. Social media channels aren't noticeboards where you stick up a postcard advertising your cut-price products; they're a place you meet, chat and share. Social media is difficult for corporations with a complicated party line to toe. Where it performs brilliantly is for businesses that trust their people to speak for themselves – perfect for small businesses, and for bolder bigger ones too.

It's really important to remember that you need to be a person as well as a business to get the most out of social media. Yes it is a publishing and distribution tool, but it's a very human place. So, if someone in your network tells you their dog has died, for example, do respond with something personal. Had you learnt that information around the water cooler you wouldn't respond by pressing a sales brochure into their hand and walking away. You'd say you were sorry. It's just the same on Twitter or LinkedIn. It sounds obvious, clunkingly so, but you'd be surprised how many people fall down at just being plain nice.

Having really valuable content to share gives you a great head start on social media, but it doesn't give you a free pass to use social media channels purely to promote your own content. Because we're living in a world of content overload, any kind of content that is over-promoted starts to grate. We see good businesses that share great stuff, but it's always their own content, over and over again. Unless you're sharing other people's, and truly engaging, you won't get the most out of all the social media landscape can offer.

Follow the valuable principles, and just like Fforest, Wriggle and Sands Beach Resort, you'll see your business thrive.

We'll leave this chapter with one more story of social media awesomeness in action. Here's a business that's found their social media voice and is getting great results.

CONTENT STORY   How Novatech's 'Stig' became a social media hero

---

Novatech builds PCs and laptops for UK schools, businesses and individuals. Here's how they're using social media to great effect.

We were very lucky in that we had a member of the IT team with a super-dry wit, who had done his thesis on Twitter for business. He posts anonymously on both Facebook & Twitter as our social media Stig and he just 'gets it'. I rarely have to give him specific instructions but we do talk a lot about our approach generally and that, in a nutshell is to run against the grain and be different to other companies.

We are adamant that social media is not a marketing tool, but a customer contact channel so we try and avoid overt promotion in favour of wit and comment. Honestly, there's a large amount of making it up as we go along, which means reacting to customers' questions and posts – either to deal with an issue or to prolong witty banter. Generally if we like it and find it funny there's going to be a good chance others will too and all of that reflects our brand motto that it's about the people who make technology work.

As a UK tech company we need to remind our customers that there are smart people behind the hardware. The personal touch trumps soulless brands' product-led marketing. On Facebook you can let your followers drive the story, but on Twitter it's more important that you maintain a semblance of control and assert your personality. Our Stig uses our followers like a comedian uses the front row – for banter, and to get a real-time connection with the audience. In Stig's words:

'I'd rather someone un-follow us for not being their cup of tea than un-following us because we're boring.'

We looked at the demographics on Facebook (80% male and under 35) and decided that we'd just treat everyone as smart and as the probable IT managers of the future.

Engagement and brand perception are wonderfully hard to measure, but we have hatfuls of anecdotes about customers who have progressed from occasional shoppers to devoted advocates, purely from irreverent banter on Facebook and Twitter. We also sit back and watch as members of our community answer technical questions before we do, and even suggest upgrades and improvements.

Tim LeRoy, Marketing Director of Novatech Ltd

The future of social networks

No one knows what the future holds but as big users of social media we notice a couple of things:

- It's getting more and more crowded out there. Playing by the valuable rules will help you stand out, find followers, be listened to, and liked.

- Free platforms are becoming increasingly advertisement driven. Remarketing, sponsored content, native advertising – you're being tracked wherever and whenever you are online, and someone somewhere is paying for an opportunity to sell to you. Fans of this approach would say it's delivering tailored and targeted content direct to consumers; others would say that an ad's an ad, however you dress it up, and consumers will treat it accordingly.

Social media is here to stay. Whichever way platforms rise and fall hold firm to the valuable principles. Respect each new platform – every one is different – and communicate in the way that suits them best, and which feels right to you.

Take action

- Join LinkedIn if you are not already there. Update your profile if you are.
- Join Twitter if you are not already there. Connect with us @sonjajefferson @sjtanton. We'd be delighted to make contact.
- Get a profile on Google+ if you haven't already, and create a business profile too.
- Decide if Facebook is right for your business.
- Play by the valuable rules whichever network you're on.

CHAPTER 6
EMAIL NEWSLETTERS

Stay in touch. Too many businesses chase new business when existing customers and contacts are far more valuable.

Mick Dickinson

In this chapter:

- The importance of keeping in contact.
- Email newsletters the valuable way.
- Email marketing tech – your options.
- Build a community.
- How to build an engaged mailing list.
- Tips on launching your newsletter.
- Autoresponder emails.

Social media will help to keep you in the public eye, but social media platforms are shared, rented spaces. You need a way of communicating that's all yours too. And that jewel in your marketing crown is your email marketing list. That's something you own.

All your social media efforts, your blogs and the rest of your valuable content should be geared towards building and nurturing this list. Importantly, your list is permission based – people have opted to subscribe. It's a list full of people who are happy to listen to you, who like what you say, who like what you're selling, and who find you useful. Customers, potential customers, referrers, advocates – these people are worth their weight in gold, so value their attention.

Printed newsletters delight and surprise in a digital age but can be expensive and time-consuming to produce. Email is a cost-effective and very powerful way to automate the process of keeping in contact, if you do it right. This chapter shows you how to build an engaged mailing list and keep in touch with valuable email content to help you win more business.

Let subscription be your goal.

The importance of keeping in contact

Not everybody is ready to buy at the first contact. Research suggests that only 2 per cent of deals are struck at a first meeting. The other 98 per cent only happen once a certain level of trust has been established. Contacts that don't turn into sales straight away are often forgotten but this could be big opportunity lost. If your company Christmas card is the only time old contacts hear from you each year then you are undoubtedly missing out on business.

Contrary to a popular myth, marketing is not just about generating new leads. Effective marketing nurtures existing relationships too. As one of our favourite US marketing bloggers puts it:

> So many businesses think 'marketing' is the same thing as 'lead generation'. In other words that marketing equals chasing down strangers so you can wrestle them through the conversion process and turn them into customers.

Sonia Simone[1]

Many professional businesses devote all their time and a considerable amount of budget to lead generation when there's a far more cost-effective and rewarding way to boost sales. Super-smart marketing coach (and master of the valuable email), Ian Brodie makes the analogy that some companies treat marketing like a one-night stand. They pour all their energies into pursuing the next big contract; finding out everything there is to know about their prospect so they can say the right things to impress at a pitch, but then moving on straight away if they don't win the work. Or they finish the job as fast as they can and never look back.

Instead of leaving in a cloud of dust, use your knowledge and creative energies to build trusted relationships over time. Be patient. If you keep in contact regularly in ways people appreciate and find useful they will reward you with their business.

Email newsletters, the valuable way

Email remains a very powerful method of communication with current and future customers. But our inboxes are under siege. We delete about 75 per cent of emails that land in our inboxes without opening them. Email newsletters will only be read and acted upon if the content they contain is consistently valuable enough to the reader. In fact, the term 'newsletter' is a bit of a red herring. Customers don't read for your 'news', they read for the useful ideas that you give them. If you make your email communications valuable, you turn contacts into customers, and motivate customers to buy again.

How it works:

- You build a permission-based database by inviting people to join your email mailing list.
- You motivate people to sign up on your website, blog, via social media, even your email footer.
- You create an email newsletter using an email marketing tool.
- You send regular communications to your database by email.
- These usually include engaging articles, resources, stories and ideas, linking to content on your site and others.
- You distribute this weekly or monthly.
- Make sure you include plenty of valuable content.

How it doesn't work:

- You buy a list of people based on their job titles.
- You email them without introduction or permission.
- You just send them your latest offers.
- You send them your latest news.
- You tell them the plans for your business expansion.
- It's all about you. You don't give them anything useful.

However tempting it is to think 'Way-hey! I'm talking to 10,000 people,' if you're mass emailing without permission you can pretty much guarantee that means that nearly 10,000 people have just deleted you, reported you as spam, or just find you a bit annoying.

Far better to build your list slowly with people who want to hear from you. Sign-ups from your blog articles, contacts you've met while networking, people you've clicked with on social media – this is a far better place to start. Invite this group to join your list, not an anonymous crowd.

> People rave about 'targeted' lists. I'll take a warm community of people who feel seen any day over 'targeting'. (Sure, maybe this isn't the best way to sell, but I don't write emails to sell. I write emails to connect and be helpful. If I'm selling you something, it's because I think it'll help.)
>
> Chris Brogan

Email marketing tools – you have options

The valuable approach to your newsletters works whatever system or email platform you choose.

You can go for a more basic system such as Mailchimp or AWeber that will provide a lot of the functionality you need (newsletter and auto-responder emails, sign-up forms, statistics and subscriber info), with costs ranging from totally free up to a certain number of subscribers, to an affordable monthly fee. These options are popular with those starting out, but also a valid platform for larger firms with many thousands of subscribers. More integrated systems such as Infusionsoft or Ontraport give you email marketing functionality alongside other online tools such as landing page set-up, web forms, e-commerce, membership sites, reports and web activity monitoring. Or you can select a full-blown marketing automation system such as ActOn, Hubspot, Marketo or Eloqua for more advanced automation, and integration with CRM platforms such as Salesforce.com – more cost, with advanced functionality. You'll find more on marketing automation in Chapter 12.

Have a look around and test some of the main systems to see what's right for you.

Build a community

The only difference between an audience and a community is how you face the chairs.

Chris Brogan[2]

Think of your email list as a community, or as a special club of your most important individuals, and treat the people in it well. These are your best-loved contacts, your potential biggest customers, your advocates, your referrers, your biggest fans.

Look after this group, make them feel welcome, ask questions, listen carefully, and find out as much as you can about how you can help to serve them better. These are people to nurture, not a list to be 'marketed at'.

How do you do that? By sharing your most valuable content with them. Don't fire out constant sales messages – create content for them that's going to really help with the challenges they are facing. Remember, whatever you write is going to be going straight into their inbox, or even directly into their hands. These are people who have opted to give you the time of day – a privilege in our over-busy world – so treat them with respect. Make the most of this opportunity to engage directly with your community, and that community will strengthen and grow.

CONTENT STORY   Project One generates a great lead two months from newsletter launch

Business change consultancy Project One's new 'Real Change Club' email newsletter is delivering early results. Content Director Geoff Mason explains their approach:

We wanted a way of staying in touch. Our initial intention was just to send stuff to the 4,000 names we've gathered over the years. We soon realized that this blanket bomb approach would not work. We decided to create something special and build a community around it. The Real Change Club was born.

Our focus for the immediate future is to send content in a monthly email that is relevant, helpful and makes people smile. We think we are different and we want a way to explain our approach to change but importantly, we're promoting different ways of thinking about real change; we're not pushing the company.

We've launched carefully and slowly. We wanted to be sure we had the technology working well and that we could feed the beast once we had started. So we launched by focusing on a small number of specific clients and then once we were more comfortable, we encouraged firstly the management team and more recently, the whole consulting team to invite their contacts personally. Some of the management team and consultants get it, and are busily telling people and encouraging them to join – others don't, yet. This doesn't matter – as we grow, they'll come on board and even if they don't, we know our list will grow.

After two months membership of the Real Change Club stands at nearly 300. We've only just scratched the surface. With more advocates internally we should be up to 2,000 by the end of our first year. I'm happy with the numbers but it almost doesn't matter. We just want to engage with people that are as excited by change as we are. We now have several CEOs, CIOs, COOs on our list – just the kind of people we want to do business with, but it's not just a matter of seniority. I want to talk quietly to people who want to listen.

We're promoting the Club in all face-face conversations. Month two and we've had our first inbound lead from the newsletter – a really good one from someone who found the Club independently; from a big corporate we've never done business with before. The content built her trust enough that she felt comfortable getting in touch.

What is more, I'm delighted that our current clients are finding our emails useful. One of our contacts at a large retailer sent this note out to the rest of his change team. 'Hi all. The Real Change Club was started last month by Project One. There is good content on here and it's a fab resource to utilize, so feel free to sign up and contact Geoff if you have a topic you'd like covered.' That's real advocacy for you.

We now need to live up to this with each newsletter in the future.

Geoff Mason, Content Director, Project One **www.projectone.com**

How to motivate more sign-ups

- **Invite existing customers and contacts to opt in.** It makes sense to start with the people you already know.

- **Make all roads lead to your newsletter**. Joining up your blogs with your website via social media should get you a stream of interested readers who like what you say. As well as a retweet button to help them share your valuable content with their followers, make the sign-up to your newsletter loud and clear.

- **Make it really easy.** Have a clear and accessible sign-up form. (Take a look at the master of the valuable email newsletter, Chris Brogan's site, **www.chrisbrogan.com**. See how easy he makes it for you to join his list.)

- **Give them a preview.** Show them what they'll get, so they know it's going to be of value.

- **Use an ethical bribe.** You can use your most valuable content to motivate more newsletter sign-ups. The promise of a free download written on key subjects will tempt some people to want to hear more from you. (Make sure your site has lots of absolutely free valuable stuff too.)

- **Promote your list widely.** Whenever you meet people or speak to new contacts, in the real world as well as online.

- **Cross-promote.** Encourage sign-up from your Facebook account, your Google+ page, and through your Tweets. Engaging headlines that offer little snippets of the stories can tempt people to sign up and read more.

Valuable Tip

Simple processes to build your list really help. Each month, we invite every new contact to opt in to our email newsletter list. Here at Valuable Content this process is automated to a degree. We tag each new contact in our contact database to ensure they get sent our invitation. 60–70 per cent sign up to our email list.

Pop-up boxes – yes or no?

Call us old-fashioned, but we're not big fans of boxes that pop up in our faces as soon as we land on a website, obscuring our view, asking us to sign up for anything at all. How about you? It feels like a pushy sales assistant jumping on us as soon as we enter a shop, and makes us want to turn round and walk straight out again.

There's a smarter, subtler road you can take here to make these work. If the sign-up boxes feel intuitive your audience will like them. If a box appears containing the next thing you were looking for, then that's helpful. Well-worded 'subscribe now' boxes can increase sign-ups, if you create them with care.

It is possible to tailor the pop-up boxes to appear in particular places on the site – not instantly and everywhere, but in relevant areas. Link them to your most popular content, for example, or your 'About us' page, and people will be more likely to sign up to hear more from you.

What should your newsletter say?

The content of your newsletter is down to you and your business. However, there are some principles that will help you shape the content and set the right tone.

Five qualities your newsletter needs:

1 a clear aim;

2 authenticity;

3 a voice;

4 relevance;

5 simple but effective design.

The valuable 'help, don't sell' notion is still in force, and here more strongly than ever. Leading hard with a sales message in each and every newsletter will undo all your blogging efforts and social media schmoozing in an instant. Sign-up to your list doesn't give you permission to sell, sell, sell – it gives you permission to keep talking.

Here, as with your blogs and the rest of your content, you're looking to make yourself useful. You know the challenges facing your customers, and here's your chance to tackle them head on. Make your content as valuable as it can be. Share your most useful tips with this special group of people – it's a privilege to be invited into their inbox, so do it thoughtfully.

Four different types of valuable content newsletter:

1 **The blog article round-up:** wrap up your recent blog articles in a monthly newsletter communication. This is the easiest form of e-newsletter to deliver.

2 **The themed newsletter:** pick a topic and deliver the best information from you and other sources.

3 **The laser focus newsletter:** go into depth on one issue only. More work but seriously valuable content on one subject each month.

4 **Personal letter:** write as you would to a friend. Share your thinking around a subject, relate it to life outside business.

Which style is right for you and your audience?

Why we changed our newsletter style

At the time of writing the first edition of the book we produced a monthly newsletter that looked like an online magazine page. It was nicely designed, with a picture, a selection of stories in columns, and lots of links to content that we'd written and some from elsewhere. We were quite proud of it. It did okay.

If you opened the email, it looked like many other company newsletters. Although we included heaps of useful content, it was clearly branded, and looked at a glance like news from Valuable Content. The trouble is, other people's news is very easy to ignore if you're busy, and even if you're not busy it's not top of your things to do list. (It's like listening to other people's dreams. Tiresome.)

We experimented with stripping out all of the design features. No more pictures, no branding, no columns. Instead the email newsletter was created in plain text, like an email you'd send to a friend.

We wrote differently too. The newsletter became more personal. We wanted it to feel more one to one, not one to many. (We started to include stories of things that had happened to us, snapshots of what was going on in the office – not client wins – things like 'Lizzie's brought in a cake', even what the weather was doing in Bristol that day.) There was a change of tone. The opening paragraph became chattier – like taking the time to say hello properly.

Then we launched into the body of the newsletter, which took a more personal look at a challenge we knew clients were struggling with. Rather than writing as 'this is what this means to content marketing/business/the world', we wrote it as 'how does this feel for you?' Basically we upped the 'You' factor ten-fold, and that made the newsletter more engaging and harder to ignore.

The change made a big difference in terms of the way people engaged with the newsletter. People started writing back to us, conversations were sparked, leads followed, and our list has increased. We hope people get a lot from it – we love the community it creates.

Our newsletter list helps us enormously too in ways we could not have predicted. Responses to questions we've posed have been hugely valuable, not least with writing this book. We value having a community who are happy to share their ideas with us.

Should you ever sell directly in your newsletter?

Your newsletter has a business purpose. It's part of your process for generating leads and sales, so it is a sales tool. If you approach your newsletter with your valuable marketing mindset, you'll already be thinking of how you can best serve your community of clients. You'll be sharing useful content, and that content may well include things that you sell. Use your newsletter space to point people towards things that you know will help them on the journey.

As in all these marketing decisions, you need to tread carefully. If people have signed up for 'free useful tips' they will probably baulk if the free tips are buried under tips with a hefty price tag. It's a question of balance, and you'll need to find your way. As a rough rule of thumb, keep any sales pitch or special offers to less than 10 per cent of your email content.

Copywriting supremo Andy Maslen (sunfish.co.uk) talks about content marketing and the Bank of Trust, and this analogy is really useful when thinking about your email content strategy:

> *Every time you give people something that they find valuable, your account is credited and your balance of trust increases. And every time you ask them to do something that YOU find valuable, your account is debited, and your balance decreases. This is the basic content marketing equation and we ignore its unforgiving maths at our peril. Let's look at the Bank of Trust concept in action when marketing with email.*

> *Having built, acquired or otherwise assembled an email list or database, it's natural that you should want to see some return on investment (ROI). Preferably as soon as possible. This is fine and commercially very sensible. After all, who invests in an asset and then doesn't expect an ROI? The question is, how soon is 'as soon as possible'?*

> *An easier question to answer is 'how soon is too soon'? And the answer is, before you've built up enough credit to make a withdrawal. In practical terms, that probably means at any point before you've sent your newly acquired email contact two or three pieces of content.*

If you're selling something, be very clear about it. Don't try and hide it. Accept that you will get pushed back sometimes. It is a tricky line to walk; you really can't please all of the people all of the time, and that's okay.

If you're very generous with your helpful content you'll build a growing list of fans, and a proportion of them will be happy to become your customers.

Valuable Tip

Archive old newsletters on your website so they can be found by potential clients, and by Google.

What is spam, and how can I make sure I'm not sending it?

Spam is unsolicited and unwanted junk mail, almost always for products or services that you don't want, and so often coming from companies you have never heard of. You will never be at risk of sending this if you have followed the guidelines in this book:

- always ask people's permission to email them;
- give the recipient an easy option to unsubscribe;
- only send information they will find valuable.

Being asked for, and delivered from a trusted source, will ensure your email marketing gets through, but there's still a chance it can feel like spam if it's written in the wrong way. Write it without a real reader in mind, and it won't hit the target. Fill it with sales messages, and it might as well be a pharmacy ad. If it's useful, people will remember it, and keep hold of it until the time comes to contact you. If it serves no purpose, you might as well not send it in the first place.

Autoresponders – a valuable addition to your email strategy

An autoresponder is a sequence of automatically generated email marketing messages that gets sent to subscribers in the order and frequency that you decide. Autoresponders are handy to master if you want to convert more contacts into leads. They are an underused lead generation tool for many in the business world and, if written well, a great addition to your email toolkit.

Here's how John Jantch of Duct Tape marketing fame uses them.

> I use an autoresponder to reply once someone subscribes. I send an evergreen issue of my newsletter so they get a taste of the value right away. A few days after they subscribe I also send what feels like a much more personal thank you note from me. This is a text email that is very simple and tells them I am glad they subscribed. I get constant feedback from people who, while they may know it's not really a personal note, love the personal feel. I suggest you adopt this approach.[3]

Autoresponders are a way of leading potential customers to the information that will be most valuable to them, and converting interest into sales. They can be part of your email newsletter campaign, as described by John above, or as a way of targeting different sections of your audience.

If you have more than one niche, autoresponders are a useful way of addressing your different audiences. They can feel more personal than newsletters, and can guide people through the maze of things you know towards the bits they are most interested in. Good email autoresponders confirm that you're in safe hands, and that you've come to the right place.

Business coach Lee Duncan, author of *Double Your Business*, uses autoresponders with great results:

> *My goal with every email is to offer some robust insights that my type of client can use to improve their business. It's my aim to educate and inspire in a practical and valuable way. For example: how to improve cashflow through better credit control; why giving employees shares doesn't motivate most of them; why business grinds to a halt when the owner goes on holiday. Six months after I first put this autoresponder sequence into play my coaching client base had more than doubled!*[4]

Launching your newsletter

Launching your email newsletter list is a key stage in your content marketing journey, and something that will be part of your ongoing content life for many years to come.

Choose a format that your customers will appreciate, and one that's sustainable for you to maintain. (Your newsletter will be going out every month – so all-singing all-dancing formats will quickly become a burden to produce.)

Remember it's better to start small and develop an engaged and enthusiastic community, than spray and pray that you hit as many people as possible. Begin by inviting your own clients and contacts to join you.

Make your newsletter valuable, and you'll be welcomed into people's inboxes for many years to come.

Take action

- Think about the newsletters you subscribe to. Which do you read avidly and which do you ignore?

- Would your customers appreciate a monthly round-up of your blogs, or a focused 'one key message' type of communication?

- Put together a list of your existing contacts and invite them to sign up.

- Create a landing page on your website to motivate people to sign up for your email newsletter.

Four great companies with email newsletters to inspire you:

- **www.newfangled.com** (all things web)
- **www.chrisbrogan.com** (for business owners)
- **www.trustedadvisor.com** (on trust in business)
- **www.projectone.com** (on real business change)

CHAPTER 7
SEARCH ENGINE OPTIMIZATION

Valuable content + best practice in web design = good SEO.

Jon Payne, founder of SEO company Noisy Little Monkey

In this chapter:

- Why it's smart to get search engine savvy.
- How people use search engines.
- What search engines want from you.
- Five steps to visible visited content.

Valuable content is the basis of all effective search engine optimization (SEO). If you follow the advice in this book, consistently publishing and sharing high-quality valuable content on the web, search engines will reward you and point those searching on the web in your direction. The days of thinking about SEO as a separate discipline are over.

If you want your content to be found, follow valuable content marketing principles. Write for real people, always and unwaveringly. Write about the subjects your readers are looking for. Create the kind of content that is exactly right for your customers, and you'll go a long way.

But there are a few simple techniques you can you use that will get you even further, and faster; a few search engine fundamentals that will help your content to be found. And that's what we want to cover in this chapter. Put these principles into practice when it comes to your content and you'll boost traffic to your site.

Without traffic from search engines your website will likely fail. To protect your business, your online marketing investment and to see maximum return, you must learn the essentials. Learn how people use
search engines and how to get the basics right on your site. Then sit back and allow your valuable content to do the rest.

Jon Payne, founder of SEO company Noisy Little Monkey

noisy littlemonkey.com

Why it's smart to get search engine savvy

Successful websites attribute over 50 per cent of their visitors to search engines. If your content is valuable enough when these visitors arrive on your site you'll build their trust, generate a lead and ultimately win their business.

SEO is what you do to make your website and content as search engine friendly as possible. This gives it the best chance of appearing at the top of the listings when someone searches for your business or the products and services you provide.

As we've discussed, there are various other ways to get people to your website: you can tell them about it, giving them a link to your URL; you can entice them there by sharing links to your useful articles on social media sites; you can share links back to your site in your email newsletters; you can write a blog so valuable that people will link to it from theirs. These are the tip of the iceberg. But whether you are B2C or B2B, e-commerce or professional service it doesn't matter what business you're in: visits from search are where it's at for maximum profitability and results.

SEO has brought Hinge Marketing a massive leap in leads

At Hinge we have always created valuable educational content for our clients and it has consistently brought us good results. But when we started taking search engine optimization seriously a couple of years ago we saw a massive leap in inbound leads. We used to get 10 per cent of our leads through the fresh content we posted on the site. With our new focus we now get over 70 per cent!

Sean McVey, Online Marketing Manager, Hinge Marketing[1]

The key to success is to always be intentional: hold search engines in mind whenever you're creating valuable content. For if you help Google, then Google will help you.

How people use search engines

Search engines like Google are getting better and better at learning how to anticipate what we're about to search for (Google maps shows up when you search for *restaurant* even if you don't add the name of your town) and new devices are being released all the time, so the way people search changes. For example, it's fair to assume that at the time of writing this book half of all smartphones[2] are running the Google app. The Google app reports that it sees 30 times more searches activated by voice than by typing.[3] Which means that in the future Google will be listening and talking to us, not simply putting up a list of websites that might help us.

If that's the near future, how can you win now and in years to come?

Typically, traffic from search engines arrives via one of two routes.

1. Branded search: someone searches for your business

For most sites the biggest portion of traffic from search engines arrives via 'branded search'. Say you run a legal practice called Ham & Cheese Legal and you have an off-the-shelf subscription service for employers called Cheesy HR Support'. If you're optimized right, you receive traffic to your website via branded search when people searched for *ham & cheese legal* or *cheesy HR support.*

SEO works with your valuable content (and your social media strategy) enabling you to dominate the search engine results pages (SERPs for short) when someone searches for you. No pesky competitors can show if your website takes up the top of the page. Your Google+ page covers the right hand side and the valuable content (both yours and other people's) that you share on other social channels takes up the rest of the page.

Noisy Little Monkey ranks for branded search

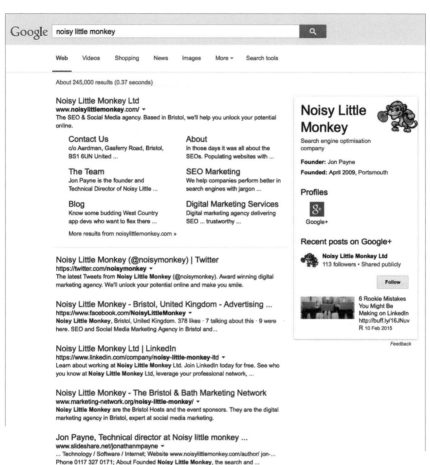

Valuable Tip

Make the most of your company Google+ page by getting your web developer to add the verification code to your website (**https://support. google.com/business/answer/4569085**). Your Google+ page, along with your most recent posts, will show on the right-hand side of Google search results. The more content you post, the stronger your Google presence will be.

2. Non-branded search: someone searches for a solution to their problem

Continuing the example of our Ham & Cheese Legal firm, maybe the Cheesy HR Support product gives employers a 24-hour hotline to help them deal with thorny HR issues. A search engine user may search for something like *HR help employee disciplinary*, and this is where your valuable content comes in.

Assuming you've got some useful, relevant content on your Cheesy HR Support page that matches this searcher's intent – blogs, or a useful guide to HR support – then you're in with a chance of ranking highly in the results. If you're in the top three results, you're in good shape.

Use keyword research

One of the most important things to understand is what sorts of words or phrases your potential customer types into the query box of a search engine. They probably don't use exactly the same language (and jargon) as you and the rest of your competitors when they describe the sorts of problems your organization can solve. The content that most accurately matches the keywords used in a search has a brilliant chance of ranking, so make sure your valuable content is written using the same phraseology your customers use online.

To give you a hand with this, Google lets you compare volumes of search using two tools: a) Google Trends **http://www.google.com/trends/**; and b) AdWords Keyword Planner **https://adwords.google.com/KeywordPlanner**.

Spend a few hours logged in and playing about with these tools to get a feel of the sort of information you can get.

Once you're used to analysing the trends and volumes of search in your sector, you should add 'target search phrase' to your content planner so each time you write a blog post, you know what phrase you want the post to rank for and then you can use it and synonyms throughout the post.

But it's not always about search

Having said this, we don't want the focus on search to paralyse and preoccupy you. Sometimes, ranking for search engines doesn't matter. You may want to create a provocative headline that you know will get widely shared on social media, but isn't optimized for search; or write a post with one specific prospect in mind, and that's fine. SEO is important but it's not the only way people will find your content. You'll create a balance of content in your library, with different goals and aims. As long as you always know why you're creating the content, and have search engines in mind, you'll do well.

What search engines want from you

Think from the search engine's perspective for a minute. It wants to provide brilliant results for its customers (the people who search) so that they don't go and use a competitor. It needs your help with this.

We'll come on to how you demonstrate this from a technical perspective later but first you need to understand that basically all search engines want from you and your content is relevance, honesty, freshness and clarity. They're trying to determine if your website is a more trusted resource than that of your competitors.

Here's how to help search engines do their job and point to you.

Trust signals

Trust signals that search engines measure include (but are by no means limited to):

- How many trusted websites link to yours (because they reference your valuable content).
- How often you're mentioned in the press (local or national).

- The freshness of your content (weekly or monthly blog posts are essential).

- How many times your content is shared on social media and the velocity of that sharing.

- How much of your content has been copied from another website (hopefully, none!).

If you're engaged in PR, then think how you can lever this for maximum SEO value (NB: it's not just about press coverage, it's about links to further resources on *your* website). Further, think about your day-to-day: is there a way to 'seed' your content with the people you already know who have influence over your target market? You'll find more details on PR and guest blogging in Chapter 10.

On-page signals

Google likes a bit of spoon-feeding. This means acting like a good librarian and setting your content correctly so search engines can understand it easily.

On-page signals include:

- **Page titles**. Use the search phrase you're targeting in your page title. This is the blue link that appears on the Google search page. Keep it short – up to 72 characters will be visible (though more likely to be 56 characters **http://moz.com/blog/new-title-tag-guidelines-preview-tool**). Convince the searcher your content is relevant. This is your 'title tag', crucial when optimizing for search.

- **Meta Descriptions**. While these don't have an effect on the ranking of your page, Meta Descriptions are crucial for SEO clarity – the 150–160-character summary of your page or article using key search terms. This is what appears on Google's search results and it needs to be informative, relevant, interesting and succinct. This is 'prime advertising space' so make it compelling enough that someone will click on your link and not your competitors'. Also, include the keyword(s) you're targeting. **http://moz.com/learn/seo/meta-description**

- **Headings**. Important for the reader scanning your article or page, and for Google too. Use them to show what the page is all about. Focus on H1, H2 or H3 tags, and include your search phrases here as best fits the content.

- **Images**. Google can't read an image so help it by labelling the images you use. This is called the Alt Tag. Again, include the phrases you're targeting.

NB – use natural language in all these areas. Don't be tempted to stuff search phrases in repeatedly, Google doesn't like this anymore than your readers.

Content that can be indexed

If you want to give your content the best chance, most of it should be in HTML text format. Images and other non-text content are not as easy for search engine crawlers to parse so if you're using video make sure you add a text transcript beneath the video when you embed it on your website. To make sure the words and phrases you want to rank for are visible, make sure they are in HTML text not embedded in images.

Valuable Tip

Tools such as the MozBar (**moz.com/tools/seo-toolbar**) show you what elements of your content are visible and indexable to the engines.

Target one phrase per page

To win the medium- and long-term battles for organic search ranking you need to think about the purpose of your website, then the purpose of each page and the search phrase (see above) for which each page should rank. Write content around that phrase and its synonyms. Keep the focus.

Design your website for search

Not all websites make it easy for search engines. There are technical aspects of web design/development that help both search engines and human visitors too. Talk to your web designers and developers and make sure they construct your website following best practice guidelines.

The SEO architecture

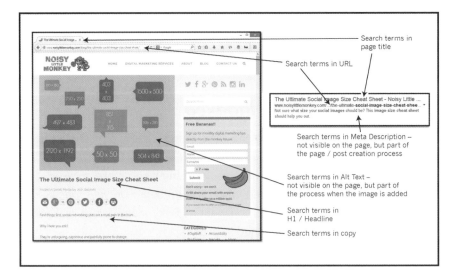

Five steps to a website that's built for search

1. Make your website faster

Search engines and human visitors want fast, reliable websites. Tell your new hosting company that you want an 'A' on this test: **www.webpagetest.org/** for 'First Byte Time'. That will focus their minds.

2. Optimize architecture on every page

If you're short on time, then maybe you only want to optimize your fresh new content as part of the writing process. This is good practice, but if you want to get the maximum rank you need to optimize every page, every category, every product on your website. It's time well spent if you're looking for a return.

The architecture you'll need to optimize for each page is as follows:

- URL
- Title
- Alt Text
- Copy
- Meta Description
- Headlines

To optimize these architecture elements ensure that your target search phrase for this page appears at least once in each of these areas.

3. Encourage people to share your valuable content

Your content is awesome and helpful, right? So, encourage the reader to share it. Add share buttons for the main social channels right next to it. Call the reader's attention to the buttons and say something like 'Find this helpful? Please share it and help others'.

4. Get responsive

If your site doesn't change layout and size so it looks great on smartphones and tablets, then you're missing a huge and growing audience. Search for anything on Google from a phone and you'll often see the words 'Mobile friendly' come up next to the results. If Google thinks it's important, so should you. It's not expensive and a good web designer can use a free responsive WordPress template to give you something that does the job for very little cost.

5. Measure what works

Google Analytics is an invaluable tool that will give you an understanding of which content on your site is acquiring visitors and converting into leads/ sales. It's free for sites with less than 100,000 pages and is something no marketer should be without. Get your web developer to install the code on every page of your site and get your graph on!

Getting the right help with SEO

There are some fantastic companies out there who will help you do the right things with your website and content so people can find you fast online. There are also some companies who still try to convince their customers that SEO is a black art, and they are therefore best avoided.

Here are six signs you need to look elsewhere for SEO support.

SEO alarm bells (or, how to tell the difference between an expert and a charlatan)

1 They're advising you on link building in isolation, without alluding to how you need great content to help you acquire them.

2 Banging on about 'meta keywords' – Google doesn't care about these any more (and hasn't since 2001!).

3 They recommend keyword stuffing (not natural, not required). Keyword density is not a part of modern ranking algorithms.

4 They focus on the latest Google Updates – Pandas, Penguins and the rest of the ark usually don't matter if you're sharing enough valuable content.

5 You can't understand what they are saying. Good SEO is no more complicated than creating good content and getting your web design right.

If you're evaluating an SEO company or freelancer, in addition to the points above, try asking them Ian Lurie's 10 questions: **www.portent.com/blog/seo/ 10-questions-to-evaluate-an-seo.htm**

Never opt for manipulative SEO techniques. While this sort of gaming of the system might work in the short term, it often results in search engines like Google imposing penalties on your site which can be extremely hard to reverse. If you don't trust what the SEO company is saying then walk away.

What's new for search engines?

If your business is a location that people can visit (an office, restaurant, concert hall) then Google wants you to mark up your website with Schema to enable it to display more relevant results in search. For local businesses, it's crucial to add your name, address, phone number, opening hours and social media profiles using Schema. It's something you'll need your web developer to do for you – so educate yourself in the basic principles here: **https://support.google.com/webmasters/answer/99170** so you can brief them properly.

Search engine rules will continue to change and evolve. One thing we're sure of is that the very best thing you can do to make your content findable online is to write the stuff your customers are looking for. That's not going to change.

What does Google love? Google loves the content that answers the questions people are asking. So focus on providing just that.

Take action

- Use Google AdWords' keyword research tool to investigate the target phrases customers use to find services like yours.

- When thinking about new content, add 'target search phrase' to your planning criteria.

- Look back over your previous blog posts. Have you included keyword-rich headings? If not, add them now.

Further reading on SEO:

- The Moz beginners guide to SEO:
  http://moz.com/beginners-guide-to-seo

- Google's Intro to the Webmaster Academy:
  https://support.google.com/webmasters/answer/6001102

- Distilled U: **https://www.distilled.net/u/.** It's a paid service but worth it if you want to learn more than is available above.

CHAPTER 8

DEEPER WRITTEN CONTENT, E-BOOKS, WHITE PAPERS, SLIDESHARES AND PUBLISHED BOOKS

There's a place for shallow, and a place for deep. Twitter is shallow; blogs are deeper. Articles are deeper yet. Or books – books are real deep.

Charles H Green[1]

In this chapter:

- Stock and flow – the value of going deeper.
- The most valuable content of all takes work.
- Your deeper written content options.
- What to write about in key content pieces.
- Deeper content demands great design.
- The importance of a strong landing page.
- Should you make people fill in a form to download your content?
- Repurposing and the value of integrated content campaigns.

Stock and flow: the value of going deeper

We want to introduce you to an important metaphor for your content. The concept of stock and flow originates from the world of economics but can also be linked to the production of content.

Flow is the feed. It's the posts and the tweets. It's the stream of daily and sub-daily updates that remind people that you exist. Stock is the durable stuff. It's the content you produce that's as interesting in two months (or two years) as it is today... And the real magic trick is to put them both together. To keep the ball bouncing with your flow – to maintain that open channel of communication – while you work on some kick-ass stock in the background. Sacrifice neither. It's the hybrid strategy.

Robin Sloan[2]

This is a useful picture to hold in your head when it comes to your content. To market a business effectively today we need to commit to both stock and flow content and get the balance right.

We've concentrated so far on flow content. Blogs, short articles and social media updates are your bread and butter content – easier to throw together, easy for people to consume quickly. You also need to provide something more sustaining – good stock content with more flavour, more nutritional value and a longer shelf life. These are your key sales pieces – the killer content you need to open new doors, motivate good referrals and win you business.

Doug Kessler who wrote the foreword to this book calls this kind of content 'Home Run Content' – the kind of content that reaches way further than your everyday stuff, content that fires your ideas out of the park and into the stratosphere. Copyblogger call it 'Cornerstone Content' – the lynchpin content that supports everything else that you do. Whatever you call it, we mean the kind of content that can really raise your profile and set you apart. Content that motivates people to pay you some serious attention. Content that people can't tear their eyes away from. Content with the power to tip people over the edge from just aware to definitely interested. Campaignable content that sells.

In terms of topic, we're talking serious lead-generating material. Ten top tips are all well and good but there are times when your customer wants something meatier, something that cuts right to the heart of the main challenge and problem they're facing (that you can help solve).

In terms of format, you want something with a bigger wow factor – gorgeous guides, superb SlideShares, awesome animations, entertaining e-books, rigorously researched papers and brilliant business books all fall into this category. They take more time and thought to produce, but when it comes to driving long-term profitable sales for your business, they're worth the effort. This is the biggest content opportunity for your business.

Ten reasons to invest in deeper stock content:

1 **Attention grabbing** – it raises you above the competition.

2 **Authority** – it shows a powerful grasp of the issues in your field.

3 **Invaluable sales tool** – it is solid proof of your capabilities.

4 **The perfect referral tool** – it does the job of answering the big questions when you're not in the room.

5 **Super shareable** – people love sharing brilliant stuff so make something brilliant.

6 **More engagement** – it pulls more people to your business, gets more eyes on everything else you've written.

7 **Value for money** – costs more to produce, but lasts for ages, gives you fuel for many more blogs, tweets, videos.

8 **Demonstrates your expertise** – deeper content really is 'show not tell'.

9 **Opens doors** – the really credible stock content like books can take you and your business to the next level.

10 **Closes business** – knocks the competition out of the water. No contest.

This chapter explores the deeper content options to you, and we'd really like to inspire you to create some of this content. Yes, it is the most time-consuming, but it's also the most powerful and the most fun.

Producing deeper content can push you to your limit, and that's a good thing. Obviously writing a book is a huge commitment of time, but creating a fantastic guide can make you think 'Can we really give this away for free?' Coming up with a fabulous rant that you just know will work brilliantly on SlideShare is exciting, but it can also makes you nervous.

> The one where you think 'there's no way I can say that, or there's no way the company will allow me to do that', then that idea is at least worth exploring – thinking really, well, why not? Go ahead and push it.
>
> You've got to have the workmanlike stuff that answers questions clearly and well, you've got to have that bedrock, but some people stop there, and I think their programmes would do way better if they threw in a few home runs.
>
> Have ambition and aim really high.
>
> Doug Kessler

Ideas that excite you and push you are really worth exploring. Of course, creativity needs to be shot through with a big dose of common sense. Neither Doug nor we would suggest going AWOL with your brand but aim high and have some fun.

The most valuable content of all takes work

Real value for your business usually comes from the content you put the most effort into. Its success is rarely a surprise (it's never 'oh that thing I spent five minutes on went viral' or 'I threw it out to a cheap content farm and it just flew'). Really valuable content takes effort and thought. So if you want to create really deep and seriously valuable content for your business you've got to do the work. You'll know when it's right.

The most valuable content invariably takes the high ground – new rules, predictions for the future of your industry, the go-to research, a list of leaders – this is bold content which takes a strong stand, states an opinion and positions you as the leader in your field. This deeper content is absolute proof of your passion and expertise. Bragging that you're a passionate exponent and expert doesn't build trust. This type of content shows without telling – far, far more believable.

These deeper pieces are about your customers of course, but they are also about you and your business. The work you do on your content gets you clearer on who you are as a business. Truly valuable content nails it – a clear communication to the outside world of what you represent, and why that matters to them.

There's a lovely quote about writing, from Pulitzer Prize-winning journalist and author David McCullough:

Writing is thinking. To write well is to think clearly. That's why it's so hard.[3]

This deeper stock content is your thinking made manifest; it's a place for your best ideas.

Because it takes longer to produce, and demands more thought and planning, creating deeper written content isn't a one-person job. Unlike your blogs and Tweets, you'll almost certainly need some assistance. Help with research, help with design, help with editing – if you're planning on upping the ante with deeper content, a team effort will take your content to the next level.

Your deeper written content options

- Research and surveys.
- E-books and guides.
- SlideShare.
- White papers.
- Published books.

Research and surveys

Undertaking research in your field that answers a genuine question that your customers are asking is an excellent use of your time, and the basis of some powerful research-based deeper content. The act of doing the research is useful for your business – we find people like being asked, so it's a good conversation opener. The content that you create from it will almost certainly turn out to be a useful sales tool. Depending on your field, original research is probably one of your easiest ways of winning some valuable PR.

Global marketing implementation agency Freedman International went out to clients and key thinkers in their field and posed the question, 'What's the biggest challenge you face when it comes to global marketing?' The responses formed the basis of a research report which they made available as a free download from the website. It positions them right at the centre of the global marketing community, and demonstrates not only their empathy with their clients (it's a tough field to work in) but also the practical help they can offer. Immensely valuable stuff that's led to business for Freedman International.

Research is a tried and tested content approach for bigger businesses too. Here's Richard Fray, Digital Marketing Manager for HSBC's Expat Banking Division, talking about the most valuable content they've ever created:

Our most valuable piece of content is our Expat Explorer survey – one of the world's largest surveys of expats – which asks our target audience what it is like to move, live and work abroad. This provides us with an incredibly rich amount of data and insights, which we have been able to repurpose endlessly in our content. The insights have been used to generate global press coverage, interactive data visualizations, videos, infographics, curated forums and country guides, populate our social media feeds and train our employees.

With the survey data, we are able to infuse our content with the voices and views of our customer base and target audience. This vastly increases the breadth of content we can create, as well as its depth and authenticity. Our content has enabled over half a million users in 200 countries to compare which countries are the best places to live, and to get advice on everything from finding accommodation to fitting in to a new culture. The feedback from customers and our social media community has been fantastic, with expats sharing our content widely and telling us that this is content they cannot get elsewhere – and that it changes the way they think about us as an organisation.

Richard and the smart team at HSBC Expat have recognized the benefits of crowdsourced content. As well as their annual survey, they regularly collaborate with their customers and social media community, exploring the question, 'what's it like to live abroad?' On the back of this simple question they've created irresistible content that's widely shared – crowdsourced hints and tips, and most recently a video and series of country-specific guides to expat life. Genius content that's as useful internally (as a training tool for new staff) as it is for marketing purposes.

Valuable Tip

Collaborate with your customers and contacts. Get them to provide the raw material to create fascinating crowdsourced content, like HSBC Expat's.

White papers, discussion papers

Positioned somewhere in between a magazine article and an academic paper, these powerful forms of content can supercharge your thought leadership efforts. They are authoritative, educational reports or guides that show the reader how to solve a particular issue.

White papers are the geeky big brother of the deeper content family. They have been published for years. While they might not have the glamour of a video or the wow factor of a brilliant infographic, white papers continue to play an influential role in purchasing decisions, and are particularly useful in technical and consultancy fields. Truly valuable white papers are widely read and passed on from person to person making them well worth the investment.

During the past year research by CMI and Marketing Profs shows that white paper use has increased by 8 per cent[4]. From 2012 to 2014 copywriting agency Radix Communications[5] have seen a 229 per cent increase in client demand for white papers.

E-books and guides

There has been an explosion in e-book publishing. E-books are a great vehicle for spreading your ideas far and wide. They're substantial enough to go into useful detail, not so long as to feel like a chore to read. You can embed video so they are great if you're teaching something. Guides are perfect in e-book form. Emailable, and very shareable with no printing or distribution costs, once you've written an e-book you can quickly get it out to the people who matter to you.

Fitness coach Mark Durnford, founder and owner of CreateFit.com, is always on the lookout for ways to help people swim better. Create Fit started sharing concise video tutorials that showed detailed instructions to help people improve their techniques in the pool. The Create Fit channel library has grown to over 110 clips with current average daily channel hits of over 7.5k. Their success inspired Mark to launch of the world's first interactive swim coaching e-books available on all platforms on any smart device. The e-book format is brilliant for this – written tips are supported by detailed video clips – and it's winning them lots of work.

How do you create an e-book?

Once you've written the content you have a couple of options. Either get a designer to turn it into a PDF that can be downloaded from your website, or go to an e-book publisher. There's a choice here, and it includes Amazon's own Kindle Direct publishing service, Lulu.com, Smashwords and a host of other options.

Where can an ebook take you?

The New Rules of PR e-book (downloaded over a million times) directly led to a book deal with Wiley for The New Rules of Marketing and PR, my international bestseller now in its 4th edition with more than 300,000 copies sold in English and available in over 25 languages from Bulgarian to Vietnamese.

David Meerman Scott[6]

SlideShares

SlideShares have sneaked in on the inside track to become one of the most influential forms of deeper content currently doing the rounds. Visual, easy to read but not shallow, a good SlideShare is brilliant for spreading big ideas.

No longer the place 'where PowerPoint decks go to die' (Doug Kessler), SlideShare was bought by LinkedIn in 2012 and turned from what was essentially a bit of fun into a legitimate business tool for spreading great content. At the end of 2013 SlideShare recorded 60 million unique visitors a month with 215 million page views. 15 million uploads have been registered with 400,000 being added each month. SlideShare is now one of the top 120 sites on the internet.

SlideShare rewards the brave and the bold. The stuff that really flies is well-written, imaginative, thoughtful, entertaining, visually exciting. There's something about the way you read them and the pacing of the content that makes them deliciously easy to consume. The presentation style lets you give weight and emphasis to the words, and allows space to think, so you can communicate ideas with more impact than other written formats.

Winning with SlideShare

Small law firm Clutton Cox become has big fan of the format. Owner Paul Hajek explains:

Great content is not just one dimensional. We've turned our most-read blog on 'the arcane rules of Chancel Repair Liability' into first an Infographic and then a SlideShare deck which coincided with my appearance as the legal expert on Rip Off Britain talking about this subject.

We're mere novices on SlideShare really but can see its potential to create great legal content and grow our reach exponentially.

Paul Hajek

Published business books

If blogs are the kings of valuable content, business books are the Masters of the Universe. Not for everyone, and by no means essential in your valuable content tool kit, but extremely worthwhile for the minority of people who relish the challenge. Consultants and advisers will certainly benefit from writing and publishing a book. A book is a power-charged business card; proof of the credibility of your ideas, and it can allow you to lift your rate as a result of the increase in inbound enquiries.

Whether you get a publishing deal or self-publish, being an author of a published book gives your ideas authority and positions you as the expert in your field.

> *It's mechanically very simple to assemble a book but somehow your fame, your respect goes up considerably if you have a book to your name. If you give someone a book it's five dollars of paper and cardboard marked up triple yet somehow it has this patina of 'Oh my gosh, that's wonderful! You gave me a book! Thank you!' People respect it.*

Charles H Green[7]

CONTENT STORY   *The 7 Secrets of Money* book raises the authors' profile and wins clients too

A few years ago, a group of four investment advisers got together as part of a study group. Quickly finding a common bond, they decided to collaborate on writing a book on their shared approach. In 2011 Simon Brown, Ben Sherwood, Richard Stott and Bruce Wilson self-published *The 7 Secrets of Money: The insider's guide to personal investment success.* They wanted to tell the truth about investment as they saw it. They also saw the book as a marketing tool – a way to boost their profile.

> **Simon:** *'We wanted the book to be a big fat business card, a PR device. Often, the first thing we do after we meet someone at a networking event is to send them a copy of the book. It's very powerful. People see you in a different way – they think that guy must know what he is talking about! The book has definitely given us gravitas and made us more believable.'*

Simon Brown, BpH Wealth Management, **www.bphwealth.co.uk**

Richard: *'There's no doubt that it has given us a real advantage. A book immediately lifts people's perception and makes them more comfortable with you. It has opened doors in terms of getting new business, which we may not have got without it.'*

Richard Stott, Connectum, **www.connectum.no**

Ben: *'It has given us a competitive advantage. We all run relatively small businesses and we are competing with large private banks – so we need to impress. And being able to show people the book makes a very good first impression. We can draw direct links from the book to increases in business. It was well worth the work.'*

Ben Sherwood, Hillier Hopkins LLP, **www.hillierhopkins.co.uk**

Simon: *'The book gave us the opportunity to clarify our own thinking and get to the essence of what we were about and what we believed in.'*

Richard: *'It also led to me getting a regular column in Norway's biggest circulation personal finance magazine.'*

(Richard is based in Oslo.)

Simon: *'The book has helped us win clients – it gets you a warmer reception. And it has helped us keep our clients too – we haven't lost a client that has read our book. Also, clients are more inclined to refer us because of the book.'*

Valuable tips for writing a book from *The 7 Secrets of Money* authors

1 Write as if you were writing for someone with very little previous knowledge of your business.

2 Get a non-industry insider to review the book.

3 Ask a client to review drafts and give frank feedback.

4 Lose the jargon.

5 Allow enough time to write the book.

6 Get professional editing help.

There used to be only one way of publishing a book, and that was through a traditional publishing house, but that's no longer the case. Self-publishing is now a serious option for any author. This route has shaken off its 'vanity publishing' connotations and produces some really high-quality publications. A third way has emerged in recent years, sometimes known as 'self-publishing with help' – these partnership publishers as they are known collaborate with authors to work together on shared goals for each project, and combine the best of both a traditional and self-publishing approach.

Whichever publishing route you choose, writing a book will bring you many business advantages. It is in no way the simple option as any author will tell you, but it's an investment that will bring huge benefit – to you and your business. Is it time you wrote it all down?

What deeper content to choose when?

Which format is right for you? It depends on your goal, your content, your business and your customers.

Some of the above are only really relevant for those whose products or services require a 'considered purchase', eg consultants, advisers, software products, etc. Selling hamburgers or other quick purchase commodities? White papers are not really for you. But there is no reason why you cannot still up the value of the content you deliver. Get creative – recipe books, calendars, interactive games. If you understand your customers well enough you'll be able to come up with content of real value that they'll treasure for far longer than a blog or a Tweet.

- Write a white paper if you're in a competitive technical field. Especially good for consultants, getting your message read at board level and influencing a highly educated clientele.

- Write an e-book or guide if you are communicating to a wider field in a conversational tone. Particularly good for social sharing.

- Publish a book if you love your subject, you're an expert in your field, and you know there's a gap in the market for what you want to say. If you really want the stamp of authority, this is the option for you.

What to write about in your key content pieces

Deeper content pieces are places where you can tackle the really big questions and challenges that your clients (and customers) are facing. You'll be building up layers and layers of content, constantly looking at new ways of saying things, but creating deeper content is where you make sure customers' key questions are answered head on, in an engaging way.

A good way to think about it is in terms of referrals. What would you really love a potential new client to have from you in the first instance? It's probably not a piece of sales literature – you know the dangers of trying to sell too early. So what's the most useful thing you can give them? What's going to have the biggest impact? What's really going to make them think, 'These are people who can help me'?

Devoting time and resources into content that answers the really big questions will strengthen your content toolkit.

You'll find more detail on uncovering your content sweet spot so you know what to write about in Chapter 11.

Deeper content demands great design

As wordsmiths, you might expect us to argue for the supremacy of the written word. But the deeper we go into the world of valuable content, the more strongly we realize the inseparable link between content and design. The greatest words in the world won't get read if the design is all over the place. The smoothest design in the world will trip up if the words don't make good sense.

When it comes to creating your deeper content, commit to quality. People won't take your ideas seriously if they're not professionally presented. And they will be equally disappointed if your design makes empty promises. If you are investing in creating deeper content, don't forget to invest in some great design too. Hire a professional designer. Use good-quality photographs or illustrations that augment, not distract from your words. Ideally, it's a partnership.

And don't forget print

Printed content is not dead. Not by a long shot. In our digital age, a well-designed, useful or inspiring printed piece is a gift – a welcome change from the online deluge. Create printed copies of your deeper content – your papers, guides, slide sets or books – and send them to your contacts if you want to make your mark.

The importance of a strong landing page

If you're up and running with social media you'll be tweeting about your deeper content, tempting people towards your website, and trying to persuade them to take the next step in a relationship with you. To motivate people to download and read your deeper written content you will need a compelling pitch or 'landing page' for each piece of deeper content where you convert that spark of interest into action.

Landing pages are crucial – you have a couple of seconds to convert that 'hmmmm maybe' into 'give it to me now'. So how do you do that?

The best landing pages are clear, focused and economical. Good sales copywriting is key. You need to get one message across, clearly and succinctly.

> *Get rid of half the words on each page, then get rid of half of what's left.*
>
> Steve Krug[8]

Key to remember with landing page copy is to focus on the benefit your deeper content will bring the reader. You're not offering a 'free 10-page report', you're offering '30 ways to save money on accountancy fees'. No one is interested in your free report (however hard you've worked on it); they want something that's going to help them now.

Henneke Duistermaat gives excellent advice on writing great landing page copy (enchantingmarketing.com):

Follow these three simple steps to planning landing page copy:

1 Create a list of benefits. If you struggle with defining benefits, list features first, and then ask yourself, *So what? Why does my reader care?*

2 Create a list of objections to taking the required action. What might stop people downloading your report, signing up for your free trial, or buying your product?

3 List the benefits and objections in order of importance; mention the most important information first.

So, clear and benefits-driven will win the day. Is there anything to steer clear of when it comes to landing page copy?

Five landing page no-nos:

1 Dull headline. They're interested but that interest could easily evaporate if the page doesn't live up to its promise.

2 Too much clutter. Your blog post feed and lively sidebar are a distraction here. Just give them the information they want.

3 Too much choice. You only want them to do one thing – sign up – so get rid of anything else on the page.

4 Bad design. Don't lose your head and start jazzing the page up with loads of colour and fancy images. Keep it clear and professional.

5 Overestimating your audience's interest. We're all lazy, too lazy to even scroll down a lot of the time. Get your message across quickly in the top half of the page.

Should you make people fill out a form to download your content?

Deeper content takes a lot more work, and costs more to produce. So should you 'gate' it – getting people to register for the privilege of downloading your content – to make sure you get a good return on your investment?

Whether or not to get people to complete a form on your website in order to download your deeper valuable content is a contentious issue in the world of web marketing. For many, gating your content by asking the reader to hand over their email address in exchange for strong content is a fair exchange. You are offering something valuable that you have sweated hard to produce. They are obviously interested in your subject, so you want to keep talking to them. Collect their email address in return for your valuable content and add them to your mailing list or to a series of useful targeted emails, and you can 'nurture the lead' towards a sale.

The opposing view is that you shouldn't gate anything you produce. If someone is interested in your content, let them have it and set your content free. They will choose to come back to you and buy from you if it is valuable enough when the time is right. The most important thing is to give them a good experience of your brand.

> *For your ideas to spread... you've got to give up control. Make your information on the web totally free for people to access, with absolutely no virtual strings attached: no electronic gates, no registration requirements, and no email address checking necessary.*

David Meerman Scott[9]

Most content is freely available on the web now. Video, for example, is probably your most expensive content option, freely available via YouTube so why restrict the rest of your content?

Gate your content with care. Here at Valuable Content most of the content on our site is free for anyone to download, talk about and share, and share they do. We believe that giving generously and freely is the best way to build your reputation and your business. If your content is valuable enough, trust you will get plenty in return. Motivating people to sign up to our email list without forcing them is our approach.

You will need to weigh up the pros and cons for your own business. If you gate your content you will add people to your mailing list, but you'll lose a proportion of potentially interested customers who will click away once they reach your electronic barrier.

If you do decide to gate your content make sure it's only for the really, really valuable stuff; exceptional content – detailed surveys, unique studies, substantive research, webinars or really useful guides that can't be found elsewhere on the web. Make sure the gated stuff is more valuable than your free content so it feels like a fair exchange. You have to earn the right to ask for people's email addresses in a world where inboxes are already overloaded. So your gated content better be worthwhile.

If you do gate your content make any sign-up fields as straightforward as possible. The fewer fields, and the more compelling you make this call to action, the more likely people are to fill them in. A 20-field form to fill in will turn away all but the most doggedly determined.

If you ask for people's information be very clear what you will and won't do with the information they give you. Jason Mliki, owner of US-based professional services marketing firm Rattleback sets out a valuable approach:

You will add this person to your email database if they ask to do so. If they don't sign up for your newsletter, you might send them an email to invite them to do so. But, you'll only do it once. And, you'll never do it again if they don't respond. You won't call them five minutes after they downloaded the content assuming they're ready to hire you. You might call them at some point in the future to make your firm available to them as a resource. But, you won't translate this small extension of trust from your potential client as a chance to rush into a sales conversation.

Jason Mlicki, Rattleback

rattleback.com

Repurposing and the value of integrated content campaigns

Deep content is the bedrock of valuable sales campaigns. You'll find more on using valuable content to sell in Chapter 14. Unlike a blog post that lives mainly on your website, deeper content crosses channels. It's one idea, communicated in a mix of formats.

A great example of this is the hilarious Joy of Fix campaign from moulded glue manufacturers Sugru (**www.sugru.com/joyoffix**). It lives as a video, as a poster, as written content, as pictures, as tips – shared widely and with a big smile by customers across social media platforms. The strength of the big idea means that it can stretch with ease across different media.

Before you launch multi-channel campaign like this, test if the idea behind it is big enough. The really good ones lend themselves to many forms of content – a SlideShare and a video and a blog post, a video, a manifesto and a guide. They are ideas that are too big to be tied down.

CONTENT STORY Pensions and benefits advice firm Hymans Robertson win more business than ever with the integrated Guided Outcomes campaign

Hymans Robertson wanted to shake up the workplace pensions market with a new approach – 'Guided Outcomes' – that would benefit employees and employers alike. They had a strong idea and story but needed great content as a means of explaining it. Director of Marketing Strategy Terri Lucas wanted to build a daring and creative campaign that would really bring the new concept to life and connect with clients and prospects on a very human level.

> *We were up against much bigger names in this market so we knew we had to do something different, to be imaginative and stand out creatively. It's a route we can pull off because as a steadfastly independent firm we have the freedom to be bold and daring, even if we don't have the budgets of the bigger business. A straightforward literal presentation of Guided Outcomes wasn't going to be enough.*

Mr Feelgood was born.

> *As well as working it into our main corporate website we developed a **stand-alone microsite** as a base for the Guided Outcomes message – guidedoutcomes.hymans.co.uk. A big part of bringing the website content alive was through animation and we developed four fun little Mr Feelgood **videos**. Alongside this we crafted regular content to educate the market and tell the story plus a more traditional film where we got industry contacts and potential clients talking about how excited they were about Guided Outcomes. We wanted testimonials and endorsements so we worked that into the video.*

> ***PR** was important for making the case and for building profile and awareness. We got national, broadcast and trade coverage – the story was in* The Sunday Times, *the* Daily Mail, *the* FT, *the* Telegraph, *Radio 5 and lots of trades. The Pensions Minister Steve Webb found the new thinking so thought provoking that we know it is now on his radar as another solution as he considers pensions reform.*

> *We hosted a series of in-house **events** around the topic too. We placed **ads** in the trade press. Ads, PR and social media are good for awareness and familiarity. We find that things like direct marketing and events are better for prospecting and getting meetings.*

> *Our sales and marketing teams are really tightly integrated. We worked hard to make sure that our marketing messages and sales pitches were consistent and joined up. It all needs to be linked and follow-up conducted by the business development team in a timely fashion.*

> *We don't shy away from **direct marketing** here at Hymans Robertson, as long as it's creative and genuinely helpful. We crafted a creative mail-out campaign using mini iPads that looked brilliant. The iPads were sent to carefully selected prospects with a pre-loaded presentation (starring Mr*

Feelgood of course) with links to the microsite content, which our new business people could follow up.

***Social media** played a part too. We set up a #FeelGoodFriday hashtag and had a bit of fun on Twitter and LinkedIn using the Mr Feelgood dude kind of feel and tone. This helped us to spread the word and extend the news to our networks. We got conversations going through Twitter with journalists and got a bit of coverage that way.*

This is a valuable, multi-channel approach that has really paid off. Five months on from campaign launch Terri said: *'We made 315 calls and from that secured 78 meetings so far. We have 52 opportunities in the pipeline and we've won five major new clients to date.'*

Repurpose for efficiency

Integrated content campaigns are well worth the investment when it comes to sales results. This is also about efficiency. Once you've put the time and resources into longer pieces of content there is an awful lot you can do with them.

Repurpose your deeper content to squeeze maximum value from it.
One e-book can become:

- 10 blogs;
- 50 short tips on Twitter;
- a short series of guides;
- a SlideShare;
- shared graphics on Pinterest;
- a targeted email marketing campaign;
- the basis of a webinar;
- a series of podcasts;
- a video.

Aim for efficiency and make the most of all your hard work. The thinking and writing that you do for your deeper written content can be stretched and tweaked in many directions, to fit the needs of different audiences and the styles of specific social media channels. It's well worth the investment.

Take action

- Prioritize the creation of some deeper content, eg *in the next quarter we are going to create a guide/e-book/white paper.* Plan to promote this hard.

- To help you decide what content to create, consider – what's the most valuable idea you can share with your customers?

- Consider what you want this deeper content to do for your business.

- Think about your customers and decide which format would work best for your message.

CHAPTER 9
VIDEO, AUDIO, INFOGRAPHICS AND MORE

Humans are incredibly visual and powerful. Moving images help us find meaning and understand the world around us. Video helps capture and contextualize the world around us.

Dan Patterson, Digital Platform Manager for ABC News Radio[1]

In this chapter:

- Different formats to connect with more people.
- The rise and rise of video content.
- Where to start with video.
- DIY versus working with a video company.
- Wonderful webinars.
- The power of infographics.
- Podcasts for business.
- Online games as sales tools.
- Mobile apps.

The right words will get your message across, but written content isn't the only way to connect. Think about the smart infographic that says it so simply, the video that captures the sense of a person more quickly than 50 words could do, the podcast you can listen to on the train. Making your website truly valuable means embracing many different ways to communicate. It means getting your message into different formats to inspire, guide and educate your website users; making it easy for people to get to your valuable stuff, in whatever way suits them best.

We are all now used to receiving content in a wide variety of formats. And there are myriad different options today – fuelled by new technologies that make it even easier for you to connect with customers and clients in engaging ways. In this chapter we cover video, webinars, podcasts, animations, infographics and online games and apps but there are more and more options coming through; endless possibilities to get your message across. Mix it up, play around with them, have some fun. See what you can create.

Different formats to connect with more people

However good your writing, sometimes there is a better way to say it. Some people find it easier to grasp information visually; others find it easier to listen to get a sense of a subject. Not everyone will want to read your white paper, or even your blog. Understanding that different people have very different learning styles – seeing, hearing, doing – is a useful way of making sure you're giving your business message the best chance of a warm reception.

It's also good housekeeping to try and get the most value from every piece of content you create by reusing your content in different formats. Cross-referencing case studies and blog posts, creating downloads from guides, infographics from research, posters from infographics, videos from events, podcasts from research – dig deep into your subject and present it as creatively as you can.

Video, audio, webinars are more tools you can use to get the most out of what you're doing. If you were giving a talk, it would make sense to get professional help to film it or record it. The 50 people in the room listening to you swells to an unlimited number of people who will be able to hear what you're saying, via the content on your website. Imagine: you can still be talking to potential clients while you're lying on a beach somewhere!

Of course, valuable content principles apply to these formats as tightly as they do to the written word – only the highest quality will do.

The rise, rise and rise of video content

YouTube dominates web usage, and is a fantastic business tool. YouTube is now the world's second-biggest search engine – so getting smart with video should be high on your agenda.

Why is video such an important marketing tool? Over the past few years online video has become a key way for people to satisfy their information and entertainment needs. Video is a fantastic way to tell a story online. Video content adds another layer of richness, credibility and accessibility to your website. When we are surfing the web there are times when it's easier to watch and listen than it is to read. Many small businesses are already getting good results from their video content, and it's easy to see why.

There are a head-spinning array of statistics that show that video is the way to go. Nielsen claims 64 per cent of marketers expect video to dominate their strategies in the near future. Video is 98 per cent more likely to put you on the first page of a search engine. Forbes Insight found that 59 per cent of senior executives prefer to watch video instead of reading text, if both are available on the same page. Video in email marketing has been shown to increase click-through rates by over 96 per cent.

And by 2017, video will account for 69 per cent of all consumer internet traffic, according to Cisco. Video on demand traffic alone will have almost trebled.

Video is a gift for content marketers who want to build their brands, connect with more people, and deepen their credibility. (That's all of us.)

Your video options

Video covers a lot of bases, but there are a few types that are most useful to the small business content marketer. They are:

- **Case studies and testimonials** – including talking heads of your clients.
- **Creative brand stories** – could be filmed or animated.
- **First-meeting videos** – you talking, just as you would in an initial client meeting. Good for ice breaking.

- **'How to' videos** – explanation, screen grabs. Perfect show don't tell material.
- **Presentation videos** – film of you giving a client-friendly presentation.
- **Interview-style videos –** talking heads.
- **Slide walkthroughs** – you talking through a presentation.
- **Vlogs** – video-based blogs.

As with any other type of content, pick the vehicle that will help you get the meaning across most clearly. Would a three-minute 'how to do X' video be most useful to your customers here, or would they get more from a video case study? Is it important to your business that people get to see your face and hear your voice, or would an animation tell the story of what you do more effectively?

Remember, people will give you more time the further they are on the road to a sale. If they're in early research mode, you probably have a minute or less of their attention. Serious evaluation time? They'll give you longer – up to three minutes. And if they really want to learn – as long as it takes!

Some video formats can be tackled by the enthusiastic DIYer, others are best left to the professionals. You'll find tips here for getting the best out of both approaches. But first, why is video such a powerful addition to your content toolkit?

Why video is so good for content marketers

Video helps people find you

A good video will get more people to your website. A study by Aimclear shows that people are more likely to click through to a website if the search throws up video results:

> *Videos in universal search results have a 41 per cent higher click-through rate than plain text.*

Aimclear[2]

Video encourages people to stick around longer too (on average two minutes more on your website). Longer visits aren't just good news for keeping people interested in you and your business, they give you extra SEO oomph too. Google places more value on longer visits, so anything that encourages visitors to spend more time on your website will improve your ranking.

Google ranks 'informational' videos most highly, which is just the kind of content that any business can produce well. Remember Google loves content that answers the questions people are asking. So approach video content in the same way as written content: produce something useful and you'll please both your clients and search engines.

Video helps people get to know you

Video is great for capturing your approach and giving people a real sense of you as a person. If your personality is absolutely key to your business success, and particularly in a business where potential clients might be nervous of working with you – for example divorce lawyers, driving instructors, or dentists – a video can be an excellent way of showing what you're like, and helping people get a powerful impression of what it would be like to be working with you.

Video helps make an emotional connection, fast

When someone visits your website for the first time, you're aiming for a fast emotional connection. Your content needs to be factually accurate, but it's also got to feel right.

Woolley and Co is a firm of family law solicitors that has embraced video as a great way to break down barriers between clients and lawyers. Teresa Harris explains why they created a series of videos on divorce for their website.

Our website gets a lot of traffic, and there's a lot of content there. We're good at blogging and producing written material, and we've created a huge bank of articles, but we know that sometimes it's difficult to absorb that amount of text. Not everyone likes to receive information that way. We wanted a way to bring the material to life, and we saw video as another way of getting our message through to potential clients. Divorce is the area where we get most enquiries, so it made sense to create some video content that would answer the questions people have around this highly stressful area.

We worked with a specialist video company and shot seven films in a day, which you can find on our website and our YouTube channel. They're very simple films, just one of our solicitors talking as they would during a first meeting. We cover some of the most commonly asked questions around divorce and children, divorce and finance. The most popular one is 'How to get a divorce' followed by 'How to save money on your divorce'.

They work very well for us; clients appreciate them. People are nervous about talking to a solicitor, divorce is a difficult process, but the videos show our human side. It puts your mind at ease when you can see the person you'll be talking to, and hear the way they speak. It makes a first meeting easier.

Video is an important part of our marketing mix. For us, blogs serve a different purpose – they're good for profile raising, increasing our search engine ranking, demonstrating our expertise and the fact we're up to date on current issues – but our blog readership tends to be our peers and the media. The videos are firmly focused on what clients want to know. Different people like their information in different ways, you need to do it all ways for the best results.

Teresa Harris, Woolley and Co Solicitors, **www.family-lawfirm.co.uk**

Video entertains

Content that makes people smile always goes down well. We're not suggesting we give over your website home page to pictures of cats falling off things, or pugs dressed as ballerinas, but creating feel-good and entertaining content will serve you well.

For downright smiling from ear to ear you cannot beat the Dollar Shave Club: **www.dollarshaveclub.com**. Salesy and in your face, yes, but hilarious. Packed with personality and self-deprecating humour, their videos are so entertaining and commercially extremely successful.

Video tells stories

For telling stories and sharing big ideas, video is hard to beat. We doubt the TED Talks would have taken off and flown so high if they'd been the TED White Papers. Video lets you get quickly and deeply into subjects, and there is real power in hearing a brilliant speaker just talking. The format doesn't have to be complicated – the simpler the better.

Where to start with video

The possibilities of filmed content are huge, and it can feel a little overawing. More and more corporations are weighing in with high production value films; the news is full of videos that have gone viral – some amateur, some corporate – making real money for the film owners. Serious businesses are investing heavily in video content, so how can you possibly compete? How do you start?

The first decision to make is to decide what kind of video you want, and why, and whether it's something you can tackle alone. Look again at the list at the start of the chapter. If what you're looking to say can be communicated by a vlog, or a very simple presentation, it might be that you can create something yourself.

DIY video production

Sometimes the message you're trying to get across doesn't need expensive, production-quality video. It's possible to make good video content without a big budget.

> *I'm always on the lookout for situations that I can video and share – athletes training, swimmers pounding the pool, cyclists touring the island – there's a lot of good visual stuff happening here that makes good quick video content. I can share it online instantly. Video really helps me promote Sands Beach Resort.*
>
> John Beckley, Digital Marketing Manager, Sands Beach Resort, Lanzarote

There's something to be said for the authenticity of low-tech video, and it can work really well for small businesses.

Remember that brevity rules. Two-minute videos (or even shorter) get much more play, and are much more likely to be played all the way to the end than long videos.

Working with a video company

For many types of video though, it helps to get some expert support. Case studies, brand stories, client testimonials, more complex presentations or interviews – these are all bigger projects than a one-person band can handle. Luckily there are lots of great companies around, and they'll help you with the creative as well as the technical side of the production.

For a small business used to the relatively low costs associated with blogging and other types of written content creation, the costs associated with making video feel much higher.

> In order to create high-quality video content, you're going to have to spend money. The proper equipment is essential to all aspects of video production, but more importantly, hire the right team.[3]

Costs aside, the key thing for you to remember is that you want a video that will be useful to your clients. There is no point in investing your entire marketing budget in a big glossy advertisement for your business. Remember, everyone skips the adverts. If you want potential clients and customers to watch, create something that interests them, and answers their questions. Make that clear to your director when you're explaining what you want to achieve – it's not 'a film about us', it's a 'film for our clients'.

How to get the best out of your video company

- **Be clear** – know the key message you want to get across and assemble your ideas into a storyboard.
- **Give them lots of background** – tell them about your customers, your business, and the unique way you help.
- **Do your research** – point them towards content you like, and tell them why that approach feels right for you.
- **Be open** – making a video is a chance to try new things, so be flexible and prepared to go out of your comfort zone.
- **Practise presentation with a webcam at home** – get used to saying it out loud, sing it in the shower, bore your kids with it!
- **Set aside enough time** – you don't want to have to rush on the day, so clear the decks for the time your producer suggests.

Valuable tips for being at ease on camera

Ann-Marie McCormack, a film director at AmmAFilms, makes videos for companies to use on their websites, and has dealt with many people who feel nervous at the thought of being filmed. Here are her tips to help you relax:

- Just be yourself. Wear something you feel confident in and don't act. Be natural.
- Be reassured that it is not live. Only 10 per cent of what is shot is generally used, so if you don't like what you have said, it can be cut out and you have control.
- Focus on chatting directly to the interviewer and ignore the camera.
- Remember the camera crew and interviewer are there to make you look good and feel at ease, so relax and let them do their job.

- If you feel you didn't get what you wanted to say across, you can do it again... and again... and again.

Awesome animations

While there's a benefit to showing your human side and appearing on camera, there's also an argument for creating animations that explore ideas and tell stories more creatively. Animated videos are a brilliant tool for businesses with a tricky proposition to communicate, and for businesses on a mission to make big change.

Some firms have gone big budget on their animated content. The stunning animation *The Scarecrow* was produced by Mexican Grill brand Chipotle and created by Academy Award-winning Moonbot Studios. This is brand storytelling at its very finest, a beautiful and haunting tale of a quest to bring real food back to the people. *The Scarecrow* film achieved over 11.6 million views on YouTube, more than 12,000 Facebook posts, and more than 31,000 tweets from more than 26,000 unique users. Take a look at **www.scarecrowgame.com**.

Animations allow you to tell your company story in a simple compelling way. Just as infographics are a great way to communicate complex data with impact in a way that's easy to understand, animations are an alternative means to tell your story. Even Google likes video animations, recognizing and ranking highly for strong, rich and original content.

There are many types of animation to explore and many uses as part of your content marketing too – you could animate the company story, use this format for explainer videos and teaching lessons, product demos, whiteboard illustrations or to get the big idea across.

And you don't have to have a Hollywood-style budget to make animations work for your business. Hire a local professional animator, or look at some of the many online tools arising to help you create animations cost-effectively – Powtoons, Wideo, Go! Animate, VideoScribe and many more. Animation deserves pride of place in your content toolkit and it's getting easier to produce.

Wonderful webinars

Webinars are another non-written tool that businesses can use to connect with clients, and demonstrate all-round valuable usefulness. Good webinars generate leads, and raise your reputation – perfect valuable content fodder!

A webinar is a seminar conducted over the internet. It is a great chance to connect with a range of people and teach them something useful. It's a workshop without the expense of hiring a huge meeting room. It's connecting with people worldwide, all without leaving your chair.

Webinars confer some of the same benefits as events – the sense of joining together with others at the same point in time (albeit at a lower key), but webinars have the advantage that they can be recorded and packaged as content after the event. Webinars are a good addition to your content library.

There are many webinar and web conferencing platforms and services to select from, including GoToWebinar, AnyMeeting, Fuze and Adobe Connect, with a range of functionality. Before you select one, think carefully about your long-term goals. How many events, how many attendees, how much flexibility do you need in terms of customization and branding? Your own speaker or are you inviting guests? When and how does your audience expect to receive the content? Build a list of questions to help you select the right platform to host your webinars without a hitch.

Here are some tips for good webinars.

Valuable webinar tips

- **Be prepared.** Thoroughly prepare what you want to cover and test the webinar software before the big day.
- **Trial it.** Do a trial run of the entire presentation to friends or family to familiarize yourself with all the controls.
- **Remind people.** Send out plenty of reminders beforehand, up to and including the day itself. It's surprising how many people leave it to the last minute to register, or lose the log-in details.
- **Get there early.** Show up at least 15 minutes early so you can test the audio etc and greet people. Display a holding slide until the event starts.

- **Don't forget to say hello!** Be friendly, introduce yourself and say why you're qualified to talk about the topic.

- **Let people settle.** Don't launch straight into your first point; give people a chance to get comfortable.

- **Record it.** Make the most of the webinar by creating new content for your website or blog.

- **Be valuable.** Give great, high-value information and don't oversell (if you are selling something).

- **Follow up** after the event. Webinars are an excellent way to make new connections.

The power of infographics

Information portrayed graphically, instead of in pure words or numbers, can say a huge amount in a small space. It appeals to people who prefer visual over verbal explanation, and opens up your message to more people. Check out 'Information is Beautiful' (**www.informationisbeautiful.net**) to see how big ideas and thoughts can be expressed succinctly with creative design.

If you have a complex idea to get across, a lot of figures to express, or processes to explain, it might be worth speaking to a graphic designer and commissioning some clever visual representations instead of relying on straight words and numbers. Your brief to the designer should include: '*Make this really easy to understand... I want people to see what we do straight away... I want it to look stylish and add value to my website.*'

Infographics have become a very popular form of online content, much shared on social media. There are many different styles you can use to get your point across – from the more traditional data-driven infographic to the simple and fun, like our Content Marketing Snakes and Ladders (page 249).

Podcasts for business

I'm a huge podcast fan. Without exaggeration, I can say that I spend more time listening to podcasts than I do listening to music (at least, not ambiently) or watching TV. If I'm running, or working out at the gym, or driving, I'm probably listening to a podcast.

Chris Butler, Newfangled, @chrbutler, **www.newfangled.com**

Boring commutes, long training runs, quiet lunch breaks are opportunities for people to use their smartphones for entertainment, research or connecting. Aural learners love audio content, so your podcasts could be welcome, if they're valuable. A good podcast will help potential customers to feel like they know you and the way you think – an easier decision then to hire you.

We hope we've stressed the importance of ridding your content of sales messages strongly enough already, but where video or audio is concerned then it's even more crucial. If you're creating content you'd like people to give their valuable downtime to, then it's got to be useful, beautiful or entertaining. A straight sales message just won't cut it. People will turn off.

Podcasts are great for delivering concise information without your users having to download documents, or read through lots of text, and creating one is fairly straightforward. All you need is your computer, a microphone, and a connection to the internet, and you can get going.

An MP3 player, or a computer that enables audio is all your clients need to hear your recordings, so you could make one today, and be broadcasting worldwide tomorrow.

Three basic podcast styles:

1 **Interviews.** Hearing a real conversation rather than reading a transcript of it makes ideas come alive. Talking with a client, or colleagues, about a subject you know is of interest to your market makes for a good podcast. If you're the interviewer, keep the talk on track. You know what will be interesting to your listeners so ask questions that steer the conversation back to the really important stuff.

2 **Tips.** Not all blog ideas will work as podcasts, but the Valuable Content stalwart of five ways to do this and 10 ways to do that translates well to a podcast. It works for all the same reasons it works as web copy – it's quick, rewarding and feeds the hunger for information now – but it widens your reach to people who'd rather listen and learn, than read.

3 **How-tos.** Accessible audio guides that teach people things they really want to know are very valuable content. How to talk to children about divorce; how to win a planning appeal; how to prepare for your first marathon. Whatever line of business you're in, there will be useful nuggets that you can record and share with your audience.

Online games as sales tools

Entertainment is one of the key reasons people use the web, so smart companies are creating branded entertaining content to keep their company name in front of clients. Companies that need to give personality to technical products are leading the way. Hewlett Packard is one example. David Nutley of Nutley and Nutley who designs and builds online games for HP explains why:

> It's a great way for companies to show a human face, rather than bombarding clients with constant sales messages. We build a game, something fun and highly competitive – leader boards are good motivators – with a good prize, and invite a targeted list of people to join it. People really enjoy them. You can tell that people are logging on every day, updating their scores, and completing additional tasks for extra points. Online games work far better for some of our clients than straight advertising. You've no way of knowing if your message has been read with a print ad. But with a game, you know that Mr X played the game six times last week. You're definitely on his radar.

www.nutleys.com

Mobile apps

Our love affair with our mobile phones has led to an explosion of mobile apps. Want to know the weather? Find your way round Barcelona? Translate your email into Polish? There's an app for it, and millions of others offering informative, entertaining and useful content. Businesses are harnessing this technology to create apps that take their brands straight into the hands of their customers. Is there an app in your business?

Calvium, the makers of App Furnace (**www.appfurnace.com**) highlight the following characteristics of successful apps:

- They serve a single purpose. Unlike websites where visitors are happy to explore, app users want to meet their goal in as few taps as possible.

- They provide linear navigation. From top to bottom, like a book page.

- They embrace the technology on offer. GPS, camera, QR codes – all make apps more engaging.

- They're tactile. People will hold, tap, stroke, spin, shake an app. The best ones use this to enhance the user's experience.

- Designed for fingers (or thumbs). They're easy to use.

A good app is one that fills a genuine need, is designed well, is accessible and is highly useable.

Apps that help your customers are another form of valuable content. More and more of us are using our phones to access services that we used to access through our laptops. Providing a mobile-specific version of your service is a useful thing to do. It's a way of being in the right place at the right time for your customers.

Mix it up

When it comes to deeper content, there are no hard and fast rules on format. Don't restrict yourself to the written word. Give yourself permission to be creative, and the ideas will start flowing. As well as the suggestions in this chapter you could put together posters, cartoons, or quizzes. How about manifestos, maps or magazines?

There are so many more ways to create content that connects with people than we have highlighted here; the possibilities are endless. Borrow ideas from the things that inspire you – books, films, music – and use them to shape valuable content that lights your fire, and that your audience will love.

Take action

- Research videos, podcasts, webinars and infographics that have been produced in your sector. Which approach would delight your customers?
- Use your network to identify recommended video companies or freelancers you could work with.
- Test the waters with your audience – what form of content would they most appreciate?

CHAPTER 10

WIDEN YOUR REACH: PR, GUEST BLOGGING, EVENTS AND PAID ADVERTISING

Content is your champagne and, when used appropriately, PR can pop the cork.

Hubspot[1]

In this chapter:

- How valuable content wins you PR opportunities.
- Getting your content published in industry-leading media.
- The etiquette of guest blogging.
- Making the most of events and speaker opportunities.
- Paid advertising options – the valuable approach.

Follow the advice in the previous chapters and you will build a great foundation for your marketing. All this valuable content will be proving your expertise and sharing knowledge that people are hungry for, drawing leads into your business. Now is the time to really widen your reach by getting your ideas in front of a new and bigger audience, establishing your authority in your chosen niche.

This chapter explains how to use PR, guest blogging, events and paid advertising options to amplify your content for even greater success. Think of it as taking your content on tour.

The value of getting your content published in industry-leading media

Once you've built up a bank of valuable content on your website and blog, it makes sense to bring it to a wider audience. Hunt for opportunities for writing and publishing your articles on well-respected and relevant websites, blogs, journals and publications. Key influencers and authority sites will have more clout and a far bigger audience than yours. They can help you to spread your ideas and get the word out to groups of people who have never heard of you before.

Search engines will reward you too. Links back to your site from influential websites with a lot of traffic will build your authority in Google's eyes and that will help your ranking.

> *Inbound links are links from pages on external sites linking back to your site. When the links are merit-based and freely volunteered as an editorial choice, they're also one of the positive signals to Google about your site's importance. Relevant quality inbound links can affect your PageRank (one of many factors in our ranking algorithm). And quality links often come naturally to sites with compelling content or offering a unique service.*
>
> Maile Ohye, Developer Programs Tech Lead[2]

Most publications and media – web or print – are hungry for great content. If your content is relevant and of high enough quality you have a good chance of getting your articles published.

Build relationships with the publishing team or journalists on social media and via their blog if they have one before you contact them.

Even when you are writing for other websites, all the valuable rules apply. Write articles that are helpful and inspiring, not self-oriented. Answer the questions you know people have in your field. Your regular syndicated spot will swiftly vanish if you write a thinly disguised sales pitch!

We are firm believers in quality over quantity. Blasting the same article to a thousand article directories and low-grade link farms is a manipulative technique to boost website authority that is thankfully losing its power thanks to recent search engine algorithm improvements.

Here is Google's take on article marketing on article directory sites:

> *Honestly, I'm not a huge fan of article marketing. Typically the sorts of sites that just republish these articles are not the highest-quality sites.*
>
> Google's Head of Web Spam, Matt Cutts[3]

Instead provide genuinely valuable content on your site and other sites that buyers find useful.

Valuable content wins you PR opportunities

Regularly sharing valuable content in a variety of formats attracts the attention not just of prospects but also of influential people and publications in your field. The connections you build can open new doors for you and widen your marketing scope.

Niche web development firm Newfangled have been asked to speak and write very widely in their industry on the strength of the content they share:

> *Because the content on our website does such a thorough job of documenting our expertise on a continual basis, it has attracted the attention of many prospects, but also other key influencers in our field whom we are able to foster relationships with. These relationships open doors which enable us to start engaging in a wide array of off-site marketing activities such as speaking at key industry events, publishing in industry journals, and publishing books through the right industry publishers. All of those opportunities originated because of the strength of our website and content.*
>
> Mark O'Brien, President of Newfangled

Ascentor's focus on providing valuable content is building their reputation as recognized experts in their field, and quickly landed them an opportunity with the BBC:

> *Only a couple of months after launching our new content-rich website we were approached by an industry-leading body to post our articles on their site. This was a real coup for us: we had a growing list of followers but they have thousands of readers every day. It gave us far more exposure, boosting our credibility and expanding our reach. The following month we were lucky enough to be featured in an article on information security on the BBC news*

website. These opportunities all stemmed from the authoritative nature of the valuable content we share, and business is coming in as a result.

Dave James, MD, Ascentor

Whether it's an opportunity on the web, in print, on TV or radio, this kind of free publicity is invaluable. It is an inexpensive way of getting your message out far wider than you can do alone, building awareness, respect and interest in what you do.

> **Valuable Tip**
>
> It is flattering to be asked but with each new opportunity check whether this is the right forum for you. Writing content takes effort so be mindful of how you're using your time. Does this opportunity meet your business goals and reach the kind of people you want to attract? Use your time judiciously and measure the outcome too.

The etiquette of guest blogging

Guest blogging is a fantastic opportunity that is often neglected. Of course, you should never lose your focus on regularly producing valuable content on your own blog. But if you make guest blogging (or blogger outreach as it's also known) part of your marketing strategy you'll improve your reach, your site's search engine authority and overall awareness of you and your brand.

Posting your articles on other relevant blogs builds trust, showing you have the respect of your peers – no one is going to share their website space with someone they don't think very highly of. If you share top-notch content and build up relationships via social networking you may well find that other bloggers find you and ask you to write a guest post for their readers.

Guest blogging has helped irreverent copywriter Henneke Duistermaat to build her business:

> *I started guest blogging to build an email list for my own blog. But I quickly found out that guest blogging was a great way to generate business enquiries, too.*

To make guest blogging a success:

1 *Consider who your target audience is – which blogs are they reading?*

2 *Study the popular posts on a blog and read comments to gain a better understanding of an audience*

3 *Network with editors on social media or in the comment section before you send a pitch email*

4 *Take your time to come up with a deliciously seductive headline before your pitch, because it'll make an editor curious, too*

5 *In your pitch email, include a reason why you think your post will be popular with readers. You could point to a comparable post with a high number of tweets or comments. Editors like to know you've done your homework.*

6 *Follow up after publishing a post – help share your guest post, reply to comments, and see whether you can agree another guest post with the editor.*

Some people think guest blogging is simply a method to build links for search engine optimization. But guest blogging is much more than that. It's a way to market your blog and business to a wider audience, and it's an opportunity to build valuable relationships with readers, bloggers, and editors. For me, blogging, guest blogging and email marketing have been the foundation of my online marketing.

How to court the influencers

We get hundreds of cold approaches to supply a guest post for the Valuable Content blog. We've never accepted one of them. We do feature guest posts on our site but they are only ever people who we have built a strong relationship with, people whose ideas we respect, whose content we know our readers will like and learn from.

So if you're thinking of approaching an influential site, journalist or blogger, know that you've got to do the work. There's etiquette to follow here, a right way and a wrong way to win the attention of the big guys. No different from any relationship really.

Work at building the relationship gently first, before you pile in and pitch. Connect on social media, share their stuff and leave intelligent comment on their content before even thinking about making an approach. Offer to do something of value for them – review their book or latest research for example on your site. Flattery gets you a long way. Perhaps ask them for expert comment on a topic and feature it on your site with links back to theirs.

Ideally you want the relationship and respect to be strong enough that they ask YOU to feature on their site. If you want to be more proactive, then here are some rules to follow

What not to do:

- Don't blanket-bomb the same message to multiple sites.
- Don't be pushy or beg.
- Don't promote your own services in the article you write.
- Don't misspell or worse miss their name off completely when making your approach!

How to find the right websites and blogs to guest on

You know what keywords and phrases you want to be found for, so search online and see what sites and blogs come up highest. These are the kind of influencers you want to reach. Dig further by asking your clients or readers what other websites and blogs they like to visit too. Do you respect and value the ideas and content on these sites? If the site is influential and respected by your customers then this signals it's a good place to guest for.

Events as content marketing

Content is as another way of educating and inspiring an audience through sharing valuable ideas so we make a strong pitch for giving a talk at an event as a form of content marketing. Talks are just a different, but very powerful, way to get your story across.

A talk gives you the opportunity to present your ideas to a receptive audience. Presenting on stage is one of the few places where you're likely to get a slice of undivided attention. It's quite a luxury these days to give yourself permission to focus on one thing (mobile switched off) and consequently the talk gives both speaker and audience a chance to make a real connection.

In a recent survey of professional firms, Hinge Marketing found that face-to-face events top the chart in terms of perceived marketing effectiveness (85 per cent see them as effective) but are used by less than two-thirds of professional firms. That gap presents a real opportunity for businesses.[4]

A good speaking gig can prove credibility, initiate new connections and relationships and generate leads fast. It certainly works for us that way.

Making the most of speaker opportunities

Spreading your valuable content wider and raising your profile as an expert in your field can lead naturally to speaking opportunities, or if you want to actively pursue speaking engagements as a way of expanding your network it gives you credence.

As we well remember from when we were first asked to speak at an event (neither of us could even touch our lunch beforehand!), your first speaker opportunity can feel absolutely terrifying at the outset but there's really no need to panic. You don't have to be a professional speaker to give a valuable talk. Start small before a friendly audience and work your way up from there. Before you know it, you'll feel confident speaking at conferences you had only dreamed about before.

Tips for perfect presentations

- Remember, it's not all about you. Know your audience and talk about how they can solve their particular challenges.
- Be clear on the purpose of your talk. Build it around a clear central message.
- If you speak with passion people will find it fascinating. Talk on subjects you care deeply about.
- Tell stories if you want to be engaging. Unless you are appearing on *Dragon's Den* this is not a platform to pitch your services.
- Ditch the bulleted PowerPoint slides. Slides are great for sharing images, charts, perhaps quotes, but never read off your slides.

- Illustrate your points in a creative, colourful, interesting way. A short video often works well.

- Presenting is about relationships – there needs to be engagement and interaction.

- Think of it as a conversation with your audience, not a lecture.

- Prepare. Don't wing it. Practise, practise, practise. Record or film your rehearsals.

- Get a professional to video your speech and post this on your website. This is really valuable content. Share your notes and handouts too.

Notice how many of the points above echo the valuable principles in Chapter 3. Spoken or written, remote or face-to-face, valuable communications are the ones that hit home.

Paid advertising options

When it comes to distributing your content and driving traffic back to your website there are more paid digital advertising options than ever before. These include Google Adwords, pay-per-click and sponsored advertising options on social media, affiliate marketing, remarketing, native ads – the list goes on. And many businesses are taking advantage of these options, not to publicize their products and services, but to promote the valuable content they're producing instead. Paid advertising is another way to amplify your content's reach.

CONTENT STORY   LinkedIn advertising brings Conscious Solutions sales results

The Conscious Solutions business development team (conscious.co.uk) advertises its valuable guides with pay-per-click LinkedIn adverts. David tracks the results of each campaign carefully to monitor return on investment and to learn what works best. For three months Conscious ran a LinkedIn ad campaign targeted at people whose LinkedIn profile said they worked in the legal sector. The total spend was £3,636. Conscious's target ROI, based on other marketing campaigns, for this spend was £28,800. The campaign was promoting one of their valuable content tips booklets – 1,214 clickthroughs generated 104 downloads; 50 effective conversations generated 12 sales opportunities, which resulted in £35,050. A successful campaign by any measure, and the valuable content was a key part.

The paid route can definitely extend your reach but never lose sight of the customer experience. You'll know the kind of advertising that annoys you, and your customers will feel just the same. Respect your audience – they are as busy, as cynical and over-sold to as you. The right advertising – entertaining, useful or emotive – opens up your content to a whole new audience. The wrong advertising approach can backfire in the long term and erode people's trust in your business.

Native advertising, for example, is facing a backlash. Seen as a way for businesses to get their message in front of people who ignore traditional ads, you pay a publication for publishing your content on their website or offline. Native content sits within the flow of all the other content on a site, and looks and feels indistinguishable from it. Often there is only a very veiled reference to the fact it's an advertisement. Many readers have no idea that it's paid advertising, rather than valuable content that's earned its place in that publication.

Fans of native advertising argue that if it's high quality enough, and it's feeding readers' needs for information, then it's fair game. People want the information, and they don't care where it's come from. What's the problem? However, it's the deceptive quality of native advertising that can make hackles rise. If you disguise your ads as independently written editorial and trick people into reading them, they won't thank you for it. Honesty is the best policy.

There are some very interesting new paid options arising, like Vidlinkr – a clever approach to video advertising that spearheads a new breed of relevant, useful and discrete advertising tools (see Coull.com). Ads can be useful. If a piece of content has prompted you to want to buy something it's helpful to be directed straight to the place where you can make the purchase. Valuable advertising – that has to be the future.

Take action

- Research the websites where you'd like to publish a guest blog. Sign up for their feeds, and connect on Twitter.

- Which bloggers would offer value to your clients and customers? Ask them to guest post for you.

- If you're working on deeper content with a strong message, keep your eyes open for speaking opportunities where you could spread the word.

- Sign up for some talks, and watch how the speaker keeps (or loses) your attention. What really engages the audience? Get inspiration for talking brilliance from some of the greats. Watch some TED talks.

- Consider paid options but tread carefully to amplify your content's reach.

PART THREE
HOW TO SUPERCHARGE YOUR BUSINESS WITH VALUABLE CONTENT

When it comes to making the valuable content marketing approach work for your business you have a choice. One option is to adopt the range of content creation and distribution tools and techniques as set out in Part Two. Start blogging, engage in social media, create a monthly email newsletter, get search engine savvy, write deeper stock content, diversify with different formats and take your content wider with smart PR. These are the fundamentals that every business needs in place to market their business today. Many of our more experienced readers will have taken this route with their content marketing, up until now.

Part Three of the book is for people who are ready to get serious about their content – who want to use the valuable content approach to drive real competitive advantage for their business. Read this section in detail if you are determined to set your business apart.

This last section will show you how to think strategically about the content you're creating, and the processes and skills you'll need to put in place to make it work and keep it going. If you're new to content marketing then this research-led approach will position you quickly as a thought leader in your field. If your business is already content marketing but wants to see better results then this strategic approach is also for you – an opportunity to step back, think hard and figure out how to make it work better.

You can supercharge your business with the valuable content marketing approach and this final part of the book will show you how. In a world where more and more businesses are getting in on the content act this is the section you need to help you really stand out from the crowd. The advice in this section will help you continuously create and share truly *valuable* content – the kind of marketing people love.

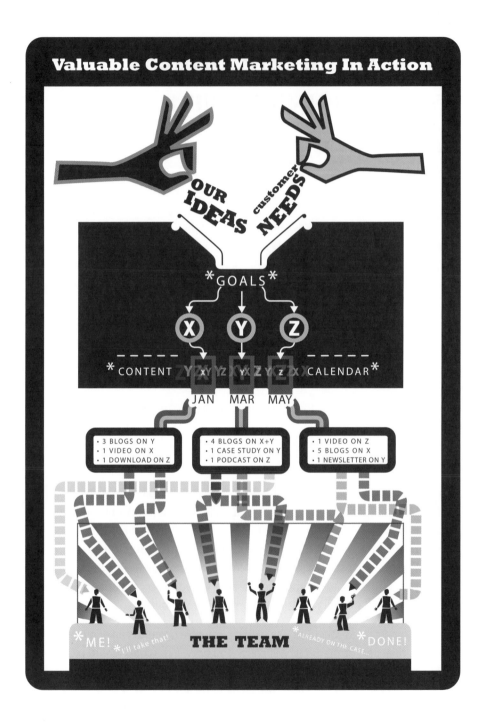

CHAPTER 11
PULLING TOGETHER A VALUABLE CONTENT STRATEGY

An ounce of strategy is worth a pound of tactics.

Andy Crestodina[1]

This chapter is your step-by-step guide to a well-thought-out content strategy – guidance for those getting started with the valuable approach; a strategic refresh for those looking to up the ante with their content efforts for greater success.

This process will help you nail the biggest question of all when it comes to content marketing – what exactly *is* your valuable content, for you and your customers? This considered 10-step approach will help you work it out.

In this chapter:

- How to create a valuable content strategy in 10 steps.
- The importance of writing your strategy down.
- Step 1: Get clear on your goals.
- Step 2: Know your business.
- Step 3: Know your customers.
- Step 4: Find the story behind the content.
- Step 5: Your content sweet spot and vision.
- Step 6: Setting your content commitment and plan.
- Step 7: Platform and tools.
- Step 8: Organize to make it work.

- Step 9: Measuring for success.
- Step 10: Work out where you are now and plan to make it happen.

NB: You'll find a companion workbook on our website to work through each step. See: **www.valuablecontentmarketing.com**.

Your valuable content strategy will become a living, breathing document that you can evolve and refine over time. We'll walk you through all the elements you need to consider – but the progression is not necessarily a direct route from A to B. Revisit each of the steps as you need to; refine as you go. Get as clear as you can upfront – and then start. When you begin to write and create content the big picture will get clearer still.

Creating and documenting your valuable content strategy

Without strategy, content is just stuff, and the world has enough stuff.

Arjun Basu[2]

So what is a content strategy? A content strategy is the means by which you make your website and content *work* for your business. It forces you to make decisions on all the big questions – why, who, what, when, where and how. It helps you focus all your content activities around a clear goal.

In short, it's a research-based thinking process to ensure your content is valuable to you (delivers on your business objectives) and valuable to your readers (answers their questions): win, win.

An effective content strategy starts with objectives and ends with results – a process and a plan to get you from A to B using the content on your website and beyond.

The benefits of a strategic approach

- You will have a clear picture of what you want to achieve. This will help as you work to get everyone behind it.

- You always have something to talk about in your content.

- You will be able to create a plan for the blogs, videos and guides that you need to create over the coming months, and a plan for who is responsible for creating them.

- You will understand your audience, and be clear on the best places to engage with them. Your people will know what they should be doing on Twitter, Google+ or Instagram so social media becomes a purposeful and manageable activity.

- You will have an essential reference point when planning your content so you'll know which ideas to say yes to and which to decline.

The importance of writing it down

Research shows that documenting your strategy will make a big difference. A study by the Content Marketing Institute at the end of 2014 found that 35 per cent of B2B marketers have a documented content strategy in place, meaning the vast majority of marketers are sailing without a compass. They also found that those who take the time to write up their content marketing strategy are far more effective than those who do not.

> *Of those who have a documented strategy, 60 per cent consider their organization to be effective. In contrast, only 32 per cent of those who have a verbal strategy say they are effective, and only 7 per cent of those who have no strategy at all. To take it a step further, 62 per cent of the most effective marketers also say they follow the strategy very closely.*
>
> 2015 B2B Content Marketing Benchmarks, Budgets and Trends – North America by Content Marketing Institute[3]

The lesson is clear – if you want to be more effective at content marketing, take the time to document your strategy and follow it closely.

But before you get writing, recognize that your content strategy doesn't start with topics – it starts with thinking and research. In fact, coming up with ideas for content is only a small part of your content strategy as you'll see.

Time to do some homework. You'll find a companion Valuable Content Strategy Workbook online to document your decisions as you work through all 10 steps in this chapter.

The 10 elements of your valuable content marketing strategy

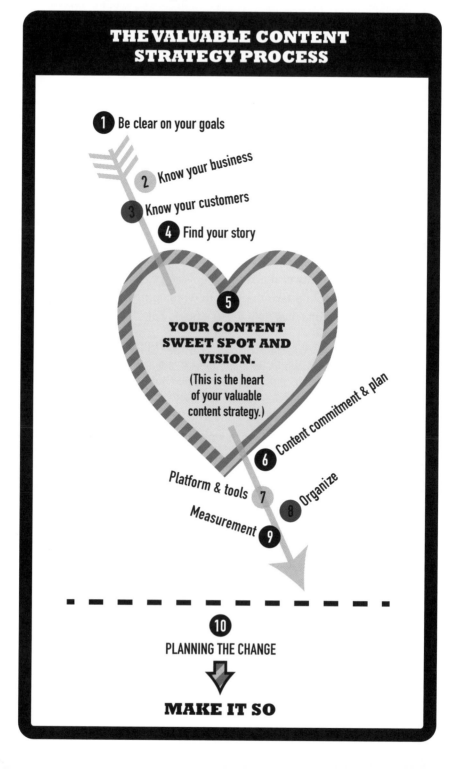

THE VALUABLE CONTENT STRATEGY PROCESS

1 Be clear on your goals

2 Know your business

3 Know your customers

4 Find your story

5 YOUR CONTENT SWEET SPOT AND VISION.
(This is the heart of your valuable content strategy.)

6 Content commitment & plan

7 Platform & tools

8 Organize

9 Measurement

10 PLANNING THE CHANGE

MAKE IT SO

Step 1: Get clear on your goals

Questions you'll need to consider:

1 What is your ambition? Your business goals for the next 1–3 years?

2 Why valuable content marketing? What's the driver, the pressure for change? What exactly are you trying to achieve with this approach?

3 What happens if you do nothing?

4 How important is this compared to other things you are doing as a business?

5 What are the goals and objectives you'll set for your content marketing?

As with any change, the first step is knowing what you are trying to achieve and why. Jane Northcote, author of *Making Change Happen*, comments: *'A change makes things different. There must be a From and a To.'* So what is the difference that marketing the valuable content way will make to your business?

For many, the switch to marketing their business this way is a big change. Spending time upfront getting clear on your goals is essential if you want to make that change happen.

Be specific about the areas of your business you want to make the biggest difference to. Is it:

- To build greater awareness of your firm – so more people find you.
- To drive more interest and engagement – so more people connect with you.
- To convert interest into action – so more people contact you.
- To improve the quality of sales leads – more of the right people contacting you.
- To speed up the sales cycle – more sales, more quickly.
- To delight your current customers – for happier, more loyal customers.
- To drive more referrals – more warm leads and easier sales.
- To make the recruitment process easier – more of the right staff.
- To lower the cost per lead – increased marketing efficiency.
- To build a better business – for a happier, more fulfilled life.

The clearer your focus, the more targeted your content marketing efforts will be. It will be easier to track and measure your success further down the line.

Set SMART objectives (specific, measurable, achievable, realistic, timely). For example, if your overall goal is to grow by 40 per cent and to do this you want to generate more inbound leads, then set a target, eg attract five more clients worth over £xxxxxx in revenue per year. We will look at some simple, effective measures and tools to help you chart your progress towards these goals in Step 9.

> **Valuable Tip**
>
> This is where content strategy meets business strategy. If you are not clear on your goals and objectives as a business we'd recommend addressing this by talking to a good business adviser or coach.

Step 2: Know your business

Questions you'll need to consider:

1 What do you want to focus on selling?
2 To whom? Where's your niche? Who are your ideal customers?
3 Why do they buy from you? What sets your business apart for them?
4 What do you want to be famous for?
5 What geography do you serve?
6 What are your competitors up to? What content are they creating?

The clearer you are from the start about who you are as a business, what you are selling and what you want to be known for, the better the valuable content you create is going to *work* for you.

Valuable content is found at the intersection between your customers' needs and your business expertise. A big part of your strategy is to uncover this content sweet spot.

Valuable content sweet spot Venn diagram

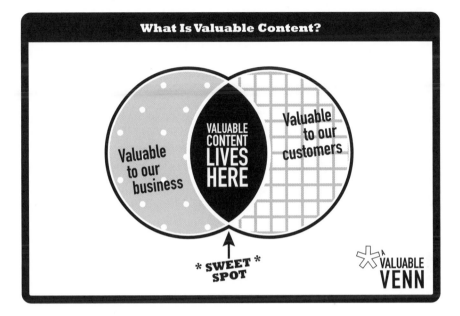

If you miss out the 'know your business' step there's a danger that you'll create content that meets your customers' needs (and they will have many) but will never win you any business. Your content should not be a library of everything. It has to clearly focus on the challenges you can solve.

So before we drill down into your customers' needs, make time for a bit of naval gazing and look inside your company. This will help you to position your content firmly in your area of expertise. Write the answers down.

Step 3: Know your customers

Questions and actions to consider:

- Who are your ideal customers?
- What do they struggle with? Why do they need you? What do they value about your product or service? What do they want to know?
- What questions do your customers ask at each step of their buying journey?

● What content can you provide to answer their questions and solve their challenges at each step?

The better we know our audience, the better we'll be at writing content they're likely to read and respond to.

Chris Butler, Newfangled, **www.newfangled.com**, @chrbutler

You've looked inside your business. Now it's time to look out. Knowing what to talk about with your content relies on knowing who you are talking to and what they care about and value. You'll know stuff about your customers of course, but to create content that really hits the spot you'll need to go deeper.

We've highlighted two stages in the process here – the real research and a creative persona exercise.

Do some real research

Get out of the office and ask your customers directly; call them up; spend some time interviewing them to uncover their real needs. Their answers will always surprise you.

Walk a mile in your customers' shoes to help you decide on what sort of content they would find valuable. Don't just make it up. Ask them. What information would they appreciate?

Heather Townsend, author of *The Go To Expert*, @heathertownsend

The data you get from tools such as an online survey is very useful but it will only get you so far. You need real insight.

The research process:

1 **Pick a sample of your ideal customers** – your best customers or contacts; the type of people you'd really like to work with, sell to again or get referred by.

2 **Make sure the customers are happy to help you** with this research (most people appreciate being asked – it shows you value them and their opinion).

3 **Devise a list of questions that will help you understand them better**, going into as much detail as you can (you'll find a list of questions in the resources section).

4 **Call them up**, book a meeting.

5 **Ask open questions** then let your interviewee speak. Listen hard and record their answers in as much detail as you can.

6 **Listen to the words they use to describe their world**, their challenges, their hopes, and their fears. Record their answers verbatim: this is really important – for these are the words and phrases you should reflect in your content.

7 **Remember to thank them too**!

You'll find more idea-starters for your research questions in the 'Get to know your customers questionnaire' in the resources section on page 277.

Valuable Tip

Try using an independent person to conduct this research – someone not directly involved in the project but who understands your business. A skilled researcher can get often get more from the interview as the customer may feel more willing to open up to a third party.

Create customer personas

One of the most useful exercises you will ever do when it comes to your content is to create a detailed picture of the typical customers you want your content to serve. In content world these are often called **'personas'** – the term we're going to use here – but you can think of them as pen pictures, profiles, avatars, whatever you like really.

A persona is a profile of your ideal customer or client – a rich picture of their goals, challenges, aspirations and needs, and the things they need to know and feel about you to select you as their supplier of choice. Personas help you target your content accurately so you know it will hit the spot, and give you and your team a way to quickly reference what has been learned about your customers when writing and creating content in the future.

How will creating personas help?

- You will know who you are talking to with your content.
- You will better understand their challenges and needs.
- You will create better content – more empathetic and in tune with customer needs.

Identify a few profitable groups in your target markets that share common needs, interests and concerns and create a profile of an ideal customer in each group. You'll undoubtedly have more than one persona but try not to create too many: 4–5 maximum if you want this exercise to be workable.

Don't be scared to exclude some people with this approach. Have confidence that the right people will like what you have to say. Content works best as a filter, not a magnet.

> *The biggest change I made to my digital presence is that I stopped trying to please everyone and I started serving the very specific community I've had the pleasure to serve.*
>
> Chris Brogan[4]

Developing a detailed picture of your ideal customer(s) will help you develop exactly the right content for your niche community. A good persona captures a whole person, not just that person for 7.5 hours of the day. Rounded personas will help you talk more directly, and engage with people more deeply, so think wide here. What do they want and need? What are their anxieties and motivations? Why do they typically select you ahead of the competition? What do they need to know and feel about your business to feel comfortable selecting your business or product?

> *Basing your work on buyer personas prevents you from sitting on your butt in your comfortable office just making stuff up, which is the cause of most ineffective marketing.*
>
> David Meerman Scott, author of *The New Rules of Marketing and PR*, **www.webinknow.com**, @dmscott[5]

Creative persona exercise

Creating personas is a mix of fieldwork and creativity. Talking to your ideal clients and customers is crucial, but there's an element of creative licence too.

This is one of those exercises that benefits from big sheets of paper, coloured pens and post-it notes a-plenty. It works best in a room full of your keenest people who are in the right frame of mind. If you're bigger than a one-woman band make sure you've got customer-facing people as well as directors around the table. Make space for it, buy biscuits and make it fun.

Hold a real person in mind when creating each persona – maybe a customer you've really enjoyed working with and would like to work with again – and answer the following questions.

- **Background information.** Who are they? Male or female? Which company? What's the sector and their role within it? What do you know about their education and background? Where were they born and where do they live now?

- **Why are they an ideal customer for you?** What would they buy from you? What are the actions you want them to take?

- **Their world.** What's going on in the world that affects their behaviour? If they work for a company then what are the big business goals, and what targets have they been set? What's going on in their sector that affects the way they do their job? How do they feel about these pressures?

- **Close to their hearts.** Personal goals and aspirations are really important. What do they want to achieve with their lives, what's their real wish for the future? Do they want to get promoted or change the world? Think short-term and long-term goals.

- **Communications preferences.** Where do they hang out? Where are they searching for answers to their questions? How do they like to be communicated with – are they digital natives or not?

- **Top five questions on their mind.** What are the biggest challenges they are struggling with that you could help to fix?

What to do with your personas

Use this newfound knowledge and thinking to help you pinpoint your story, your content sweet spot and vision (see Steps 4 and 5).

Certainly keep a written record of the persona profiles by your side when you're planning, writing or creating any other form of content so you know whether it's on target.

Some companies go further than that. Companies like cheeky email marketing giants Mailchimp create posters of their personas to ensure the team remembers exactly who they are writing (or designing) for. See **designlab.mailchimp.com/persona-posters**.

If you do this too, it will help. Having a clear target in mind makes a huge difference to the quality of your content.

Use your personas to generate early ideas for your content

Your customers' questions = your valuable content. So what questions are they asking? What content can you provide to help them along the way?

The purpose of your content is to build and strengthen relationships at every step of the process, to motivate those all-important sales. To help you with your content planning, work out what questions your persona groups have along their buying journey. What content would they really appreciate at each step?

Your persona	Questions when researching	Questions when evaluating	Questions when they become a customer
Persona 1			
Persona 2			
Persona 3			
Persona 4			
Ideas for content you can provide at each step			

Keep a firm focus on your customers' challenges here. Using the research you've undertaken ask yourself – what are the answers that your customers really crave?

> **Valuable Tip**
>
> Keep a running list of content ideas that come to you as you're creating your strategy. Useful when you get to detailed content planning stage.

Step 4: Find the story behind the content

Questions and actions to consider:

- Why does your business exist? What's its purpose in the world?
- What's your mission?
- Can you communicate this in six words or less?
- Can you communicate this in a hashtag?
- What do you believe? Write this in a manifesto.

As we mentioned back in Chapter 3, the most valuable content of all communicates a strong story – not just a story of what a business does, or how it does it, but *why* the business exists, its purpose in the world.

> *People don't buy what you do; they buy why you do it.*
> Simon Sinek[6]

There's no clearer description of the importance of starting with why than Simon Sinek' startwithwhy.com. In his 'Golden Circle' TED Talk (listed as the third most popular TED Talk to date), Simon wisely explains:

> *Every business on the planet knows WHAT they do. These are products they sell or services they offer.*
>
> *Some organizations know HOW they do it. These are the things that make them special or set them apart from their competitors.*

Very few organizations know WHY they do what they do. WHY is not about making money. It's about purpose, cause or belief – the reason your organization exists, beyond financial targets.

Simon Sinek[7]

If you want to really inspire trust with your content marketing then the *why* of your business must be as clear as the *what* or the *how*. Stories explain the *why*. Stories help people understand quickly, and speed is of the essence in the digital world. Tell the story of why you do what you do and people will remember you. This is how to stand out from the crowd.

> ## Valuable Tip
>
> In bigger firms this is where content strategy and brand strategy overlap. Holding the content focus firmly in mind will help you ground your brand activities.

Think of the content heroes we've mentioned throughout this book:

- Jeans manufacturer Hiut Denim leads its promise of quality with the *'Do one thing well'* message.
- IBM communicates an inspiring bigger purpose with *'Smarter Planet'*.
- Surf clothing company Finisterre differentiates with their notion of *'Cold water surfing'*.
- Our own mission here at Valuable Content helps to guide our content decisions – helping good companies like yours create *'Marketing that people love'*.

All these companies lead with a compelling message that answers the question Why? Their content is the vehicle that takes the story out there. Finding the message and narrative that underpins your content is a key part of your strategy. These are the crown jewels at the heart of your marketing that will give your content real purpose.

Communicating an authentic and inspiring purpose matters. It helps you to build trust and win more of the right kind of business; it sets your company apart and galvanizes support – a story for everyone to get behind and share.

As Amy Grenham, Marketing Manager of IT firm Desynit explains, once you get the big picture right, the content just flows.

> Desynit is an IT services firm with a difference – we don't talk tech, we talk to humans. The business has evolved hugely, and 18 months ago the time had come to replace our outdated website and messages. Rather than the traditional jargon-heavy approach, we took a different route. We thought in terms of our story and core beliefs. Having spent time researching what our clients valued and what we really wanted to say as a business, we came up with 'Good Systems Change Your Life' as our core brand message, underpinned by a series of customer-centric values, our Good Systems Manifesto.
>
> Whatever platform we work on, the story and manifesto will always be true, and clear to all. Our content-driven strategy just flows from here. The whole team contributes with blogs, newsletters, podcasts, infographics, social media campaigns etc. The short powerful messages of our Good Systems Manifesto also work beyond the digital arena – at exhibitions, on T-shirts, posters, and more. The manifesto values always underpin the approach.
>
> The results have been fantastic. Since launch, 12 months ago, website traffic has almost quadrupled and is increasing all the time. Many more leads come directly to us from the web. Increased visibility and recognition has made a huge difference to our sales outcomes. Referrals too bring in a steady stream of new business. People have heard of us and know what we stand for. Putting our story and human values at the heart of our marketing has translated into great content a consistent pipeline of business opportunities.
>
> Amy Grenham, Marketing Manager, **www.desynit.com**, Desynit

Now, getting your story straight is rarely an easy job. It's one of the steps in the process you will revisit many times. Do think hard about it, but don't use the challenge as a reason to procrastinate. It took us several years and a few attempts to get the Valuable Content story totally straight. We've written our way to it – thinking, talking, listening – circling round, getting clearer about the things we don't like and what we're in business to do. The message has come out of work on our business strategy, and is tied to our mission to create marketing that people love.

Some questions to help you uncover your story:

- What inspired you to set up in business? What was the idea behind it? What did you set out to achieve?
- What does your company stand for? What are you for? What are you against?

- What bugs you about your industry – your biggest frustration?
- How do you make the world better for your customers?
- Why should anyone care that you exist?

What are you looking for in your story?

You're looking for something that inspires, that makes you feel proud, with a single message at its heart to connect all your content. You're looking for something that nails the emotional connection with your audience. That's the vision for your story and if you can find it it will make a huge difference to your company too.

A good business story:

- **Is customer-centric, not company-centric.**
- **Is not a sales pitch.** As Simon Sinek says, 'It's about purpose, cause or belief – the reason your organization exists, beyond financial targets.'
- **Makes you memorable.** It sets you apart from your competitors, and helps the right people choose you.
- **Doesn't aim to attract the whole world.** It sets out to attract the people you really want to work with.
- **Is not about putting on an act; rather it's about being more of what you are.** For people inside the business, the story should feel natural, not forced. Something that's as easy to say to your neighbour as it is to a potential lead. Simple and clear. Your story should give you confidence in your identity.
- **Needs to engage emotionally,** and make the right people grasp the essence of what you're about in a few words. It's about how you make your customers feel.
- **Starts with belief** – think manifesto or crusade.
- **Communicates the happy ever after** – so talk outcomes.
- **Is a promise** – love it enough to live by it.
- **Is brave and bold.**
- **Is an idea that will stretch** – you'll know it when you've found it.

How to find your story

Where can you uncover this golden thread that will illuminate all the content you create? Start by giving it the time and space it needs. Give it some serious thought.

Soul searching is important, but like so many good stories, you will probably need to go on a journey to find the answer. The thought you put into Step 3 talking to clients and customers while doing your persona research will help you here too. Look back over the answers people gave when you asked how they'd describe what you do for them, how it makes them feel, and what benefits and value your business brings to their lives. This is the core of your story.

Tips for uncovering your story

1 **Look at what you do from your customers' perspective, not from your own.** Put yourself in their shoes (by talking to them – real research, asking great questions) and tell the story from their perspective.

2 **Think like a book author.** If you were going to distil all your knowledge into a book for your client base, what would it be about? What's the title? What would you really like to say to the world?

3 **Get some emotion into your offer.** People respond to emotion, not logic, when they're buying. What are you fighting for as a business? What's your crusade?

4 **Get some outside help.** This is really, really hard to do by yourself. Get a view from the outside and consider calling in some expert assistance.

5 **Give yourself the gift of time.** Make a stab at this and then refine over time.

Get thinking, asking, and talking. Cut out the waffle surrounding what it is you do, polish up the jewel at the centre, find your story and your content will shine.

One day I'll find the right words and they will be simple.

Jack Kerouac[8]

Write the story

You'll know when it's right when you can communicate it easily, succinctly and with conviction. Here's an exercise to help you hone your story:

- What's the six-word strapline?
- What's the hashtag #? eg #smarterplanet, #coldwatersurf.
- Write your manifesto, starting with the words 'we believe that...'
- Write it in two paragraphs for the 'About Us' page on your website.

The words *for* and *because* are useful jumping off points – eg IBM – *for a smarter planet*; Desynit – *because good systems change your life*. Try writing the message that underpins your story in this way.

Your story is important, but don't hold up the whole process by trying to nail it. We reckon if you're 65–70 per cent there, then that's fine. Be prepared to come back and refine. Your story can and will evolve.

Step 5: Nailing your valuable content sweet spot and vision

Some questions and actions to consider:

- Where is your valuable content sweet spot?
- What are the big topics that you'll talk about underneath that heading?
- What's the inspiring vision for your content marketing?
- How will you win?
- What attributes define your content?
- What are the principles you can put in place to guide your content creators?

Now we get to the heart of your valuable content strategy process. You've done a lot of research and thinking – your goals, your business, your customer needs and your story. Time to distil that into clear decisions and an inspiring vision for your content marketing.

Defining your content sweet spot

> *In content marketing, your sweet spot is the exact area of your company's expertise. It's the thing that you are uniquely positioned to talk about. The thing your company knows better than – or at least as well as – anyone else in the world.*
>
> Doug Kessler writing for Econsultancy, **www.econsultancy.co.uk**, @dougkessler[10]

This is the most fundamental challenge of all.

What is the conversation you want to own with your content? Think big here. As a business, what are you better equipped than anyone else to help people with?

If you've got the bigger story straight then you're in the ballpark. We just want you to go a little further here – the sweet spot is what's going to hit it out of the park.

Think about this in terms of why and how. Your story is the why – your purpose and belief; your content sweet spot is the how – your unique approach to solving problems for your customers.

Taking our own content as an example:

- 'Marketing people love' is our why, our purpose.
- 'Valuable content marketing' is how people do that – that's our sweet spot. Our content (including this book) shows people how to make the approach work, for them.

The answer doesn't have to be complicated. The idea that guides the brilliant content that HSBC's expat division creates and shares is simply: *'If you moved abroad, what would you want to know?'*

When it comes to your sweet spot you'll know it when you've got it. The message will hit the spot with your customers and the content ideas will flow. It doesn't have to be something new or the latest bandwagon – more what you do every day, backed up by all those years of experience.

Your content sweet spot should feel like home. Capture it in a single sentence and write it down.

What are the big topics?

Once you have nailed the sweet spot, think about the main topics of conversation that you will host throughout the year. These topics will guide the longer pieces of content you create – the e-books or white papers – and will give you a framework for your blogs. This avoids the 'what do I write about now?' and prioritization problem that can arise if you just ask your team to start blogging.

Taking our own business as an example: our content sweet spot is '*Inspiring good businesses to create and share valuable content and make marketing that people love.*' We're on a mission – what we really want to do is inspire, teach, build great businesses, change the world! Under this headline the topics we talk about through the year include: content marketing strategy; website planning; writing valuable content; selling with valuable content etc (all the sections in this book!). We're very clear about the message we want to get across and the things we want to write about. This makes planning our content every month so much easier.

Questions to help you plan your topics:

- Look at the questions people were asking when you did your customer research. Can you group these under a few headings?
- Think of your blog – what categories would you set up?
- If you wrote a book, what sections and chapters would you include?
- If you were presenting, what are the main topics you'd like to talk about as a business?

Use this thinking to write down your main topics. Aim for no more than six or seven.

Valuable Tip

Once you have selected your themes, think SEO. Use keyword research to look at the terms people search for online. Refine the titles of your categories on your website accordingly.

Setting out the vision for your content marketing

Build clarity and pace in that order. You need to set the vision then make it happen.

Geoff Mason, Project One UK[9]

So you've defined your sweet spot. Now you need to pull together a clear and inspiring vision for your valuable content marketing. One that (if you're a business of more than one person) you can use to keep everyone engaged.

For many, the switch to a valuable content marketing approach is a really big change. Getting the vision clear and agreed upfront is vital, whatever the scale of your operation. For larger businesses, aligning everyone around that vision is key, for this is a change that will touch many parts of the organization.

Think back to the story you want to tell as a business and the information you know that your audience craves. Set out the attributes that will make your content valuable. Combine this knowledge to craft the vision for your valuable content marketing efforts.

A simple formula to help you communicate the vision for your content marketing:

- We will become the go-to resource for... (*your ideal customers*).
- Who want to... *(ultimate outcome or value that you can help them achieve)*.
- By learning about... *(your content marketing sweet spot)*.
- What sets our content apart is... *(what attributes make your content particularly valuable?)*.
- This will help us to... *(the goals you've defined in Step 1)*.

Step 6: Your content commitment and plan

Questions and actions to consider:

- What's your schedule? What commitment will you make to valuable content over the next 12 months?
- What's the distribution plan to promote your content?
- Set out your publishing plan – your content calendar over the year.

Your aim is to work towards a bank of high-quality, valuable content that you can distribute effectively throughout the year. Now you have your sweet spot nailed and your vision clear it's time to work out how to make it happen.

Remember: consistency and quality are always more important than volume. Aim for an achievable pattern – something you can stick to as a business.

Prepare your content calendar

To make your content strategy actionable you'll need to create a detailed content calendar. What content are we going to publish when, how, and where? Think like a magazine editor when you're doing this. Plan your schedule and themes you want to talk about throughout the year. You can vary this as events arise – hot industry news, for example, that demands a fast response. The plan can flex but it really does help to start with a plan. (You'll find more detail on monthly content planning in Chapter 15.)

Here at Valuable Content we make a detailed plan for the next month and a high-level plan looking forward 2–3 months further than that. You'll find more details on this in Chapter 15.

Here is our commitment to content creation. We will:

- tweet every day;
- update our company LinkedIn page with fresh content every week;
- post on Google+ three times a week;
- post a new blog four times a month;

- send an email newsletter to our subscriber base every month;
- publish a deeper piece of content every quarter;
- post a fresh case study every quarter; and
- write a book every couple of years!

And here is what a year's worth of content looks like for a consultancy firm we worked for.

A consultancy firm's annual commitment to valuable content

Quarter	Month	Activity						
		Social media	LinkedIn	Blogs	Newsletter	Case studies	Discussion papers	e-book
1	Jan			●●				
	Feb	Every day	1-2 per week	●●			●	
	Mar			●●		●		
2	Apr			●●●	●			
	May	Every day	1-2 per week	●●●	●	●	●	
	Jun			●●●	●			
3	Jul			●●●	●			
	Aug	Every day	1-2 per week	●●●	●		●	
	Sep			●●●	●	●		
4	Oct			●●●	●			
	Nov	Every day	1-2 per week	●●●	●			
	Dec			●●●	●	●		●

How will you distribute your content so it gets read?

You'll know by now that creating valuable content is only half the job. Once it's created the hard work of distribution and promotion will begin. For without some serious promotion your content could well languish on your website gathering cobwebs, like a dusty old book in the corner of a library no-one cares to visit and nobody loves.

Make a plan for the channels you will use and prioritize to promote your content, so it gets into the hands (or onto the screens) of your ideal customers.

Step 7: Prepare your platform and pick your tools

Questions and actions to consider:

- What types of content will you choose to create?
- What content creation tools will you need to support this?
- How will you distribute your content? What distribution tools will you require?
- What functionality does your content strategy demand from your website?
- Other marketing tools to support your strategy.
- Do you need a fully integrated marketing automation system to support you?

You have defined the vision for your content marketing. What kind of platform will you need to support you in making that work?

What types of content will you choose to create? With blogs, a huge variety of social media, newsletters, SEO, video, webinars, podcasts, e-books, infographics, SlideShare, guest blogging, traditional PR, talks and paid media you have a plethora of content creation and distribution options and formats to select from. Remember: you'll need to plan for a mix of stock and flow content, as you learned in Chapter 8.

How will you create it and how will you get it out there? What content creation and distribution tools will you add to the mix to support your strategy?

A summary of some of the main distribution options:

- Social media – Twitter, LinkedIn, Google+, Facebook, Instagram, Pinterest etc.
- Search engines – optimize each piece of content so it gets found.
- Direct contact – sending it to your personal contacts, clients and network if it's relevant – getting the whole team to do the same.
- Your subscribed email list.

- Paid media – advertising, online advertising, remarketing.
- PR – traditional media, online sites, guest blogging.
- In-person events and talks.

Your website is the hub for all the content you'll be creating. What functionality will you need from your site? You'll find much more on this in Chapter 12.

Other marketing tools you'll need to make the strategy fly? A good email marketing platform, analytics, a CRM/contact management system are the fundamentals. There are more and more tools on the market to help you with content curation, creation, distribution, analytics and tracking, and planning and management. (Check out The Humungous List of Content Marketing Tools, a crowdsourced list from Doug and the team at Velocity Partners (**www.velocitypartners.co.uk**)).

Will you opt for a mix of separate tools or a fully integrated marketing auto-mation system to support you?

Step 8: Organizing to make it work

Questions and actions to consider:

- Who will have overall responsibility for your content?
- Who are the best people to create it?
- Who and how will you distribute and promote it?
- What other skills do you need on your team?
- Do you have these in-house? Need for outsourced support or additional skills?
- Training needs for your team?
- How will you manage and control the process to make it work?

To make your content strategy work you'll need a team, a budget and an efficient process. But who will be involved? What roles do you need in place to make the process work? How will you organize, work together and manage and control what you do?

If you really want success the work goes very deep – turning old structures upside down, and involving many more people than just your marketing team. No small task and not for the fainthearted, but a very exciting journey nonetheless.

How to structure your business to make it work

Senior-level buy-in is vital. Whether you do it in-house or outsource, someone in your business needs to take overall responsibility for content. For bigger firms this person needs the support and commitment of the board. Every company should now employ someone with overall responsibility for your content initiatives.

But where should they sit within the organization? Who owns content? If you're a one man or one woman business that's an easy one – the valuable content marketing buck stops, starts and rests with you. This *is* your marketing, so make it the priority.

For bigger businesses with established marketing functions, where ownership of content marketing lies within the organization is often a contentious question. Should it sit with marketing, PR, digital?

We're going to make a strong stand here. Your organization's story and message is king; marketing, PR, digital – these are all ways of taking it out there. If prime responsibility for content lies in one of these channels, then your message will get muddled and lost in these silos. Instead, put someone senior, skilled and passionate in charge of content, with a reporting line straight into the board.

How you organize around this is of course up to you. One of the most sensible organizations we've found has a Head of Content and Communications in charge of the message and media and a Head of Marketing Operation, bringing marketing rigour to the process, with responsibility for tools like the website. These two roles work very closely together to bring their content-fuelled marketing strategy to life and make it work.

Remember, in today's world your customers have the power. Content cuts through old structures with an internal focus, and forces you to organize your business in a way that makes most sense from a customer perspective.

Who are the right people to tell your story?

The most effective people to create the content are the people closest to your customers – those who have the experience, not marketers who hear things second hand. It's a fabulous content opportunity if those on the ground are the ones who tell your story. They'll have the passion and the knowledge. Your job is to equip them with the skills and confidence to create the content your business needs.

CONTENT STORY   From one engineer to another at Indium

The Indium Corporation is a true leader in valuable content creation at scale across a B2B firm. Indium Corporation develops and manufactures materials used in the electronics assembly industry. Not the richest vein of writing material to mine, you might think. Yet Indium's team of engineer bloggers manages to create immensely valuable content that draws in interest, builds relationships and absolutely drives sales results.

Our customers are engineers. Our technical staff are engineers. Engineers like other engineers: they understand them; they trust them. They speak the same language. The Indium Corporation developed our practice of 'From One Engineer To Another®' *when I realized that we needed to turn our company inside out. We needed to eliminate the 'corporate spokesperson' role (me) and facilitate our customers speaking directly with our engineering staff – no middleman, no noise. Consequently, the CONTENT that we share is absolutely THE information an engineer requires to optimize their process, to address their opportunity, to solve their problem, and to make their breakthrough. It is experimentally derived data, it is optimized process recommendations from the engineer who did the actual work in the field, it is the performance characteristics of a new assembly material by the engineer that developed the product. It includes information-rich papers from the people who authored them and it is face-to-face presentations by technology professionals who got their hands dirty creating the concepts and testing them personally. This strategy produces world-class CONTENT that is highly sought after by our target audience.*

indium.com

Your crack content marketing team

A commitment to valuable content marketing means new skills for many: customer research, design, SEO, social media, email marketing, design, web development and mainly writing. There's a lot to learn and do.

> *The marketing department of tomorrow looks very similar to a publishing department of today, so managing editors, storytellers, and producers are key to success.*

Joe Pulizzi, the godfather of Content Marketing, @joepulizzi[11]

In a small business, one person will probably wear many content hats, with an outsourced team at their beck and call where necessary. Here at Valuable Content it works like this:

Sonja takes the role of content strategist and content manager, gets content up on the website, looks after measurement and events. Sharon takes the role of chief writer, queen of VC social media, PR and outreach, coordinates the design work. Shared roles include subject matter expertise, editing, writing, community management and content distribution. Roles we outsource are design, web, video, email marketing, SEO support and analytics.

In a larger organization, you will be able to spread the load more evenly. Whatever size of business you're in, the key is to make sure people are clear on their roles, and have all the support they need to do a great job. Sort that, and you'll be away.

Here's an overview of the whole gambit of content roles that you're likely to need to draw on.

People to direct and oversee your content strategy

- **Director of content (chief content officer).** Senior person who owns the strategy and process, oversees all content marketing initiatives and is responsible for its success. Internal role.
- **Content strategist.** Takes responsibility for creating, documenting and driving forward the content marketing strategy, taking the learning and refining the strategy along the way. Internal or external role.
- **Content manager.** Manages the content process to ensure that it delivers the aims of the content strategy and content plan and meets

the needs of the audience. Ensures all content created lives up to best practice and is managed effectively over time across all channels. Internal role.

People to create the content

- **Editor in chief.** Responsible for quality – does this content meet the real needs of our customers? Makes decisions on what content gets created (and what does not). Manages the approval process. Final sign-off on all content – the valuable stamp of approval. Internal role, someone who knows the business and the subject matter well, with editing skills to boot.
- **Subject matter experts.** Knowledgeable experts in the business who are tasked with coming up with ideas for content, writing first drafts and of course distributing the content to their networks. We suggest this team includes both technical experts and frontline salespeople who know the questions customers are asking. Internal roles.
- **Content writer.** A skilled writer on your team who turns drafts into polished content. This role can be internal or outsourced.
- **Website expert.** Design, development, UX – complex web enhancements that cannot be addressed via the CMS, responsible for UX as content builds, keeping up with latest web trends and developments, marketing automation adviser. Internal or outsourced.
- **SEO expert.** Looks for keyword opportunities and ensures all digital content is optimized for search. Internal or outsourced.
- **Content designer.** Produces web and blog illustrations, design of guides (printed and digital), infographics, SlideShare presentations, photography etc. This role can be internal or outsourced.
- **Video producer.** Creates and edits quality video content. This role can be internal or outsourced.

People to distribute the content

- **Community manager.** Curates and posts up fresh content on social media, makes connections and answers questions, notifies subject matter experts of queries and opportunities, thanks those who share content. Responsible for getting new blog articles up on the site (checking they are labelled correctly for SEO). Ensures email newsletters go out on time. Responsible for the CRM. In charge of content distribution – communicates all new content around the organization. Preferably internal role.

- **Content outreach and PR.** This person seeks out and manages media relations and opportunities, including traditional media and online, guest post opportunities, events. Internal or outsourced role.

People to help the business learn

- **Measurement officer.** Tracks measures on a monthly basis and reports against goals. Internal or external role.
- **Skills trainer.** Ensures that all areas of the organization have the skills required to carry out the content strategy, eg content marketing awareness training, blog and content writing skills, social media skills, selling with content. Internal or external role.

When setting a budget for your content marketing efforts take these roles into account. Factor in the cost of any external support, or hiring new people to your team, changes to your website platform and cost of any tools you need to make it work, the cost of design and production and more than anything else, the cost of your time.

Marketing with valuable content is cost-effective, but it means allocating marketing budget differently.

> *While you may cut media, printing, mailing, and call centre costs from your marketing budgets, plan to replace them with well-paid writers and analysts.*
>
> Christopher Butler, author of *The Strategic Web Designer*, **www.newfangled.com**, @chrbutler

The biggest cost of all is wasting effort on content that misses the mark, so the strategic thinking you're doing upfront is vital.

Getting your people working together

Getting your business communicating the valuable content way means big change. It relies on people doing things differently. If you're the one driving this new approach you'll need to inspire people to take on new roles, and set out what it is you want them to do differently.

You'll need your people on the ground – your subject matter experts and your sales people – to help you create content. Listen hard to what customers ask them, look for opportunities to create great content, to come up with ideas, and to help create these.

Good sales people will be listening already, but it might be that you're asking them to collaborate more. Not just to remember that X asked for information on a certain part of the process to help their next sales call, but to share that information with the content team who then produce a guide to help a hundred Xs who may be struggling with the same part of the process. You want them to use this content to help them build relationships. And to tell you how things have landed. What's worked, what's not, what could work better next time?

You want your marketers to make 'help, don't sell' the founding stone of the marketing department. You want your business leaders to back this strategy, create content of their own, and share it; take advantage of their own fantastic networks, and adopt a long-term view. Understand that this takes time, and hold your nerve.

Step 9: Measuring for success

Questions and actions to consider:

- What meaningful measures can you align with the goals and objectives you defined in Step 1?
- What measures will help you track progress towards your goals?
- What outcomes demonstrate results?
- What content is driving conversion?
- Where should you be spending your time and focusing your efforts?

You've done your research, crafted the story and made your content plan. You're nearly ready to start creating all that content, but before you press go work out how you will assess whether your new strategy is working.

Today, you can measure lots of things. The most important metric though is 'how is business?' For companies that live and breathe how business is, you will see an immediate tie to growth and what you are doing online.

David Meerman Scott, *The New Rules of PR and Marketing*[12]

The difficult thing when it comes to measuring content marketing is that there is usually a gap – in the case of complex sales, often a very big gap – between you publishing the content and the eventual sale. So what should you track to show if the strategy is going in the right direction?

Content marketing measurement is not an exact science. Marketers have struggled for years to capture these metrics. However, as measurement tools and marketing automation have advanced, it is getting easier to attribute sales and new opportunities to specific content initiatives.

So embrace your inner data geek, or surround yourself with others who love the numbers more than you. Here are a few things we've learned about content measurement along the way.

You can't measure without a clear goal

Well, you can, but it's pointless. You've done the thinking about your objectives and goals in Step 1 so refer back to the decisions you made here. Create a set of meaningful measures that are aligned to your ambitions as a business.

> *First go to bat knowing what your business objectives are. If your content answers first to your business objectives, you can measure its impact where the executives need to see impact. Retweets, likes and comments don't matter to business objectives. Design your content measurement around SALES, REVENUE and COSTS and you'll keep executives (and clients) happy.*
>
> Jason Falls, **jasonfalls.com**, @jasonfalls[13]

Measure what matters

Marketing on the web gives you easier access to an awful lot of stats – visitors, page views, bounce rates, referral sources, email open rates, click-through rates and more. On one hand this is great – there are many free tools to help you analyse the impact of your investment in content marketing – Google Analytics, your website or blog software, email marketing tools, link shorteners like bit.ly and social media management tools like Hootsuite all enable you to capture a lot of data. There is so much to measure that there's a temptation to get sucked into obsessing over data for data's sake.

Reports lifted straight from Google Analytics confuse most people: 2,345 page visits in the last month – so what? An overload of meaningless data can cause paralysis, stopping you from doing anything at all. Bombarding your fellow content team with data can make for some pretty pointless meetings too. When it comes to making sense of the data you're going to have to do some clear thinking and a bit of extra interpretation too.

Measure progress along the journey to a sale

It's helpful to recognize the difference between leading and lagging measures. Lagging measures track the eventual outcomes. Leading measures look further upstream – early indicators of progress towards your goals. A good content marketing measurement system tracks both.

> *Revenue is the mother of all metrics. Everything else is either a vanity metric, an early indicator or both. Of those, I'm a big believer in shares. Shares by your target audience are the ultimate endorsement and are invariably a leading indicator that wonga is on its way.*
>
> Doug Kessler, @dougkessler[14]

Bryony Thomas sets out a useful framework in her book, *Watertight Marketing*, that focuses measurement on three things: volume, movement and outcomes through the sales process. If your goal is profitable sales, then don't just measure awareness. Pick out measures that show how you are developing leads and building relationships on the way to a sale.

Performance at each step in the buying process can be tracked when it comes to your content marketing. For example:

- **Awareness.** Who is coming to the site, how are they finding it? You can track this by measuring the number of unique site visits each month. Watch where the visits are coming from (referral traffic).

- **Interest.** How many visitors are engaged with your content and interested in what you are saying? Shares on social media? Site visits longer than three minutes? The number of people who opt to download your stock content? The number of new sign-ups to your email list? Watch your bounce rate.

- **Evaluation.** How many people want what you are selling? Number of visits to your FAQ page or price comparison page for example; numbers who sign up for a webinar; numbers who sign up for a trial step in the process, eg free trial; and ultimately inbound leads – people who email or call your company to see if you're right for them.

- **Adoption.** Suggested measure is the number of people who become clients.

- **Loyalty.** You can track feedback from customers delighted with your content; or even tools such as NPS score (send customer feedback questionnaire. 'How likely would you be refer to this company to a friend or colleague?' For more on NPS score see: **www.netpromoter.com/why-net-promoter/know/**). The ultimate measure is the number of people who sign up for more than one product.

(Steps adapted from Philip Kotler's 'Model of Rational Decision-Making', with measurement guidance from *Watertight Marketing*, Bryony Thomas.)[15]

Conversion is the key

Content that converts is king and you can measure this in a number of ways. In our business we look at sign-ups to our blog digest and mailing list. We use this to indicate the visitor's interest in our content. It's a crucial step in our lead development process. It's useful to pick out the content that drives conversions (sign-ups in our case) – that's the really valuable stuff. Not every blog post will motivate mass sign-up and that's okay. We know that success is more about our content mass as a whole than it is about one specific post.

Marketing automation makes you smarter

Smart marketing automation systems (such as Hubspot, Act On, Marketo for bigger firms or new players such as New Rainmaker for smaller firms) make content measurement easier (you'll find more in Chapter 12). They show you which online content a lead has visited – a picture of what content might have influenced them on the way to the sale.

But even automated systems like these can't measure everything. Its limitation is that it doesn't show which influenced a buyer most of all, or what other content, eg on social media or real world events (sales meeting, talk, referral), made an impact too. That's why the data as a whole is more informative than the data on any one piece of content.

Create a bespoke measurement report

There are a variety of goals and metrics for your content marketing – you need to find a set that's right for you. Understand exactly what you're looking to achieve as a business and build your own set of measures to track progress. Google Analytics and other analytics systems are extremely useful but you'll need to translate the results to make it easy for people (and you) to understand and track progress over time. Where should you be spending your time and focusing your efforts? Build a short, simple report that you share at your monthly content planning meeting to track your progress towards your goals.

You'll find an example measurement report structure in the Resources section.

The purpose of measurement is to check that you are going in the right direction. So stick a stake in the ground now, before you get going, and track indicators of progress. Tally the results up every month and chart against these goals. Measure the change.

Measure, refine and learn over time

You won't know what works until you try it. You may think that that e-book was going to be the best thing ever, but once you put your heart and soul into it, you find out that the simple checklist you created a few months back has blown it out of the water. Be prepared to learn and adapt. Measure what's working and adjust for more of it.

Unless you're a huge business creating thousands of pieces of content, it's worth looking back at each piece of content you created during the month to see what's worked, spotting trends and planning actions to improve the quality and performance of your content in the future. You might notice that content around a particular subject consistently works well, or that one form of content gets a lot of traction and motivates more sign-ups. So invest in more of this. This kind of measurement will let you adjust and refine your strategy so that the content you produce is more valuable – to your visitors, and to your business – more awareness, more engagement, more sales, and a better use of your time.

But never forget that content marketing is both art and science. Bryony Thomas warns us not to *'measure out the magic'*. Simply focusing on the hard measures will miss the intangible but brilliant metric that Doug Kessler calls 'ripples' – those serendipitous things that happen when your content hits the spot – invitations to speak, great new contacts and connections, collaborations. Difficult to measure but immensely valuable to your business.

Step 10: Work out where you are now and plan the change

Questions and actions to consider:

- What content do you have now?
- What tools and resources do you have now?
- To what extent does your website meet the needs of your strategy?
- Where are the gaps? What needs to change?
- What's a realistic implementation plan to make that change happen?

Don't jump straight from strategy to delivery – plan the journey first. Know where you want to go, and how you're going to get there.

Geoff Mason, Project One UK[16]

If you follow the 10 steps and document the results you have your valuable content strategy straight. It's time to work out how to bring it to life.

The power of any good strategy is in its implementation. What do the decisions you've made here mean for your website, how you're organized, your current content, your business? What changes must be put in place to make the new strategy fly?

The first thing to do is understand what content, tools and resources you already have at your disposal. Conduct a content audit and gap analysis. The place to begin is a detailed look at your current content. What do you have, and is it any good? Does it meet the needs of your content strategy?

With a bit of exploration most companies find they have great content squirrelled away somewhere – past presentations, guides, or articles – that can be polished off and repurposed. Make an inventory of all current content so you know what you've got and what you can reuse. Log and rate each piece of content and tag it carefully – give it a valuable score (a spreadsheet will do fine for this). Reusing as much as possible will save you money and time.

We'll look in detail at the changes you may need to make to your website in the next chapter.

Content strategy on a page

You've completed all the groundwork. Time to write up and communicate your new content strategy. We'd suggest you condense the main elements into a much shorter visual document so it's simple and easy to refer to for the future. Pin it to the wall and discuss it regularly with the full team. This is the document to refer to in your content planning meetings every month. You'll find an example at the end of the workbook – see: **www.valuablecontentmarketing.com**.

It's so easy to get pulled off course when it comes to content creation. The secret is to know where you are heading and to be intentional. Sure – it's fine to stray from strategic on occasions but it works to work to a plan. Be prepared to learn and adapt your strategy to your audience's needs as your understanding grows. Measure what works and adjust for even more of it.

Valuable Tip

Take action, but be patient. Content marketing is a slow burn not a quick fix. Give yourself six months to build up and start using your stock of valuable content, before you expect to see serious results.

In the next chapter we will look at how to put the decisions and plan you made in your content strategy to work for your business – with particular emphasis on your website.

Take action

Download and complete the content strategy workbook on our website.

Once you're happy with this, fill in your content strategy on a page template and keep it in view.

CHAPTER 12
MAKING YOUR WEBSITE VALUABLE

Even if you have stellar content such as e-books, webcasts, white papers, all roads ultimately lead back to your website. If your website is not resonating with prospects and clients, you are ultimately losing business.

Michele Linn[1]

In this chapter:

- Build your content strategy on firm foundations.
- Is your website set up for content marketing success?
- The role of a valuable business website.
- The 80:20 rule of content.
- Logic, emotion and content for every step of the sale.
- Traditional website versus valuable website.
- Guidelines for a valuable website.
- Working with your website design and development team.
- Two important web design features.
- Marketing automation and the future of websites.
- Instructions for your web designer/developer.
- Ideas for key sections of your site.

Build your content strategy on firm foundations

You can share articles, videos, e-books and Tweet to your heart's delight but if the website these pull people back to doesn't convert interest into action – to return, to sign up to your newsletter, to contact you, to refer, to buy – then your investment will be wasted. Will your current website do your new content marketing strategy justice? Can you create, upload and house all this new content easily? Will people be able to find the valuable stuff on your site? Will your website convert their interest into action and motivate them to get in touch or stay in touch? Does it help you track their behaviour along the way?

Every strategic content marketing project we've worked on over the years has necessitated some work on the company website. Most likely some change will be needed to make your website deliver the benefits of your new content strategy.

This chapter shows you how to get your website right, making it valuable to your customers and turning it into a fully contributing member of your sales team.

Evaluation time: is your website up to the job?

Before we look in detail at what makes a valuable, content-marketing ready website, here's a quick evaluation tool to give you a picture of where your own site is now.

IS YOUR WEBSITE SET UP FOR CONTENT MARKETING SUCCESS?	YES	IN PART	NO
Is it immediately clear to the visitor what your company does? Is there a clear, customer-focused message upfront so people know they're in the right place?			
Is there a strong story that anchors all the content and gives meaning to the message? Does the website answer 'Why' as well as 'What' and 'How'?			

IS YOUR WEBSITE SET UP FOR CONTENT MARKETING SUCCESS?	YES	IN PART	NO
Do you have lots of valuable content as well as sales pages on the site? Great content marketing sites follow the 80:20 rule – 80% valuable content to 20% sales content.			
Is there an active, and well-designed blog as part of the site? The blog is the engine room of the website and often the place visitors land first. Does it feel like a welcoming home?			
Is there a resources section to house the deeper content? You're looking for a library of stock content – the heavyweight, long-lasting content along side the blogs.			
How up to date is the content? Fresh content added regularly? No tumbleweed. Your visitors will look for signs of life.			
How easy is it to find all the valuable content? Think of the visitor journeys through the site. Can they find what they need each step of the way? Is the site structure and information architecture clear?			
Is there a variety of content in different formats (eg video, infographics, podcasts as well as written content)? Does your content suit all learning styles?			
Plenty of evidence-based sales content? Case studies, stories of real customers, testimonials? Can the visitor find proof that the company delivers value to real people?			
Clear calls to action? Is it immediately obvious what the company wants you to do having found this site?			

IS YOUR WEBSITE SET UP FOR CONTENT MARKETING SUCCESS?	YES	IN PART	NO
Is there a sign up for email updates – so people can keep in touch with the content? This is a key call to action so make it very clear.			
Human touch – evidence of real people behind the firm? People do business with people. People profiles with photos and links to social accounts; author profiles again with photos?			
Engagement tools eg social share buttons, commenting facility, ability to rate content?			
Links to active social profiles? Easy-to-find evidence of an active and engaged community?			
Compelling service/product information with related content showing up on each page? Is the reader enticed to dig deeper, learn more?			
Responsive website design – so the site is easily viewable on all platforms?			
Professional, distinctive modern design that brings life and personality to the content?			
How customer focused is this website overall? (Messaging, copy, layout, design.) Is it all 'we, we, we' or 'you, you, you'?			
Analytics and insight? Does your web platform give you the insight you need into visitor behaviour and content performance?			

Use the questions to help you understand where you need to focus to make your site an effective platform for your valuable content marketing efforts.

The role of a valuable business website

Over 80 per cent of buyers are looking to the web to evaluate you as a potential service provider. Whether sellers are consciously shaping their online presences or not, buyers are looking there for information.

Hinge Marketing research 2014, **www.hingemarketing.com**[2]

Potential customers and clients will be led to your website from all directions so you need to make it clear to them that they've come to the right place. Your website should feel like home to them. *Here's a place where people really understand me.*

Start with the questions your customers are asking – their concerns and problems. Your entire website needs to embody the same customer-focused attitude as your blog. Most business websites are written as if they are sales proposals or flat online brochures. Yes, the website is about you, and your business, but just like the rest of your content you need to approach it from *the customer's* point of view. Not 'Why we're great' but 'Here's how we can help you'. This is a complete turnaround in tone for many business websites.

In his book *A Website that Works*, Mark O'Brien, founder of world-renowned web development consultancy Newfangled, is very clear on the three goals for a business website:

- to attract prospects;
- to get them to the areas of the site they are most interested in; and
- to bring them into the next level of their relationship with the firm.

The role of a good website is to engage web visitors with your business; to pull them closer to you, win their trust, inspire them to spread the word about you, and to buy from you when the time is right. A valuable website is a powerful platform that independently draws in leads, builds relationships and helps convert that interest into sales. That should be your aim.

All the hard work we have done on our website and content has greatly increased our brand awareness. Now people are coming to us instead of us always going to them.

Dave James, MD of Ascentor, **www.ascentor.co.uk**, @ascentor

Make sure the content caters for visitors at each stage of buying journey – from early stage research through evaluation and selection to loyal customer. Buying is hard, and prospects are crying out for your assistance. So when it comes to your website don't just pitch.

Turn it into a veritable hub of information and resources that visitors can delve into and learn from – more library than proposal or brochure. You'll get much better results that way.

How self-oriented is your website?

Take a look at your current website and try this simple test. How much of the wording is devoted to promoting the company? How much focuses on your potential customers and their needs and challenges? To make your website valuable, talk more about your clients and customers than you do about yourself. You, you, you, not we, we, we. This is a simple way of testing self-orientation.

Give your website a customer-focused goal, like Mel Lester

Management consultant Mel Lester demonstrates this customer-focused attitude perfectly. His desire is to create content that serves his clients and he leads his website with a strong promise:

> Mel Lester is pleased to offer this website as a valuable source of 'how-to-get-things-done' information and tools. I set out with an ambitious goal: to create the best internet resource for helping managers of architectural, engineering, and environmental consulting firms succeed, both corporately and personally.

Taken from the home page of **www.bizedge.biz**[3]

Mel's statement demonstrates all the valuable attributes to aspire to with a good website. His content is helpful and focused, his goal clear and compelling. He has committed to content excellence and is evidently sincere in his desire to help. He focuses on the customer first and it gets results: by not selling so hard he elicits more sales.

If you are going to succeed with your website put your customer first, like Mel.

We've seen so many people design a website first, and then tack all the content on afterwards. The words are seen as just a filler to replace the *lorem ipsum* text, blogs are an afterthought hidden at the back of the website. By creating valuable content first then designing the website around it, you'll create a far stronger and more useful platform.

The 80:20 rule of content

How should your website content be structured? How many static sales pages versus how many pages of valuable content? It's an important distinction to make.

If you want to win on the web, weight your website heavily in favour of valuable content. This means devoting far more space to useful, educational content overall than you do to sales pages. And it means devoting more of your marketing budget to creating this type of content too.

A great rule of thumb to help you strike the right balance is 80:20. That is, 80 per cent of your website should be devoted to the helpful valuable kind of content you consistently create with your clients/customers firmly in mind, and the remaining 20 per cent should be your more static sales content.

Now this is a BIG change for many business websites, and we'd suggest you aim to change the ratio in favour of valuable content over time.

At Valuable Content, our blog is the beating heart of our website. At the time of writing, if you include our blog articles, we have 270 pages of valuable content versus 15 sales pages. More than 80:20 in favour of the valuable stuff!

Provide content for every step along the path to a sale

In a world where research is increasingly carried out online, much of the sales process is now complete before a customer gets in touch with your firm (60 per cent in B2B according to *The Digital Evolution in B2B Marketing*, Google and CEB). You'll know that your website has a major role to play, particularly if your product or service is one that takes careful consideration before purchase (rather than a snap, impulse buy).

Imagine you're trying to find a new accountant for your business. More than likely you'll put out many feelers, but whatever route you take you're likely to end up at a website with a lot of questions.

Would this company solve my problem? Do they want to work for people like me? Are they expert in what they do? Would they make a good partner? Who runs this thing? What do other customers say? What results do they get? Will they value my business? Would they be good to work with? Do their world view and mine match up? Exactly how does it all work? What's the first step? How can I test if they'd be right?

Your website needs to answer all these questions through the content you provide. Give them the answers they need to choose to take the next step forward in their journey to becoming a loyal customer. Bryony Thomas captures this journey in detail, expanding on the elements of emotional and logical needs, time taken and the third parties people talk to, in the *Watertight Marketing* framework,[4] in the book of the same name. Think through the information that the people, potential customers, will be seeking as they're looking to buy. Use your content to give them a valuable experience and a call to action at every step to move them along that path.

Imagine yourself as a potential customer. What thought processes do you go through when you're thinking about making a big purchase?

- **From research to awareness.** When someone's researching, you want to appear everywhere they look – you want to pop up in search, in their social feeds, in the press they're reading, through recommendation. Your job at these outposts is to draw them back to your website, so whether it's your tweets, headlines in Google search or the title of a podcast, present them with something short, snappy and instantly appealing that motivates them to click through to your site.

- **From awareness to interest.** You have their attention, now you want their interest to grow. Provide answers to their challenges: make them think, make them laugh, inspire them or teach them something new. Draw them closer with blog articles, videos, infographics etc. Don't lose their interest – motivate them to stay in touch by signing up to your email list.

- **Surviving evaluation.** They're ready to buy. Make sure they buy from you. Give them all the information they need to make that decision, like you would in any good brochure: up-to-date case studies (video plus written), testimonials, reviews and clear information on your company and service/product and pricing. Your deeper written content is helpful here – fantastically useful guides, FAQS etc will give you more time when the potential customer is making a decision. So give them the detail they need to make the decision process easier – and make sure it's easy to find.

- **Try before you buy.** They've decided you're probably the people or the product for the job, but how can they be sure? Give them a flavour of what it's like to work with you through the content you share. Often in the professional world this occurs through an offline meeting or call, but your website can help here too. Think webinars or online reviews, offered via your site. Make the final decision to buy from you as easy as you can.

- **From sale to happy customer.** Congratulations, you have a new customer. The job of your website does not stop there. Hold their hand as they settle in to using your service or product. A series of warm, useful welcome emails with links to blogs and content on your site will help.

- **From customer to loyal advocate.** Keep the conversation going with your content to build an experience they love enough to share. Not just how to get the best out of your product or service but a drip feed of useful inspiring content that builds their understanding and shows you continue to care. Showcasing their success is a great way to do this. Make your customers the heroes and cement your bond with them.

Logic and emotion

People usually buy on emotion, then use logic to justify the decision they have just made. In the first part of the *Watertight Marketing Framework*, Bryony Thomas shows the interplay between logic and emotion in what she calls 'The Logic Sandwich'. To catch someone's attention and hook into a need you must appeal to their emotions. Then the logical brain kicks in as they scrutinize your offer. As the final decision draws near it needs to feel right and you're back to emotion.

With a mix of marketing content on your website, from visuals to blogs, research and factual information to a heartfelt manifesto, you can make sure you hit the right emotional and logical triggers to keep someone on the path to your bottom line.

Appealing to the heart of your buyers may be harder to quantify than appealing to logic, but there are steps you can take to make sure your website hits the mark.

We often refer to this beautiful quote from Maya Angelou:

> I've learnt that people will forget what you've said, people will forget what you did, but people will never forget how you made them feel.
>
> Maya Angelou[5]

That's as true for businesses as it is for people. A business that makes people feel good will fly far. Smiling and listening comes naturally when we meet people face-to-face, but sometimes these important feel-good factors get lost when they're translated into a website. And as your website is your business by proxy, it's smart to do all you can to make it as feel-good as possible.

Feel-good means friendly – the right tone of voice, pictures of real people, good design. It also means it makes it work effortlessly. Don't underestimate the huge surge of gratitude you'll get from visitors when they find exactly what they're looking for straight away, and whose progress through the site is joyfully straightforward. We love sites that make life easy for us.

So when you're thinking of designing your website content, think head plus heart.

Traditional website versus valuable website

So you're convinced that you need a valuable website. What does that look like in practice? What elements make a traditional brochure-style website different from a valuable content marketing site? Here are a couple of different layouts to show you what we mean.

Not so valuable website

Characteristics of a traditional, brochure-style website

1 The menu doesn't even mention the customer. It's all about the company. Nothing valuable on the site to help clients solve their finance challenges.

2 No clear message. No clear story for the customer, just an anonymous stock image. Customer can't easily see what is in it for them.

3 Self-oriented wording. The copy is all about how great they are. Plenty of nonsense gobbledygook too. Also trying to be everything to everyone (and catching no one in the process).

4 Meaningless self-promotion that doesn't build trust.

5 Selling, not helping. Sales brochure is the only download. Presumes that visitors want to buy, now.

6 Company news. Internal-looking news of no real interest to the customer, and out of date.

Characteristics of a valuable, lead-generating website

1 Tagline focused on the customer. The whole website is designed and written around the needs of the customer. Valuable content is prioritized.

2 Search.

3 Simple customer-focused toolbar.

4 Clear message. Sets the scene with an inspiring snapshot of what this company is all about and what it will do for them.

5 Customer-focused wording. Engages with their issues and tells them they are in the right place.

6 Content that engages with customer challenge and pulls them in.

Continued ▶

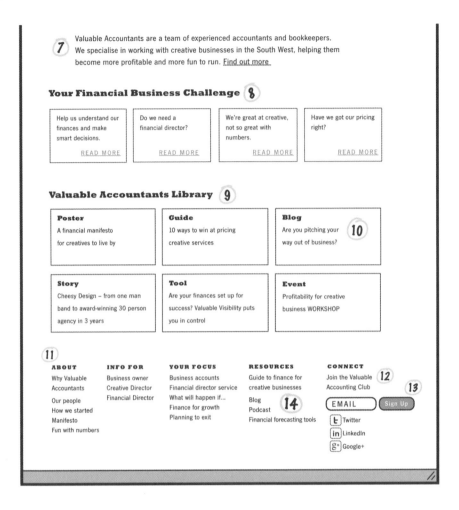

7 Valuable Accountants are a team of experienced accountants and bookkeepers. We specialise in working with creative businesses in the South West, helping them become more profitable and more fun to run. Find out more

Your Financial Business Challenge 8

Help us understand our finances and make smart decisions. READ MORE	Do we need a financial director? READ MORE	We're great at creative, not so great with numbers. READ MORE	Have we got our pricing right? READ MORE

Valuable Accountants Library 9

Poster
A financial manifesto for creatives to live by

Guide
10 ways to win at pricing creative services

Blog
Are you pitching your **10** way out of business?

Story
Cheesy Design – from one man band to award-winning 30 person agency in 3 years

Tool
Are your finances set up for success? Valuable Visibility puts you in control

Event
Profitability for creative business WORKSHOP

11

ABOUT
Why Valuable Accountants
Our people
How we started
Manifesto
Fun with numbers

INFO FOR
Business owner
Creative Director
Financial Director

YOUR FOCUS
Business accounts
Financial director service
What will happen if...
Finance for growth
Planning to exit

RESOURCES
Guide to finance for creative businesses
Blog
Podcast **14**
Financial forecasting tools

CONNECT
Join the Valuable **12** Accounting Club **13**
[EMAIL] [Sign Up]
[t] Twitter
[in] LinkedIn
[g+] Google+

---

7 Niche business, focused market.

8 Customer-focused route into service pages. Gets them to information that's relevant to their challenge, fast.

9 Heaps of valuable content in different formats. Highlights customer stories. Important credibility-builders.

10 Blog. Lots of fresh, useful content. A hit with customers and search engines alike.

11 Use footer as quick route to find what you need.

12 Monthly newsletter to maintain contact and build relationships.

13 Easy ways to get in touch.

14 Offers a clear call to action. The sign-up box is motivating and clear.

Working with your website design and development team

Your website is a work of commerce, not a work of art.

Mark O'Brien in *A Website That Works*, **www.newfangled.com**, @newfangledmark[6]

If you are thinking about designing or redesigning your company website, it is tempting to focus first on how it should look to impress your customers. This strategy prioritizes form over function, aesthetics over information. But this design-led approach fails to consider how and why people buy your services and what customers want from a professional business website.

Design is very important, but if you concentrate on colour schemes before planning the content you run the risk of creating a great-looking site that customers either have no use for or cannot use.

With a few exceptions, people visit the web for its utility, not its beauty. Having a visually appealing site is good, of course, but content is golden.

Web usability guru Jakob Nielsen, **www.useit.com**[7]

Think content first. Before you pick up the phone to a web designer, think very carefully about what you and your customers want from your site; what does it need to say to convince them to buy your services and how should this content be laid out?

A good way to get this clear is to create a 'wireframe': a non-graphical layout of each page of your site. This will enable you to organize the content and test the layout before you start building the site. Draw out a structure with pen and paper, or use a simple wireframing tool such as Balsamiq (**www.balsamiq.com**). If you wireframe first, before a single graphic is chosen or line of code written, you have a far greater chance of web success, for you and your customers, and you'll avoid expensive and time-consuming revisions at a later date. Use this to help you brief your web designer/developer. Use a tool like this to show your designer what you're looking to achieve. You'll find that many good web firms use tools like this too.

Valuable Tip

Spend as much time planning your new website as you do building it.

Two important web design features

Here are two design features to add into your plan and discuss with your web team:

1 Related content

Too many websites miss the opportunity to engage people. The problem is often not the content, but how findable it is. Related content and sidebars are your friends here. Prioritize these as part of your web design and you'll encourage people to stay longer on the site and engage more deeply.

If you're following the advice in this book you'll have both a library of valuable content, and sales pages that talk about your company and the products/services it provides. Connect the two by signposting the reader to related content in your sidebars.

Give the visitor links that match their interest. Use a related content feature to direct people deeper into the website and motivate them to stick around. 'Our services' is a key place where your valuable content can add richness, authority and depth. In addition to a clear description of how you help, signpost people towards a relevant customer story, or a handy guide. Make it easy for them to get to the information that they need, and prove your expertise in the process.

No page should be a dead end; every page should open a door to further useful and engaging content. Using related links is a great strategy for keeping people on your site (your bounce rate will drop) and earning their loyalty. Sites that offer useful suggestions encourage people to interact with them and to come back repeatedly. Maintain the conversation by ensuring that related links are relevant, well written and presented so that they get noticed.

2 Calls to action

Clear calls to action across the site are absolutely key. You've got their interest. What do you want people to do? Because people will be arriving at your website via your blogs or from any number of places, every page needs to have a clear call to action. Make it obvious what you want people to do next. Action is everything when it comes to your website.

The key actions you want people to take when they visit the site are:

- take something away – download a document they find useful;
- keep in touch – sign up to your updates or newsletter;
- get in touch.

Include these calls to action as relevant across the site. Give calls to action some emotional weight by showing you understand the client's problem. 'Wrestling with end of year accounts? Call Sarah' is better than 'Call us'.

Marketing automation and the future of websites

If you're considering a website redesign, it will pay you to look ahead at what's happening in the fields of marketing automation, CRM and new email marketing, and how these can be linked to your own site. The next generation super sites are much powerful than websites of the past, and the technology is becoming more accessible. Next generation websites are an integral part of a whole lead development ecosystem. They don't stand alone but are linked to the social web, to your growing email subscriber list, to your contact database, to smart analytics.

Joining up your website with a smart marketing automation system (eg Hubspot, Act On, Marketo and more) that connects with your email marketing tool (eg Mailchimp, Aweber) and CRM platform (eg Salesforce) will give you a high-performing content marketing base that will give you insight, knowledge and real control.

Marketing automation is a key part of this ecosystem, a way to help you power your website and manage the relationships your content builds. Initially the preserve of larger firms, with new platforms like New Rainmaker from

Copyblogger (newrainmaker.com) these powerful online and sales platforms are becoming more accessible for smaller businesses too.

Here are two powerful elements that smart automation platform like this will bring.

1. Automation platforms give better insight

In terms of insight, analytics takes you only so far. You can learn from analytics what content is driving most site traffic, where this is coming from and therefore what places are best to share your content. But there are other, important questions that are more difficult to answer.

Questions like:

- Specifically, who is consuming which content and when?
- Which types of content (both topics and delivery formats) are most likely to attract your ideal customers?
- Which valuable content is leading to the best opportunities and ultimately real revenue for your firm?

A good marketing automation system will help you answer these tricky questions by tracking visitor behaviour. As a visitor moves through the buying process and eventually becomes a customer, it allows you to track their progress back to the first point of entry and conversion – closing the loop on which content is most likely to lead to good opportunities and new business.

A good automation system lets you go more granular still, tracking how your *ideal* customers behave so you can design your content and your site around their needs. This is good for them (a better and more relevant web experience) and very good for you too (far more likely to choose you, and you'll know what content works). Win, win.

Smart marketer Jason Miliki, owner of US-based professional services marketing agency Rattleback (**www.rattleback.com**), explains more about the power of this approach:

> For most small- to midsized firms, websites are still pretty much static experiences that are uniformly the same for most site visitors. While we've

introduced dynamic elements (Twitter feeds for instance) for the most part we're still delivering largely the same information to everyone who visits the site. But, increasingly, web users expect more. I call this the Amazon Effect. Because Amazon knows so much about me based on things I've looked at or purchased in the past, it can largely drive my web experience every time I visit. I know every site I visit is tracking me, and I'm starting to expect that they're going to use that information to deliver me some value.

Automation tools like Marketo are already making elements of this possible for midsized firms and possibly even smaller firms. We're already capable of delivering smart calls-to-action on the sites we build that ensure that no site visitor will see the same call-to-action twice.

The next step is really to apply this thinking to the 'relevant content' of a site. So, you read our article? You might also like the research study we did on the same topic... You already downloaded that? Well then let me offer you the webinar we did on the same topic... and, we can do that all directly on the site page while the visitor is there (rather than through email after the fact).

2. Automated connection, no matter the size of your following

In an ideal world we'd bet you'd like to nurture each and every one of your prospects personally, wouldn't you? But as your email subscriber list grows (and it will) to a meaningful size how will you communicate with all these followers? You'd like to share content with them that's helpful and related to the content they've already read. Smart marketing automation allows you to do this through automated programs and what's known as 'lead scoring'.

Automated programs give you the ability to send out timely content and messages to a visitor based on content they've previously interacted with. With lead scoring you can score visitors based on who they are and the actions they take. As they accumulate points, you can set up triggers in your system to notify you when they reach a certain threshold.

Over time you'll see which content people are most likely to want to interact with as they get closer to getting in touch with you. And you can identify those who might be ripe for direct personal contact at the right time.

Pretty fantastic, right? While we're sold on the idea of using this technology to deliver more good stuff at just the right time to your customer, we also know it's not possible to automate trust. If you get it wrong, it backfires horribly. More importantly, we know how it makes us feel if marketers use data to target us too relentlessly (cross, that's what) so keep your customers' best interests at heart, and handle with care. You'll find more on trust and selling in Chapter 14.

The future for your website?

The right content to the right people, right time, right place – that should be the aspiration, and as we've explained here, much of the functionality is available now. The websites of the future will offer visitors an even more personalized experience, with valuable content as the default navigation.

New platforms will undoubtedly appear, and new web agencies will hopefully follow who understand the need for holistic solutions for our connected digital world. One thing is for certain though; having the right content – knowing what to say and how to say it – will remain at the heart of it all.

Instructions for your web team

Now you're clear on what you want the website to do, it's time to talk to someone who can build it for you. Most website suppliers are good aesthetically or technically, however not all fully understand the needs and functionality of a valuable content marketing site.

Use this checklist to help you guide your web team on your requirements.

Requirements to discuss with your designer:

- **A fully content-managed site**. This is a no brainer. Platforms such as Wordpress make it very easy to add and update pages of additional content. You'll be constantly updating the website so you want to be able to do it yourself.

- **A content-centred site** rather than a highly visual experience. Any movement, sounds, graphical devices, blocks of imagery should fulfil a specific purpose.

- **Simple, intuitive navigation and layout**, designed around target visitor needs. It must be very easy for people to find the information they want.

- **Fully responsive design** – viewable on all mobile devices.

- **An integrated blog** – fully functioning and well-designed.

- **An engaging home page** that highlights valuable content and pulls people in.

- **The ability to upload, store, highlight deeper content easily** – video, podcasts and other content.

- **Search engine fundamentals** – a logical URL structure and the ability to set metadata (see Chapter 7).

- **Analytics** – you want to know who's coming to your site, what pages are your most read, what's working and what's not.

- **Marketing automation** – what level of automation and integration of tools will you require?

- **Integration with an email marketing tool** so visitors can sign up for content updates.

- **Ability to show related content** and relevant calls to action on every page. No page should feel like a dead end – there's always more to discover.

- **Engagement tools** – eg social share buttons, ability to comment on articles, enquiry forms.

- **Strong visual design** – professional and interesting but uncluttered.

- **Professional page and content layout** – paying attention to typography and styling to help the content stand out and be easy to read.

- **Search capability.**

- **Clear contact details**.

Valuable Tip

Hire a web designer/developer who creates valuable content for his or her own business. This way you'll know that they understand what you're looking to achieve.

Ideas for key sections of your site

Home page

Your homepage isn't a gallery. It's a door. You need to convince people that there's a good reason to come through it.

Chris Butler, COO of Newfangled[8]

When you're trying to sell your home, estate agents recommend clearing out the clutter to show off your best features. We think the same applies to your website home page. It should make people feel at home – understood, looked after, in the right place.

Although people will arrive at your site via lots of pages, you still need a well-designed home page. It needs to demonstrate:

- Clarity of purpose. In a nutshell – what you do, what you've done, what your clients say, what you say, and why that matters.
- Clear navigation.
- Is this you? Clear pathways to get visitors to the answers they're looking for, fast.
- Valuable content loud and proud.
- Room to breathe.

About us

Potential customers will want to know what kind of company you are, so this section is important. But that's not all. They're really after information that tells them what problems you can solve and if you are the kind of team who can help them:

- See the page from your potential customer's point of view. Your team's golfing prowess might be awesome, but how does that help? Focus here on your approach to the business.
- Share your mission, your story – what you believe and why?
- Be clear about the customers you want – what kind of people can your business help?

- Don't write too much. Remember the rules of good web writing. Short and to the point, with strong headlines and subheadings.

- Make sure the whole page links well to the rest of your site. Relevant 'About us' copy will make natural links to your customers, services and stories.

Our people

Apart from figuring out if your approach to business inspires confidence, potential clients like to see who they will be working with:

- Good professional photographs of the team are a must.

- Show some personality, although still remember that potential clients are most interested in themselves and their concerns so don't go overboard with personal stuff.

- Quick Q&As are an engaging way of getting across enough information to show your human face without becoming a bore.

- Link to the valuable content they've produced.

Is this you?

Define your customers or clients and their concerns in an engaging way. This is where your customer persona profiles come to life. You'll need a place to demonstrate exactly who you serve and how well you understand their problems and can help to overcome them. An 'Is this you?' page is a useful way to do that. Direct different potential buyers to the services, products and content that is relevant to them.

Customer stories

Don't tell me the moon is shining; show me the glint of light on broken glass.
Anton Chekhov

In a low-trust world, we crave independent evidence from real people. There is huge power in hearing your story from the perspective of those who have been on the receiving end of your products or services. It's much more believable coming from others than it is from you.

Case studies, or customer stories as we prefer to call them, are particularly important when potential customers are evaluating you as a potential partner to work with. They set your services in context and when targeted right will mirror the buyer's situation.

> *Customer stories serve a role that no other promotional tools truly fill by accomplishing the three purposes at once: credibility, education and validation.*

Casey Hibbard, *Stories that Sell*, **www.storiesthatsellguide.com**[9]

Here's how to make your case studies work on your website:

- Put the client you worked for centre stage. Make them look good.

- Show how your product, service or organization solved a specific issue. Frame the business problem you solved clearly and upfront.

- Give value. Make this type of content really valuable by giving away learning points for others to follow.

- Involve the customer in the creation process. How do you know what benefits a customer got from working with you? You will only find out if you ask!

Valuable Tip

At the end of every assignment or sale ask your customer for their feedback. What did they really think? Why did they buy? What were the real benefits of your involvement? What did they appreciate and what could you do better next time?

You will find a case study template in the Resources section at the end of the book.

Our services/products

Your products or services section is the real nitty gritty of what you do, and these pages can be the most difficult to write. If your business sells technical services, for example, there is a risk they can become stilted and jargon-filled, distancing your potential clients. If you have a number of services for a wide variety of clients, your website can become confusing.

You need a brief but clear description of your services for the people in the early stages of web research. Remember to phrase your services answering the question 'How do you help people like me?' and not just 'What do you do?'.

Write a short, clear overview, and signpost to more pages for those who crave more detail. Remember to add 'Related content' boxes too.

Useful structure for service copy:

- name of service;
- who this is relevant for;
- why they need it/what problem it solves;
- what your service involves;
- results/benefits;
- call to action – what to do next;
- relevant image/photo/video;
- customer stories and testimonials;
- related valuable content.

Free resources/library for your deeper content

Call it what you will – resources, free stuff, knowledge bank or library – this is a crucial section of your site. Your valuable content will be highlighted throughout the website, but it needs a home of its own too. Showcase the valuable stuff in one easy-to-find place. Gather together your articles, newsletters, videos, podcasts, downloads and SlideShare presentations and make them available as valuable free resources for your potential customers.

Just as a library needs cataloguing and signposting, your resources need to be presented so that people searching can find what they want quickly. Organizing your content into categories is important, and linking between connected pieces is the best way to keep people engaged on your site. Dividing by format too makes it easier for clients to access the information in the way they want.

Launching your new website to the world

The process of creating a new website will stretch you, frustrate you and really make you think. It forces you to look at your business with fresh eyes and make some really tough decisions – on your message, your customers and their needs, your services, the reason you're in business.

Once the hard work is done – your new website built, your content strategy in place, your social media feeds primed and a heap of new content ready to share – the temptation may be to just *go go go!* You've created a fantastic content marketing machine, and you're going to use it! You might be feeling a bit media mogul. All that power! Bwah hah hah!

Before you launch yourself onto the world, firing on all cylinders, and all guns blazing, remember that this content marketing game is about building relationships. Listen as well as broadcast. Share other people's content, not just your own. Be generous. You do have the power. Now use it wisely.

The work doesn't stop when you've launched your website. It's a platform to build on, not an end in itself. Be clear on your content strategy, create a publishing plan for the months ahead and keep adding and sharing great content if you want to get found and loved. It takes time to build up that head of steam when it comes to driving leads from the web but hold firm. If you follow these tips and continue to add value results will come.

Take action

- Review your current website. Will it support your valuable content marketing goals? Is it the platform you need?
- For inspiration for examples of best practice check out the websites of companies who have won a Valuable Content Award:
  www.valuablecontent.co.uk/valuablecontentaward

CHAPTER 13
HOW TO WRITE VALUABLE CONTENT

Anybody who can think clearly can write clearly about anything at all.

William Zinsser[1]

In this chapter:

- Can anyone learn to write valuable content?
- Planning before you write.
- Basic writing rules.
- Striking the right tone.
- Help with headlines.
- How to stop procrastinating and just do it!

Writing underpins everything a content marketer produces. Blogs, guides and deeper content need to be well written, so too do social media profiles, headlines, video captions, the updates inviting people to listen to your podcasts and the calls to action on your website. Even in this increasingly visual age, there's a real need for the right words thoughtfully shaped.

There isn't an area of content marketing that's untouched by writing, and the ability to write well will give you extra oomph. Becoming a good writer will help you to create any type of valuable content and supercharge your business in the process.

Can anyone learn to write valuable content?

What makes a writer great? Tremendous love for the audience and the topic. You have to care a lot – about language, about your readers, and about what you write about.

Sonia Simone, Copyblogger, **www.copyblogger.com**, @soniasimone[2]

The act of writing itself can feel like a huge hurdle – you may feel you just can't do it, or can't do it well enough to make it the main focus of your business marketing.

But don't despair. We believe pretty much anyone can write. All you need is common sense and a clear sense of purpose. This chapter will ground you in some good writing basics, and help you with the less tangible aspects of writing – how to make sure what you're writing will be valuable, how to get your tone of voice right and how to be engaging. Not just how to write, but how to produce writing that people will value.

Our advice is to get stuck in and give it a go; like any skill, writing improves with lots of practice. Get to grips with the basic rules we outline here, and writing for your business should become easier. (We'd love you to enjoy your writing too, but right now we'll settle for you just getting it done.)

We guarantee the act of writing improves your own understanding of your field, and your connection with your customers and clients.

Writing is thinking, really valuable thinking, and doing it will help you build a stronger business.

What's different about writing valuable content?

Writing valuable content is different from other kinds of writing you're likely to have done. The main difference is in perspective. Your starting point is always '*How is this going to help my customer?*' Customer-centric, not self-centred, it takes a shift in attitude that can feel unnatural at the start. Its directness takes some getting used to. Likewise valuable content really benefits from showing personality and so makes people who have been trained to keep their writing measured and impartial feel on shaky ground.

There are some simple rules though, and a methodology, and once you've grasped them it will be become easier. This chapter will teach you to write valuable content with confidence.

Planning makes perfect

In preparing for battle I have always found that plans are useless but planning is indispensable.

General Dwight Eisenhower

Having a clear idea of who you're writing for, and why, will shape what you write.

Well-planned content has a much better chance of ending up as well-written content too. So here are some questions to make sure your content is on track to be valuable. Answer them first with every piece of content you create before you dive in.

Planning questions

- Who is this piece of content designed for? Who is your ideal reader?
- What's the concept or keyword you're targeting with this? What question does it answer for the reader?
- Working title for this content?
- What's your goal? Why are you doing this? What do you want the reader to learn, and what do you want them to think and feel as a result?
- What's the call to action? What do you want the reader to do having read it?

Get the answers to these questions clear first, and then start writing.

On to the rules!

Some basic writing rules to improve everything you write

Say more with shorter sentences

If we had to pick one golden writing rule that shone above all the others we'd pick 'write shorter sentences'.

Make it easy for us to get to the important bit quickly. In Victorian England your reader was happy to accompany you on a journey of immensely long and complex sentences. But your reader today is different. Where your business writing is concerned, keeping your sentences short will give your copy more impact.

Try taking a piece of copy you've already written, and count the number of words you write in an average sentence. And then cut them. Just like that. Wham.

If you're averaging over 25 words per sentence cut them in half. If you're consistently hitting about 15, cut some of them right down. Not every sentence needs to be super short. Variety is the spice of life. But on the whole shorter is better. Much better.

Why is shorter better? Because the act of reading has changed. Let's imagine our Victorian reader seated comfortably next to the fireside. You can put them in a crinoline, or a handsome beard (or both if you like, it's your imagination). They're reading your words bound in book form or in a large newspaper, turning pages at their own pace.

Today's reader will be reading your words online on a laptop, or a tablet. On the tiny screen of their phone on a packed and crowded train. It's difficult reading long sentences under these circumstances. If your reader needs to scroll too often to get to a point they will quickly lose heart. So keep it short.

Quick writing exercise

Go through your most recent blog post. Find the five longest sentences and rewrite them so they are no more than 10 words long. See what difference that makes.

Active not passive

An engaging tone of voice is rarely passive. Look at the way your favourite writers use words, and you'll almost certainly find they use the active voice.

Using the active voice gives your words authority too. Don't say 'The report will be delivered', say 'We'll deliver the report.' It's much more powerful.

Another quick-fix writing rule is change the tense of your writing. Using active verbs in the present tense gives the impression of purpose – just what you want to make readers feel they're getting somewhere fast.

Quick writing exercise

Take one of your blogs and change its tense so it reads as if it's written in the here and now. If you're yet to start writing then compare these two sentences and see which you prefer.

> A. Businesses signed up to our newsletter will be receiving tips and tricks to help them get more out of their money.
> B. Sign up to our newsletter for tips and tricks to help you get more out your money.

Hopefully you'll prefer B. (If you don't, keep reading them both again until you agree with us.)

Sentence A wanders between the past (signed up) and future (will be) which leaves you feeling a bit adrift and detached. Sentence B has more immediacy. It also employs another basic writing rule. It gets 'you' in there.

Capture the power of you

Good writing makes a connection with the reader. The quickest way to do that is to put the reader directly into the copy. Get 'you' in there and your writing will be harder to ignore.

Quick writing exercise

Compare:

> **A** Business finance is something that keeps many people awake at night. Worries about profit and loss, cash flow and forecasting are commonplace amongst the owners of small businesses. Big Red Pen Accountants can help.

B Business finance shouldn't be difficult. Would you like yours to be simple? Understanding what's going on with the figures is the key – so if you'd like help getting to grips with your profit and loss, cash flow and forecasting, we'd love to help.

Sentence B has more impact because it talks directly to you. We don't immediately identify with the 'many people' in sentence A, but we're right there in sentence B.

Look at one of your blogs. Rewrite, replacing any examples of them/our clients/people with 'you'. It should make your writing feel more immediate, and more conversational.

Ask questions

The eagle-eyed among you will have noticed that as well as getting 'you' into the sentence above, another trick we've used to give the writing more immediacy is to use questions in the copy.

Asking questions of the reader makes your writing feel more like a conversation. It's like turning to the person next to you and checking they've understood what you said. It shows empathy, and makes your writing warmer and more engaging.

Questions make it easier to develop a relationship with your reader. Do you agree?

It stops you from feeling like you're on the receiving end of a lecture, and makes it into a two-way conversation.

Quick writing exercise

Look at one of your blogs. Can you see any places where adding questions would improve the flow and readability of the piece? Try adding them, and see the difference that it makes. If it's working well the copy should feel more alive – as though you are more present in the writing – which is just what we want. Human is good.

Declutter

A good place to start if you're looking to write shorter and punchier copy is to rid your lines of slow-you-down conjunctives. So any 'howevers', or 'moreovers', or 'herebys' can hit the cutting-room floor. You can also can the cans. Don't say 'We can deliver X', say 'We deliver X'.

Metaphors and analogies

Analogies are a really good way to be engaging and make connections with your readers. Making comparisons can throw up some fantastically memorable phrases that make points quickly and strongly. For example, if I'm trying to explain how a website homepage shouldn't look, I could say 'Disorganized, chaotic, cheap, scruffy, a bit all over the place, full of tarnished sales messages, don't know where to look, invokes an overwhelming feeling of "Oh I can't be bothered"'. Or I could say 'Like the sales floor of a department store after the first day of the January sales'. The analogy says it far faster, and gives the reader an image they can quickly grasp and will be able to recall.

A metaphor is a word or phrase that is used to make a comparison. Metaphors condense ideas and feelings succinctly, so weave some in and *cut straight to the heart*. (That was a metaphor.) Pick ones with an emotional resonance to pull readers in and make them more receptive to your message.

Break some rules

It's OK to start sentences with *And*, *Because*, and *So*. And it's even OK to break some of the rules we've just set you, as long as you're clear why you're doing it. I'm thinking particularly of the golden short sentence rule. Here's why.

Be real

Mimicking natural speech patterns is an excellent way to develop a good written tone of voice. It helps break you away from writing in a flat way. Making every sentence super short can make your writing sound too staccato, and not like a real person. When we speak we vary our sentence structure. Sometimes we speak in very long sentences that meander and wind around and come back to the beginning again. Sometimes we don't. As long as most of your sentences are short, getting some of this variety into your writing helps establish an authentic and natural-sounding tone of voice.

Embrace editing

Once you've got into the swing of writing, you'll come to recognize the euphoria that accompanies the finishing of a great blog article. There will be five minutes when what you've just written is the most important thing that's ever been written in the entire world on that subject. There's not a moment to waste – you have to share it now, this very second. Your life and the sanity of the world depends upon it.

There's also a drive to be finished with it. Ticking it off your things-to-do list would make you feel better, so you're itching to upload.

The very best thing to do now is not to press send, but to save the document, close it, and go back and look at it again tomorrow with clearer, more cynical eyes.

Just a few hours' distance should make you better able to check the piece for the following common mistakes.

Stop, look, edit – six things to do before you press 'Publish'

1 **Is it on target?** You felt like it was at the time, but writing can be deceptive sometimes. Ask yourself if it is genuinely useful for your clients. It might be that some simple tweaking is all that's needed to pull it back in line, or it might be that you need to put it on hold for longer. Great ideas are never wasted, but they do need the right format to fly. Don't be scared of pulling something if you know it's not right.

2 **Have you missed any words out?** Easily done when the prose is flying. Check your copy slowly and carefully to make sure it makes sense.

3 **Is there any waffle?** Places where you've gone on too long, or talked around the houses too much. If so, cut any meandering sections and rephrase more succinctly.

4 **Have you repeated words?** Again, it's a common mistake when you're writing fast. Check again.

5 **Is it spelt right? Is it the right word?** Spellcheck picks up most errors – but it won't pick up mis-substituted words. Don't let something go out until it makes perfect sense.

6 **Is the grammar right?** Developing a natural and engaging tone of voice doesn't mean you can stop writing proper, like. Inaccurate grammar stops readers in their tracks, and it makes your writing hard to understand. If you're not sure, ask someone else to check too. Even if you are sure, a second pair of eyes is never a bad idea.

The right tone of voice for your business

Striking the right tone of voice is important. People will turn off instantly if they feel you're talking down to them, or that you don't understand them. 'Feel' is the operative word here. Tone is something we respond to instinctively.

Sometimes it's hard to put our fingers on what's right or wrong, but we sure as hell know when we don't like it. The wrong tone can make us tense, or cross, or left out – *this isn't speaking to me* – and we'll walk away.

Tone is a difficult thing to get right when you first start writing, and a lot of people worry about it. Following the writing tips outlined above will improve the tone of your writing voice, but how does your business get the right tone of voice?

There's no generic tone of voice that suits every business. How a web design agency speaks is not the same as a firm of solicitors; an HR firm sounds different from a chain of Italian restaurants. Good content shares similarities – it's clear, concise and easily understood – but the variances in tone of voice are important for building your business brand.

Start with speaking, not writing. How would you talk to a client that you're working with? What words would you use to explain what you mean if they were sitting right next to you? Chances are you'd want to make it as easy as possible for them to follow. Expertise can be a stumbling block if you just dump it in somebody's path, so see what you're saying from their point of view.

Talking first can establish the right lexicon of words for you to draw from. It should eliminate all but the most clearly understood jargon in your sector – the terms that everyone uses and understands completely – the words your clients would expect to see as part of their working lives. You wouldn't throw in something your client wouldn't understand if you were chatting through a project over a coffee – blank faces are disconcerting and don't make for comfortable meetings – so don't put them into your articles and blogs.

For example, don't say 'We facilitate training sessions to leverage optimal grassroots success': say 'We run coaching workshops for new businesses.'

What you're aiming for in any blog, Tweet or web page is connection. Don't let awkward language or unnecessary jargon get in the way.

Thinking of a real client when you're composing your content will make whatever you're writing warmer and easier to connect with.

Smaller businesses can find the tone of voice through trial and error.

> *The tone of voice for our business has evolved naturally. You have to start writing and experiment. There are some strong personalities in our office, so we're quick to tell each other if something doesn't feel right. Now we can all tweet in Wriggle!*

Larger businesses need to do the work of talking and listening to clients, and draw up tone of voice guidelines that can be shared among everyone who's going to blog and tweet.

Basic tone of voice guidelines

- **Authenticity is the key to striking the right tone of voice with your content.** Don't write something that you wouldn't be happy to say out loud. That simple rule will save you from some big tone mistakes.

- **Understanding and respecting the people you're writing for will help set the tone too.** People need to feel that you care about them.

- **Imagining the real person as you're writing will rein back any sales spiel** – you'll remember how uncomfortable it feels to be on the receiving end of pushy sales messages (and how uncomfortable it would feel to deliver that spiel) and will focus on the parts of the message that you know will resonate most with your reader.

- Lastly, **keep the big picture in mind**. Set the tone to build a community around what you do, and you won't go far wrong.

Help with headline writing

On average, five times as many people read the headlines as read the body copy so learning to write good headlines is a valuable writing skill to master. Faced with an immense sea of information, we scan for headlines that pull us in and anchor us to something relevant. Headlines matter on web pages, and even more so on social media sites like Twitter. Here's how to get people to click on yours instead of swimming past:

- **Be succinct.** Summarize the point of your article or blog in as few words as possible. Short and snappy is more appealing than convoluted. It's a good test of your content – if you can't sum up the point in a sentence, maybe you haven't got it quite right yet.

- **Use the keyword on the title.** This is useful for SEO, and potential readers.

- **Put your reader first.** Think about what they want to know. What will they be searching for? How is your content going to help them? Use the phrase they'll be searching for as your headline. *Home page design – a quick guide. Networking etiquette – what to say first. Key components of winning press releases.* These are examples of reader-focused headlines.

- **Ask a question.** Headlines that engage are good news, and conversational questioning-style headlines do just that. *Are your business cards working? Is your recruitment process up to scratch? Do your clients know how to find you?*

- **'How to' headlines.** People are searching for information, and the 'How to' headline attracts readers to click for more detail. *How to design your About Us page. How to boost e-commerce sales. How to sell your house in six weeks.*

- **Promise success.** We all want to succeed, and are tempted by people that offer it to us. Spiking your headlines with positive success words can encourage clicks. *Win more clients with smart business networking. Successful sales start with three words. Boost profits with smarter working.*

- **Raise the spectre of failure.** Fear of failure is as big a drive as the desire for success. Scare people into reading your stuff! *Five costly*

PR mistakes to avoid. How to lose customers and alienate people. Is your web copy costing you sales?

- **Offer some inside knowledge.** Who doesn't want to know a secret? It's not hard to pique our curiosity. *The secrets of successful bloggers. The trait top novelists share. Which blogger do 20 world leaders follow?*

- **Play the numbers game.** Maybe it's the promise of a quick read, perhaps because it seems to offer something easily graspable and definitive. Whatever the reason, Twitter can't get enough of the numbers headlines. *Five ways to improve your SEO instantly. Seven ways to keep readers on your site. Three writing rules you must break.*

- **Get active.** Words like boost, drive, run, leap, soar, make headlines more compelling than passive words. Injecting some energy into your headlines grabs attention. Boost sales with clever marketing. Drive customers to checkout faster.

- **Say something different.** Originality is like a breath of fresh air in the crowded Twitter marketplace. Headlines created from a different lexicon leap off the page. I'm not talking jargon, just unexpected words – nouns or verbs – that shake up the stream of salesy Tweets. *What Lady Gaga can teach you about networking. Why Puffins rock at closing the sale.*

- **And if all else fails...** Capitalize Everything. It's in your face, brash, and hard to avoid. *How To Win More Sales Overnight. Why Your Content Sucks. How To Write Killer Blogs.*

Become a confident content writer

Becoming a confident writer will make creating valuable content much easier, and much more enjoyable. As well as being able to write blogs and other deeper content, you'll find good writing skills will improve your social media presence, your presentations and your talks.

The words you choose to share with the world matter, and becoming a better writer will help you communicate more clearly wherever you are.

And finally: how to stop procrastinating and just do it!

We do know that getting down to doing writing is difficult if you're running your own business. Most of us don't have the luxury of dropping everything and getting away from it all to focus on writing alone. And even when we do get the time, suddenly other things seem more pressing. Should I check my email? Tidy my desk? Have a cup of coffee?

Here are some things that help get writing done:

- **Remember why you are doing it.** The words you are writing are part of your big marketing plan. A small step in the right direction, not a huge hurdle. Get it into proportion.

- **Don't waste energy thinking about it. Redirect energy into doing it.** Just get on with it. Open your computer, don't turn on Twitter, don't look at Facebook, don't open email, just start writing.

- **The sooner you start the sooner you finish.** Anticipate the end. Once you've done it, it's done, and it won't have to be done again. Get on with it!

- **Promise yourself a treat.** It works for small children and for grown-ups too – 400 words and I can go for a walk/have a cake/make that phone call.

- **Carve out some real time, and protect it from other demands.** Five minutes a day to record your ideas in a blog diary, half an hour to plan a blog (and write one too, once you're really up and running), an hour and a half to write something that addresses the question that keeps coming up, and get it up on your website.

- **Remove yourself.** Write somewhere different, away from the distractions of your usual working day. A quiet meeting room, a café, a library, even a different desk.

- **Make a commitment.** Deadlines work (it's the only way we ever get our writing done!). Writing really will make all the difference to your business, so set aside the time, and keep to it.

- **Tell people you're doing it.** Going public makes it more difficult to give up.

Take action

- Find a blog that you enjoyed reading, and look closely at the way it was written. Which techniques does the writer use to grab your attention and keep you reading?

- Practice headline writing. Notice the headlines that catch your eye, and try rewriting one of your headlines in the same style.

- Read more. Not just blogs but novels, poems, play scripts, anything and everything. Keep your eyes and ears open for the words that move you, and use the same tricks in the next thing you write.

- Give yourself permission to play. Good writers have fun with words.

CHAPTER 14
HOW TO SELL WITH VALUABLE CONTENT

You can't stay in your corner of the forest waiting for others to come to you. You have to go to them sometimes.

Winnie the Pooh

In this chapter:

- Outbound selling isn't dead.
- Valuable content, not brochures.
- Using valuable content to start sales conversations.
- Valuable content and the power of good sales follow-up.
- Handling leads from content marketing.
- Bringing marketing and sales closer with content.

This chapter is for salespeople. If you are in sales or selling is part of your role then we want to inspire you to embrace content as a crucial part of the business development process.

Valuable content really is at the heart of modern sales practice, and sharing it is the perfect way for you to build trusted relationships. We want to show how great content and the new digital toolset can help you to open doors, develop relationships and close more business. With valuable content in your toolkit, selling becomes easier.

We also want to inspire you to get involved in the content creation process, for if the sales team are contributing their ideas it makes for better content.

Only with your involvement will content marketing be truly effective for your firm.

Outbound selling isn't dead in the era of inbound marketing

Proactive selling is not dead. Even in our web-first era there is a place for a direct sales approach but only if it's done in the right way, respecting how people wish to be communicated with today and without annoying potential customers. People will take a call willingly if they feel they have a relationship with you. The task of sales and marketing is to work together to develop and nurture more and warmer relationships, and valuable content plays a key role.

As you will have read throughout this book, creating and sharing valuable content is an excellent 'pull' or 'inbound' marketing strategy. Executed in the right way, it is a highly effective 'push' or 'outbound' sales approach too. And often a hybrid approach works best of all.

CONTENT STORY Inbound and outbound sales in harmony at consultancy firm Ascentor

We introduced you to information risk management firm Ascentor in Chapter 1.

Three years ago they invested in a content-rich website and marketing strategy that is successfully pulling leads into their business. But it's not just about inbound for Ascentor. They use the valuable content they create to proactively engage with new prospects too.

Here's an example of how this worked for one of their valuable content-led sales campaigns. Managing Director Dave James recognized an opportunity to assist businesses who sell to government to get accredited for the G-Cloud (the new UK government cloud) and wanted to generate awareness of Ascentor's services in this field. His campaign involved a combination of activities:

- **Inbound:** creating compelling web pages describing their service, with a series of useful blog articles around the subject and a very useful downloadable guide to the process.

- **Outbound:** proactive contact with potential clients – offering them the valuable guide to the accreditation process, and prompting a sales conversation on the back of this.

The G-Cloud accreditation process is jargon-heavy and the requirements are written in government-speak. So we put together a useful guide (in both print and online format) and a series of blog articles to help people demystify the process.

Dave James, MD of Ascentor

Their blogs, web page and guides rank highly in search and pull in good inbound leads that have led to sales. And on the outbound side MD Dave James reveals: *'In the first month of our campaign I rang 25 businesses who we wanted to do business with in this area. Seventeen asked for the guide, eight meetings were arranged and we won two new clients off the back of these meetings.'* That's a very impressive conversion rate.

Ascentor adds value right across the business development process whatever way they connect with their customers and it's brought harmony to their business development activities. The senior team, sales, marketing and subject-matter experts all work together to produce and share high-quality content that potential clients appreciate – valuable to those who receive it and immensely valuable to their business too.

ascentor.co.uk

Valuable content, not sales brochures

If you are looking to engage prospects and get sales meetings, focus much of your marketing budget on creating valuable content rather than producing costly brochures. Brochures are useful, but as a credibility tool not a door opener.

Here is a story of a forward-thinking company that sends valuable content not brochures for sales success.

CONTENT STORY   Conscious Solutions' sales team lead with valuable content

David Gilroy, Sales and Marketing Director of Conscious Solutions, a specialist provider of digital marketing services for UK law firms, is a great believer in valuable content to engage prospects and initiate sales. Theirs is a niche proposition for the top 4,500 out of 10,000+ law firms in the United Kingdom and they know their market well. Conscious' content-rich website and social media activity generates leads and referrals but with ambitious growth plans they want more to meet their goals. They take their content to their market and this strategy gets them sales results.

David and his sales team produce some product factsheets and case studies, but not brochures. Instead they have created a stack of useful, well-designed guides for law firms held as downloadable e-books in PDF format on their site and in printed format too – guides such as *38 Common Mistakes Law Firms Still Make with Their Websites*, *29 Mistakes Law Firms Unwittingly Make with Their Brand*.

> *Our valuable guides – in e-book and printed format – are the only marketing materials my sales team needs. Guides, not brochures, open new doors and get us good meetings, lots of brand recognition and sales. We've even sold six guides on Amazon!*

> David Gilroy, Director of Stuff & Things, Conscious Solutions, @conscioussol

They conduct valuable content campaigns around each guide, sending carefully written emails to target contacts with a link to download the guide from the Conscious website. Each campaign builds their reputation as helpful experts in their field and generates around a 15 per cent response rate. If someone clicks the download button the Conscious website alerts the team and a salesperson will call 'to see if the booklet downloaded OK'. It's a perfect conversation starter rather than a hard sell conversation. This approach is backed by using intelligent visitor analytics software from **www.canddi.com** which also shows what other pages someone who's downloaded the guides, looks at. David's sales team can then have a guided sales conversation about what the prospect is know they are interested in.

See **www.conscious.co.uk**, @conscioussol

How to use valuable content to start sales conversations

The cold cold call is dead; the warm cold call is not. You can use valuable content to warm up cold prospects so they're far more likely to take your call.

Valuable content is the perfect relationship builder. Lead with the valuable stuff – send articles, an e-book or even a printed book – and you can earn the right to engage. This is the type of information that flies under people's anti-marketing radar, because it's interesting or useful. The key, as ever, is to start by knowing who you want to work for. Be crystal clear on their needs and interests and provide content that hits that sweet spot. Continue to deliver value with each and every contact.

If you want to meet a dream prospect then build a personal valuable content marketing campaign just for them. It might be based on two or three emails or tailored letters sent over several weeks with a different, interesting and useful article attached. Valuable content campaigns are highly effective in getting meetings with key people and in helping to build a trusted relationship.

> Don't discount direct mail. In these days where we're overwhelmed with email, good old direct mail is making a comeback. Not flyers and adverts – but well-written letters that offer something of value rather than a sales pitch. And hand addressed. Even better: send 'lumpy mail' – a package with a relevant object accompanying the letter. Who doesn't open packages?
>
> Ian Brodie, More Clients Blog, **www.ianbrodie.com**, @ianbrodie[1]

Twenty ideas for a successful valuable content sales campaign:

1 Know exactly who you want to do business with – do your homework and create a targeted list.

2 Create something they'll find useful, relevant and surprising – an e-book or guide or fascinating piece of research for example.

3 Send this valuable content to your dream prospects, alongside a short introductory email or letter carefully – remember: help, don't pitch.

4 Don't forget to send a copy of it to current clients too.

5 Put the e-book on your website too. Create a great landing page for it on your site. Promote the e-book on your home page. Make sure the e-book content is optimized for search.

6 Blog about it.

7 Tweet about it.

8 Record a podcast about it.

9 Share it as a LinkedIn status update. Mention it on relevant LinkedIn groups.

10 Turn it into a slideshow (with nice design) and get it up on SlideShare too.

11 Feature it in your email newsletter.

12 Advertise it with a targeted ad on LinkedIn.

13 Put a link to it on your email signature.

14 Put a link to it on the back of a business card.

15 Create a webinar on the subject and invite your network to attend.

16 Guest blog about it on other peoples' websites.

17 Write a press release about it (particularly if it's research with fascinating data).

18 Create a talk around the subject, and give copies of the content away at the event.

19 Track the results carefully and learn from these.

20 Create a case study to show your top management team the benefits that your valuable content strategy is delivering.

Remember that the prospects you are targeting are as busy, as cynical, as suspicious and over-sold to as you. The only way to stop people hitting the delete button or marking your email as spam is to provide something that they find interesting and of value.

Valuable content and the power of good sales follow-up

Not everyone will buy at the first sales meeting. Inertia, lack of time, other more pressing matters to deal with, budget constraints – there are many valid reasons why the first sales meeting does not immediately lead to a sale.

Yet, according to research, only 20 per cent of sales leads are ever followed up. That's a shining pile of sales opportunity lost without a trace, simply due to lack of good follow-up.

Valuable content makes for perfect sales follow-up. Instead of strong-arm closing or increasingly desperate demands for a decision, keep the dialogue open by sending your prospect information that they will value – the *'saw this and thought of you'* sales strategy:

- Send a link to industry news and research that proves the need for the approach you recommended.
- Write an article that reminds them of the benefits of your solution and nudges them towards the sale.
- Invite them to join your mailing list and send valuable newsletters and updates to build trust and keep you front of mind until they are ready to buy.

Valuable content is highly effective when used at the proposal/presentation stage and to keep in touch after putting in a proposal without seeming pushy. The content has to stay relevant. If the client feels that they have been put on a database and sent a generic email you will lose their credibility and enthusiasm. Be valuable, stay relevant. Better still, write something just for them. Do this and it'll speed up the sales process significantly.

How should you follow up content downloads?

As a salesperson you have an ever-increasing amount of data at your disposal: email newsletter opens, website visits, content downloads, social interactions. Websites are getting smarter. Automation is joining it all up – a honeypot of potential leads for the sales department. But when exactly does an action on the website make a sales-ready lead, and if you're in sales, how should you follow this up? The answer? With extreme caution. Here's why.

Here's how not to do it

A few weeks back a friend sent Sonja a link to a short guide on content marketing. She'll read anything on this subject (we know, it's sad) so thought she'd take a peek. Annoyingly the content was gated behind a sign-up form, but keen to learn everything she can she dutifully entered her details and downloaded the guide. The content was OK, worth a read, but to be honest she forgot about it pretty quickly. Later that week the phone rang. A sales-person had noticed that she'd downloaded their free guide – would she like a demo of their marketing software?

> Sonja's response: *'Er... no! Just because I'd downloaded their content didn't make me a lead. I wasn't interested in their product, just the content. I'm not in the market to purchase marketing software; I didn't even remember the company name. And I was pretty annoyed to get a cold call from someone on the back of downloading stuff. I was busy; I didn't know who they were; NOT interested!'* SLAM.

What she did next: this riled her enough to tweet about it – a quick 140-character rant about the experience. It hit a nerve with a lot of her followers too.

Is it right for your sales team to follow up your content marketing efforts? Isn't this a fair exchange? We invest all this time and effort and money in content BECAUSE WE WANT TO SELL PEOPLE STUFF. Surely it's right that we go after the ones who have downloaded it... isn't it? Or perhaps there is a better way?

If you focus your marketing efforts around creating and sharing valuable content you have to be very, very careful about how you follow up any interest in your content. The style of any follow-up has to be congruent with the customer-centred spirit of your marketing approach. If it's not your customers will spot the change in tone, and they're fed up with that type of intrusion. Cold call clumsily on the back of a piece of generously shared content and you risk killing any nascent relationship with your brand so pay attention to your tone of voice.

Know that not everyone who downloads your content will be your ideal customer. For those who leave their details you need a way of carefully segmenting this list based on a profile of your dream customer. Get your sales team to approach these people respectfully. Don't bombard them with product or service offers – you have to earn the right to sell. Prove you have their best interests at heart. Build relationships. Court them with more valuable content until they are ready to buy.

In summary, if you want to build trusted relationships with your customers don't mix helpful and pushy business development styles. Respect for your customers has to be at the heart of your marketing *and* sales activity.

Cynical marketing and pushy selling are dead. There definitely is a better way.

A better way to follow up a download:

Play the long game. In a follow-up discussion on our blog Bryony Thomas from Watertight Marketing suggested that the sales scenario with Sonja should have gone something like this:

- Sonja downloads an interesting piece of best-practice style content, leaving her contact details.
- This triggers a follow-up email in which there is a case study of someone using the software to implement the ideas in the earlier piece.
- When she clicks the link to read more on the case study, this is flagged to a sales person.
- He researches her company thoroughly and sees that she's a content expert herself. He finds her on Twitter, follows her and tweets to see if she liked the download.
- As a smart salesperson, he shares some of Sonja's great content, comments on her blog, replies to her tweets, to keep the conversation going.
- Instead of calling with a sales pitch, he calls to see if she would have time to give her expert opinion on how they could improve their software for content marketers.
- She agrees, and gives some excellent feedback which is fed into the product development.
- They subsequently hook up on LinkedIn.
- He asks if she'd like to receive their newsletter, which she does.
- The software company sends her a thank you card, which is a really nice touch that makes Sonja smile.
- She starts receiving the newsletter, which is genuinely interesting, and later that year when one of her larger clients is thinking about some marketing software, she recommends these guys.

(This idea is expanded in Bryony's article for *Winning Edge.*[2])

That may sound utopian but it's not impossible. The message we're trying to get across here is the need to accept that your buyers are in charge and to move from selling to helping as a business development approach. Use the new social and web tools available to you to build relationships and add value at every step.

Getting marketing and sales working together on content

Creating and sharing valuable content as a strategy for attracting and winning business is usually a tactic driven by the marketing department. Most often the driver is the company website, with the recognition that if you get your content right you can draw in leads from the web.

So marketing owns the content development process. Up goes a new website, with a blog at its heart and a growing library of useful resources in the form of articles, guides, infographics, videos and the like. And along comes the company Twitter feed, Facebook page, Google+ profile, YouTube channel, all managed by the marketing department. It's a lonely old task but with a lot of hard work the business starts to see results in terms of engagement and leads, to an extent.

But what of sales? Too often they're not really involved, disconnected from the content being produced. We've heard tell in more than one larger firm of marketing spending a fortune on creating a website packed with blogs, infographics and guides and the sales teams having no knowledge of what's being produced! A survey by the Institute of Sales & Marketing Management magazine found that *'About 40 per cent of marketers rarely or never include sales in content development'* (from a survey by Brainshark). What a missed opportunity![3]

If you are in sales you are in the perfect position to come up with ideas for valuable content. You hear first-hand the questions that prospects and customers ask about your industry, your products or services. Ask Marketing to help you create valuable collateral that answers these questions – FAQs on your website, articles on your blog, case studies in written or video format written from the customer point of view, a white paper or e-book that solves a pertinent problem. This is just the kind of collateral that will get you the sales results you need.

Both Marketing and salespeople at the coalface of customer communication have a role to play here. Creating valuable content is the perfect opportunity to get the two departments working closer together.

So when it comes to creating and sharing valuable content, the business needs you, Sales! Attend the content planning meetings (you'll hear more about these in the next chapter). Tell your marketing department what you require and what customers want to know. Share the valuable content that's produced with your networks, use it to help you open doors and build trust through the sales process. Help the marketing and content teams to understand the sales process. Invite them to spend time in your shoes.

Three reasons why sales people need to be involved in the content marketing process:

1 **Salespeople have the knowledge.** They are the ones who spend their time talking to potential customers – they know the questions that customers ask. It's the answers to these questions that make the most valuable content. Use their knowledge to create content that really hits the mark.

2 **Salespeople can get the content into the hands of potential customers.** A good salesperson has a large network of contacts. If salespeople (and for that matter, all departments of the business) share the content directly it will spread far wider, and is far more likely to get into the hands of potential clients. Don't rely on inbound methods alone.

3 **The sales team is the barometer of good content.** If they willingly and consistently share the content produced with their potential clients, know that this stuff is good. If they use it to help them win business (eg links included in sales proposals, useful guides left behind after a meeting) you can be pretty sure it's valuable.

Content marketing presents a huge opportunity for those who get it right. If we all work together the results the business gets from its investment in content will really start to pay off.

These are really exciting times for those who align their sales and marketing approach with the new expectations of customers and clients.

Action for sales people

- Identify the content you already have in your business. Is it valuable enough to send to potential clients and use through the sales process?

- Use your knowledge of the people you want to do business with. Plan three pieces of content you'd be happy to use to open doors.

- Write an article or get the marketing team in your business to help you create the e-book, video, download or white paper you need to kick-start more conversations.

CHAPTER 15

WINNING THE CHALLENGE OF CONSTANT CONTENT GENERATION

Success is not final, failure is not fatal:
it is the courage to continue that counts.

Attributed to Winston Churchill

In this chapter:

- Content marketing is a long game.
- The valuable content production process.
- What do you write about every month?
- Content planning meetings.
- Strategy into action – using your content calendar.
- How do you get your stuff read?
- Getting the most from the content you've created – repurposing, reimagining.
- Getting the team involved and building a content culture.

If you've got this far through the book then you're perfectly poised for your content marketing journey. This chapter will take you beyond launch, and help you find long-term success.

Content marketing is a long game. The value comes from creating content over time, and building momentum. The value is both in creating a deep and varied body of content that helps you get found and trusted online, and also in strengthening your own thinking and the relationship you have with your customers.

We know from experience that the content marketing long haul brings its own set of challenges, and that's what we're going to help you with here. It's a marathon, not a sprint. Once you've started, how do you keep going, and improving?

Here are some useful ideas to help you create a strong pulse for your valuable marketing, and a picture of the ups and downs of the valuable content approach to look out for.

The valuable content production process

Never underestimate the effort it takes to create high-quality content on an ongoing basis. It's a steep learning curve. Consistently creating content that hits the mark is no small feat.

Most likely you're busy with your day job and content production comes on top of everything else you have to do. How do you keep up that early zeal and continue to keep creating content that's valuable to your customer and to your business, month in month out?

Don't panic. Here's a simple process to follow (we know – seven steps again!).

The content production process:

1 **Think.** Come up with ideas for content – do your research, use the knowledge of those nearest your customers (often sales, consultants, customer service).

2 **Prioritize.** Work out which ideas to take forward and which to park.

3 **Plan.** For each content idea you decide to take forward, be clear who you're writing for and why you are doing so. How does this content fit with your goals? What do you want it to do for the business? Select your canvas – what format will work best, who will create it (internal, external?), how much are you investing and what are the timescales? This planning phase is crucial so don't skip it.

4 **Create.** Words plus design – think production quality (more on writing in next chapter).

5 **Promote.** For the best chance of maximum exposure use the channels that work best for this type of content. Is it a Facebook piece or best on Twitter and Google+? Communicate to all teams and contacts. Saw this and thought of you approach. Offer it to other blogs, sites to extend its reach. Is it worthy of paid promotion?

6 **Repurpose.** How can you re-use elements of this content so you get the most mileage from your investment?

7 **Learn.** Measure and review the results. What did you learn?

Hold this process in mind when it comes to producing valuable content over time. We'll explore these elements throughout this chapter so you're clear how to keep the good stuff coming as time goes on.

What do you write about every month?

If you've taken the strategic approach in Chapter 11, you'll be clear on your content sweet spot. But you'll also need to find ways of consistently coming up with relevant new ideas that mine that sweet spot, without running out of steam.

Revisiting your content strategy is important. Keep it firmly in mind. Better still, when you're planning pin the one-page overview in our workbook to your wall where you can see it, along with pictures of the personas you are targeting and the map of their needs along the buying journey too. Remember, these are real people, with real challenges that you can help with.

Here are a few more ideas to help you write, month in, month out.

Get yourself a notebook

The secret sauce to content marketing? They ask, you answer.

Marcus Sheridan, **www.thesaleslion.com**, @thesaleslion[1]

Your deepest pool of ideas will always be your customers. Your customers' questions will become your content. Every question asked is a content opportunity. So keep a notebook in your bag and write down the big questions they ask you. Write their questions down verbatim – and jot down ideas for content you could create in answer. If your firm is bigger than just you then motivate other customer-facing staff to do the same.

Balance your content – not just the attention-grabbing stuff

Be wary of 'the traffic trap'. The goal of content marketing is rarely just about attracting as many visitors as possible to your website. The real goal is most likely more leads and more sales. So make sure you're creating a balance of content that answers customer needs at every step of the sales process.

> When you look at it from the sales department's point of view, the content marketing focus is often too much on the early stage of engagement. The valuable content created tends to be seen purely as a way to build up a brand/ reputation, educate and entertain. That's fine, but at some point (increasingly later in the sales process as a result of much of this content) people (sales) will be interacting with people (customers). Valuable content is required at every stage of the sales process to support sales through to securing the business and then helping with advocate development afterwards.
>
> Trevor Lever Consulting (TLC), **www.trevorleverconsulting.com**, @realtrevorlever

Every month, ask yourself: have we got content that covers all bases? Doing this alongside creating content that answers the unique questions you get asked along the way should give you a useful baseline of ideas to use.

How do you prioritize?

> My biggest challenge is prioritization and knowing how much time to allocate to a specific piece. There's always so much to do. If it's really well received it could pay back – otherwise that's time wasted. Should I put my time into one fantastic (long) piece or quicker pieces?

You'll find that you have plenty of ideas for content and never enough time. Which ideas do you take forward and which do you park? Remember: to be valuable content must be both of value to your business and of value to your customers. This is the balance you'll need to weigh up when deciding which content to invest in with urgency.

If you're struggling with prioritization, try ranking each piece of content you think about creating with this simple calculation in mind:

Simple checklist: Is this content idea valuable?

- Does this content have a clear business goal? *On a scale of one to ten, how valuable is this content to our business?*
- Do our customers crave this content? *On a scale of one to ten, how valuable will this be for your ideal customers?*

(You'll find a more detailed How Valuable is Your Content checklist in the resources section on page 288.)

Take forward the ideas that matter most to both parties. Work out what content you need, and how much time to allocate to its creation. Make a strategic decision on the big content pieces, and on the shorter blogs and stick to it.

Creating valuable content is not an exact science – you can never predict exactly which pieces will fly and which won't. Get a few under your belt, and you'll develop a feel for it. Don't let fears about prioritization become procrastination. Experiment and learn.

Getting your content read

People can often start content marketing with buckets of enthusiasm and the very best intentions, but then they hit a wall. We've witnessed a pattern here with companies both big and small. More often than not this wall looms largest at the two- to three-month mark. The new website is up, there's some great content coming through but a couple of months down the line frustration strikes.

Where are all the visitors? Why aren't the leads pouring in? It feels like we're talking to ourselves. This stuff is valuable – and I'm under pressure to deliver results – why isn't it getting read? We need more eyeballs on our content, fast!

It's a natural reaction and a frustration we can well understand. Our advice: don't panic; check you're doing all you can to promote your content; and keep on keeping on. Here are some ideas to help you ride out the two- to three-month content marketing slump and get the success your content deserves.

First things first, be patient. Remember, content marketing is a long game: a slow burn not a quick fix. You will see some interest in the early months but in our experience it's between six and twelve months when you really start reaping the benefits, so hold firm.

Keep the faith, and definitely keep going, but also make sure you're doing everything you can to get your content read. Combining tactics to build a distribution plan as outlined in Chapter 11 is the best way to ensure your content gets the interest it deserves.

Are you doing all you can to ensure each piece of content is getting maximum exposure?

Here's a quick checklist of what works for content promotion.

How to get your content read

1. Tell people

In our digital world this might sound too basic for words but you'd be amazed how many companies forget this crucial real world step. Once you've created a piece of content, tell people!

If you're not a one-man band, tell everyone in your company, and ask *them* to take the content out there. Imagine the reach you could get if everyone in your company told everyone in their networks? Ask people to email it or post it as a LinkedIn status update if it's relevant to their contacts.

Outside your company, tell your contacts, prospects and clients about useful content. Don't be shy of this step if your content is valuable.

Of course you have to have enough people to tell. Grow your network of contacts – even in this digital era, old-fashioned meet-and-greet networking has certainly not gone out of style.

- **Do this:** Global marketing agency Freedman International paste up a copy of each new piece of content on the office wall near the kettle as well as mailing all staff a message and link they can share.
- **Don't do this:** Keep it to yourself. Hope for the best.

2. Promote your content on social media

Distribute your content to your social networks, with links to every new piece of content you create on your social channels.

Work hard on your headlines. Make them interesting and engaging. Remember, you can get away with doing this more than once on channels like Twitter (but not too much – don't be a pain!). Try posting a comment or question with a link to your content on relevant LinkedIn groups. And use hashtags intelligently to make your content more findable. (You'll find headline help in Chapter 13, and social media advice in Chapter 5.)

- **Do this:** Ask good questions, be curious, comment positively on other people's posts.
- **Don't do this:** Spam out links to your content, only drop by when you're selling, forget to engage.

3. Email

Tell those who have signed up to your list. Give them an option to subscribe to receive your latest updates and remember to pop a link to the best of your new content in your monthly email newsletter too. And how about a link in your email footer for each new piece of content you create?

- **Do this:** Invite people to sign up for your new content.
- **Don't do this:** Buy a list and spam everyone on it with everything you write.

4. Optimize for search engines

Use the advice in Chapter 7 and make sure you're optimizing each new piece of content carefully for search engines to increase your chances of getting found. This means knowing the keywords you want to be found for with the right focus for each piece of content you create. And act like a good librarian, labelling your content correctly by setting the metadata right before your publish.

- **Do this:** Write for real people but be clear on the keywords that they are searching for.

- **Don't do this:** Forget to label your content. Post and hope for the best. Or worse – stuff your content full of keywords and alienate your readers!

5. Take your content wider with PR

As we mentioned in Chapter 10, PR is a great tool to amplify your content. So work to get your content published in industry-leading media and other websites.

- **Do this:** Develop relationships with a few key influencers so that they will be happy to share your valuable content. Be helpful – not pushy.

- **Don't do this:** Send identical 'please share this' emails to everyone you can think of. Use this tactic sparingly – you'll quickly run out of people and the people will run out patience if you ask for sharing favours every week!

6. Form a content club

How about collaborating with like-minded content creators to form a content club – a group of people/businesses whose ideas you rate and content that would be useful to your audience, and vice versa? Agree to tweet out their content (if it's valuable), and they'll share yours.

Collaborate with your readers too. Seek their opinions. The more you get your audience involved in creating the content, the happier they will be to share it on your behalf.

- **Do this:** Link up with like-minded content creators.

- **Don't do this:** Ask them to share stuff that's not relevant. Or forget to share!

7. Pay

When it comes to driving traffic to your website there are more paid digital advertising options than ever before. But, as we mentioned in Chapter 10, approach with care and don't lose sight of the customer experience.

- **Do this:** Talk to the experts and find out all you can.

- **Don't do this:** Throw money away on annoying your customers.

8. Make the most of traffic

Make sure you are making the best of the traffic you do get. Is your website working as hard as it can? Make it easy to find the valuable content you're creating. Have a really clear path to buy, or to sign up for email updates. Link to other relevant content to keep people interested, lead them to other content that will really help.

Hold regular content planning meetings

One of the best steps you can put in place to help you prioritize and maintain your commitment is a regular content planning meeting (sometimes known as an editorial meeting). These will help you to organize and engage your team, spark off content ideas and keep everyone focused on your goals. These meetings will help you to make the process a strategic, structured and sustainable one for your business.

The purpose of a good content planning meeting is to look at what's worked, brainstorm new content ideas and decide which ones to take forward, planning how to make them happen. We recommend a monthly or bi-monthly get together for all involved in the content thinking and creation process. Keeping this regular will help you to get more high-quality content out of the door.

We've seen that the companies who are most successful with their content efforts think wide when it comes to content planning and creation – they embrace it as a whole team effort, not just a one-person job. They allocate resources and time to the content challenge, across a range of disciplines. If you're a larger firm, bear this in mind when sending invitations out for the meeting. We'd include the person in charge of content, your content creators, marketers and designers alongside subject matter experts and representatives from the sales team.

Agenda for your content planning meeting:

1 **Why are we here?** Introduce and position the meeting. Reiterate the importance of and vision for your content marketing. *(5 minutes)*

2 **How are we doing?** Overview of the past month's content. What content have we published, how has it gone down, what results have

we seen? Where are we against our goals? And how's the process working for everyone? *(10 minutes)*

3 **Content brainstorm.** What are our customers asking for? What opportunities for valuable content has the team spotted? What's coming up over the next few months in our customers' worlds that we can create content around? What can we produce that hits the spot? In what formats? Big themes? Newsletter plans for the next few months? Remember to strike a good balance between stock and flow content and get your ideas down. *(15–20 minutes)*

4 **Do the ideas meet our strategy?** Revisit your content strategy. Remind the group of the business goals, the needs of the customers you've chosen to serve and the commitment you've made in terms of content volume and topics each month. Have you struck the right balance with your content ideas? How valuable are each of the content ideas you've come up with? Are you missing anything – do you have enough of the right content for every step along your customers' buying journey? *(5–10 minutes)*

5 **Content planning.** Complete your content calendar (more details on this later in this chapter). What content are we going to publish when, how, and where? Here at Valuable Content we make a detailed plan for the next month and a high-level plan looking forward two to three months further than that. How far forward you plan in the meeting is up to you. It'll depend on how often you meet and how mature your content marketing efforts are. *(15 minutes)*

6 **Action plan.** Agree actions. Allocate resource and a process to make it all happen. Set date for next meeting. *(5 minutes)*

An hour to an hour and a half maximum should suffice for your content planning meeting.

Make it fun

Creativity is intelligence having fun.
Albert Einstein

Run well, these content planning meetings can be a highlight in the working week. Professionals are often scared of being creative, so put some thought into how you can make the meetings a really positive experience for all involved. People are more creative when they're enthusiastic and having fun so don't let the meetings drag. Steer discussions of analytics and data on to actionable points (*more headlines like this, this format kept people engaged on the site for longest, this guide led to four positive sales calls*) and keep the focus on '*how do we create the best content for our clients and customers?*'

You could stoke enthusiasm to fever pitch by giving out prizes for the best content of the month. Maybe not a holiday in the Caribbean for the best blog (although we bet that would work), but some companies give out t-shirts (like the fabulous content team at systems development firm Desynit – what IT developer doesn't love a branded t-shirt?), and we use our Valuable Content Award badges as rewards for our clients' content stars.

Planning and using a content calendar

To make your content strategy actionable you'll need to create a detailed content planner and calendar. We mentioned this at the end of Chapter 11 on content strategy, but we want to go into more detail now.

Updating our content planner and calendar is something we do at Valuable Content every month, both to inspire us and keep us both on track. If you're prone to over-ambition, or lethargy, either will become clear once you've written it on the calendar. (Twenty blogs each per month is probably unworkable; one blog a month by one person won't get you very far.)

Without a good planning and calendaring system, it's extremely difficult to get better at content marketing. Why? Because it never become part of your marketing routine.

The content planner we've created for our own content creation is a simple grid. Here are the headings we use, and some pointers to help you fill in your first one.

- **Publish date.** Obvious but important. When will you get it out there?
- **Writer.** Who is responsible for its completion? Commit resource.
- **Content format and destination.** Will it be a blog, a video, a printed mailer, newsletter, infographic or even a talk? And where will you post

it – on your blog? A guest article on someone else's site? Or even another site like Medium perhaps?

- **Working title.** This may evolve as you write but try out a good positioning headline here.

- **Target keyword or concept.** What challenge are you looking to solve for your reader with this content? What subject are you focusing on? Think of real people *and* search engines if you want to give the content the best chance of being found. What words/phrases would they use? Include these in your title and through the content.

- **Target audience.** Who are you talking to with this piece of content? Be specific. Have a clear picture of who you are creating this is for and what they need if you want your content to hit home.

- **Goal.** Why are you creating this? What do you want this content to achieve for your business? Probably the most important question of all.

- **Call to action.** A crucial step if you're looking for results. What's the desired action you really want from the reader?

- **Status.** Planned or in motion? Track how you're doing on the road to completion.

- **Results.** Well, was it worth it? Measure and record the results here. Then you'll know what works best and what it makes sense to repeat.

(Sign up to the Valuable Content Club from our website **www.valuable content.co.uk** and we'll send you a blank copy of our content planner to start filling in.)

The act of filling in a planner like this is useful in itself. You get a clear picture of the story you're telling, the sector you are targeting and the conversations you want to be hosting.

You'll also be able to see any gaps, to tell if you're focusing too strongly in one area at the expense of another, and if your targets are realistic.

Once the planner is filled in, put that up on the wall too. There's nothing like a bit of public commitment and a good shot of accountability to make sure tasks get completed. Attach names and dates to the content pieces, make sure everyone can see it, and you'll be able to keep on top of things.

Content calendar tools and implementation

If you're a lone ranger, then filling in a content planner and putting it on your wall might be the only thing you need to keep you on track. Adding reminders to your diary of publishing dates, or of the time you've elected to block out to write could be a useful prompt, and we know that works for some people. For many businesses, especially those with more people involved in content creation there are a growing number of online project management and content workflow tools that will help keep everyone in the loop and keep the content flowing.

One simple tool is Trello (trello.com). As easy as moving Post-it notes along a board, Trello helps you keep your content pipeline on track. You can upload work in progress for discussion, and move it along the line towards publication as it gets polished. The email reminders are handy, and make sure the right people get to see the right documents.

Whether it is Trello, more sophisticated content marketing tools such as CoSchedule (coschedule.com), online project management tools such as Basecamp (basecamp.com) or Teamwork (teamwork.com), or a simple Google calendar, a whiteboard or spreadsheet – find a system that works for you and stick to that.

Having someone in charge of making the content creation process work makes a big difference. Someone like Carmen Camacho at global marketing implementation agency Freedman International. Carmen is the driving force behind their content marketing process – their Implementation Captain as Freedman terms it – and she runs a tight ship. With the big picture in mind Carmen runs the content calendar using Trello, keeps a close eye on budget and the delivery schedule and makes sure everyone – internal people, external writers and designers – is on track.

Even if you're a one-man band, put your implementation hat on and keep to the plan, like Carmen.

Building team spirit: a culture of valuable content

What you're aiming for is not just the creation of fantastic content ideas, but the creation of a solid team of content creators. You want every member of the team to get the big picture and to understand the steps along the way. Successful content marketing isn't the sum of individual acts of brilliance; it's a sustained team effort. You don't just want people just to submit their own blogs on time; you want them to happily promote each other's content too, and for valuable content marketing to become a way of life in your business.

Show people why it matters, and inspire them with stories of businesses and individuals that find success through marketing with valuable content. If you're worried that inspiration will be hard to muster from the off, then start small. Build a modest team who are eager and comfortable with writing, and get them to contribute regularly to a blog and to share the articles with their contacts.

Demonstrate that the approach works and communicate the results across the business. Showing not telling should inspire others to want to get on board and to produce their own content. They will be able to see the personal benefits it brings – more good leads (fewer time-wasters), more referrals, more PR and speaker opportunities, more clients, deeper expertise, and trusted, profitable client relationships.

Give people time to create content

We don't mandate, but we do bake thought leadership development into annual plans.

Greg Austin, Head of Global Marketing at ZS Associates

If you recognize the importance of valuable content marketing, then give your people time to create great content. Blog writing shouldn't be something people have to squeeze between other tasks – for the best results people need thinking and writing time. And of course people will quickly run out of enthusiasm for this new content marketing thing if you expect them to work through their lunch breaks and at weekends to get it done. Make 'creating valuable content' part of their role and their performance review process. Relieve some of those billable hour pressures – you can't be writing content when your goal is to pound a time sheet!

If you're a one-man band then we suggest you give yourself time too. Recognize content creation as an important business task and set time aside for this. You need head space to create stuff that's valuable. Half a day a fortnight, take yourself away from the office and write somewhere nice.

Lead from the top

Businesses that succeed with content marketing in the long term have buy-in from the very top of the organization. That means the MD blogging alongside customer-facing people.

> *A consulting firm sells expertise. Expertise is demonstrated through thought leadership. Senior people should be expected to contribute to a firm's thought leadership. If they can't or won't, even with the help of a writer, they probably shouldn't be among leadership.*
>
> Jason Mlicki, Rattleback, **www.rattleback.com**

It's all part of creating a culture of content marketing – the ideas and processes needed to be embedded all the way through an organization.

Motivate, don't force

We've heard tell of some companies who use punitive measures if people don't produce the content they're expected to create. We're big believers in bringing people with you on the content journey, not beating them over the head – creativity is hard to pull out of the bag if it's coerced. Here's a much better approach from business change experts Project One:

> *I am now driving content through facilitating willing volunteers in Project One. I've laid out some suggested topics and sought volunteers for beer-and-pizza sessions to shape the content. Not to write – they don't have the time and it's my job. But if I can get their ideas, feeding the beast is a walk in the park!*
>
> Geoff Mason, Content Director, Project One, **www.projectone.com**

Build it into your recruitment process

Thinking further into the future, smart firms that really want content marketing success will build it into their recruitment process. Some are doing that already.

> *The Indium Corporation enjoys a very enthusiastic and dedicated team of maniacs who truly love their careers, their fields of study, their technologies, and their colleagues. This joie de vivre for semiconductor assembly materials, for nanotech materials and assembly processes, for thermal interface materials, for electronics assembly materials is the answer to the content challenge. So HIRE people who are consumed with the topics that matter to your customers. Then put the two together and let them rock.*
>
> Rick Short, Indium, **www.indium.com**, @indium

Up-skill the team

For bigger businesses, spreading the content load widely makes sense both time-wise, and because it will give you a good variety of perspectives. If all of the team are keeping notes of the questions clients ask them, you'll have a far bigger pool of content ideas. Get as many people involved as you can. Customer-facing people are a great source of content, equally as important as your technical experts.

Once people find their feet, you'll discover where the real content strengths are, and where people could do with a bit of extra support.

Training helps people become better content creators. If you're a sole trader and you want to take the learnings from this book further, a basic content creation course can help you practice some of the techniques and give you the confidence to keep going on your own.

If you've got a wider team to train, you might want to upskill one group in blogging techniques, and give your content distribution person a crash course in the best ways to share content.

Support your team

Make it as easy for them as possible to honour this new commitment. Your most reluctant subject matter experts could start their blogging career by being interviewed by a writer who turns those thoughts into blog articles. Think about hiring an internal content writer or outsourcing some of the work to a content creation agency or freelancer.

A hybrid approach to content creation will make it easier, and we're seeing more and more companies opting for this – some original content developed by in-house experts, some initiated in house and polished by an external content writer, and others initiated by your writer and vetted for accuracy by those with the knowledge in-house.

Make the process as efficient as you can. As Greg Austin, Head of Global Marketing at ZS Associates advises: *'Repurpose existing content, capture new ideas and points of view when they're fresh – like right before or after someone has presented to an internal audience or at a conference, written a white paper – and hire capable writers to ease the burden of fleshing out the bones from an interview.'*

And continue

Getting started and keeping the content going is tough work. You do need to knuckle down and keep at it. Take heart from the knowledge that everyone has to start somewhere. We know that you will be making progress on your journey, even if it doesn't feel like it.

Never forget the valuable rules in your desire to get your content read. No bombarding people or whacking them over the head again and again till they *read* it. Valuable principles and behaviours apply when promoting – even if your content is useful – so play nice!

A combination of great content and wide distribution tactics will see you through. Hold your nerve and keep going. Keep on creating, mix up the formats, keep a steady stream of stock and flow content coming. Listen hard and laser in on the big questions.

If you care about the people you want to serve and create content with them in mind success will come.

Take action

- Get yourself a notebook and keep a record of the questions customers ask you.
- Download the valuable content checklist and content planner and use when thinking up ideas for great content.
- Organize a monthly content planning meeting and get the team onboard.
- You're off! Good luck! Hold on to your valuable principles at each step of the way.

CHAPTER 16
TROUBLESHOOTING Q&A: ANSWERS TO THE BIG CONTENT QUESTIONS

> *Well, if it can be thought, it can be done;*
> *a problem can be overcome.*
>
> E A Bucchianeri, *Brushstrokes of a Gadfly*[1]

In this chapter:

- How do I find the time to write great content?
- How do I squeeze every drop of value out of my content and my team?
- How do I get over my fear of writing?
- How do I keep it interesting over time?

When writing this new edition of this book we turned to our clients, contacts and our email subscribers. We asked them a simple question: *what's the biggest challenge you face when it comes to your content?* We wanted to understand what people really struggle with. Their responses were enlightening.

So here are direct answers to the key questions that come up time and time again when it comes to marketing with valuable content. If these are in your head, know that you're not alone. These are all good questions that deserve serious consideration.

Question 1: How do I find the time to write great content?

As a creative, I'm actually not bad at coming up with ideas for content. Also as a creative, I'm not too bad at copywriting either (or at least good enough for my own content purposes!) but finding the time to create or write the content is exceedingly tricky. How can I find the time?

Christian Tait, Designer at Creative Cadence

Sound familiar? It seems there's never enough time to do all the things you have to do, let alone the things you want to do.

We struggle with it too. We faced a version of this challenge ourselves trying to fit book writing in alongside client work, day-to-day content writing and making some fairly big changes to our business. We had to make some radical decisions to make sure we got it done.

Our solution – when writing the book we shut up shop every Friday. No calls, no emails, no social media checking on a Friday. We just wrote. It gave us the time to do what we needed to do. More than that, we decided we had to make the writing a pleasurable thing. The idea was that if we wrote somewhere nice, somewhere we looked forward to going, we'd be more likely to make this a habit that we stuck to. So we wrote at the gym. We'd write in the gym café, 'treat' ourselves to elevenses on the rowing machine, and a swim at lunchtime. In the interim hours we focused on writing and nothing else. The upshot is that we really enjoyed the book-writing experience (and we hope it's made for great content). An added bonus was that we both found it easier to focus on our other work, knowing that we'd be writing the book on Friday. When you carry around a huge burden of 'I should be doing that instead' thoughts it's hard to do anything well. Committing to writing, and protecting the time to do it, helped us to concentrate better – and you might find the same too.

That was our solution. You'll need to find your own way but here are some ideas to play with if you're struggling to find the time to write:

- **Recognize the importance of your content.** Write down *why* you are doing this and what it will achieve – for you, for the business. Being clear on the goal and the benefit helps you make the time for it.

- **Understand the value of writing.** Creating valuable content is one of the very best ways you have of winning the kind of business you want from your ideal clients and customers. And writing about your area of expertise will make you better at what you do. It's not just a nice to have – it's essential work.

- **Change your mindset.** Think of it as marketing/professional development/networking. If you think of it like this you'll be more likely to consider it as time really well spent and easily as important for the long-term success of your business or your career as today's client work.

- **Ring-fence the time.** Setting aside time, and guarding it, is important. We're not suggesting you carve out a day a week necessarily. If you ring-fenced half a day a fortnight we bet you'd achieve a lot. Block it out in your diary, put a 'do not disturb' sign on your door, switch the distractions off and get down to it. Protect that time as carefully as you would if it was a key client meeting or your child's birthday party.

- **Build it into your routine.** We're all creatures of habit. It takes time to establish a new routine, so plan to spend a couple of hours a week on writing for the next three months and you'll give yourself a better chance of making the habit stick.

- **Set deadlines.** Deadlines that other people are relying on are best, because you can't let them slip. (Somehow we always find the time to write our newsletter on the last day of the month!)

- **Make writing a treat.** Gym, park, your favourite café, home – wherever works best for you. It's easier to find the time for things you're looking forward to.

- **Don't wait for the muse.** She doesn't exist. Writing is a skill that only gets better with practice. If you get to your allotted writing hour and the ideas aren't coming, just keep at it. Write notes, write a stream of consciousness babble, just write yourself into a writing frame of mind. Having said that, find a time that works best for you. Sharon writes better in the mornings, Sonja prefers the evenings. Carve out some time when you'll be at your sharpest, and focus on your writing.

- **Take a timer.** Seriously useful tool for writers, particularly the procrastinators among us. Plan your content then just write – for 15–30 minutes. Resist the urge to edit and just get the words down. (Try the Pomodoro Technique: **pomodorotechnique.com**)

- **Start thinking like a writer.** Collect ideas. Always be thinking of the next thing you'll write. Jot down notes of the questions that a client or prospect asks you. It won't take you more than a couple of minutes, but developing a habit of always looking for content will make the time you do have to write more productive. Writing clearly is strongly linked to thinking clearly, so spending more time thinking about the content you want to create for your clients will help you write it.

Half a day a week spent on creating valuable content will be time well spent – saving you time on ineffective forms of marketing and building a stronger and more robust business. Because of the results valuable content will generate, this will be your most productive half of a day of each week. Squeezing another task into your week might feel like a struggle, but it is doable. We've mentioned keeping a notebook for blog ideas, and that's one of the best things you can do to make time. A lot of the thinking around your writing happens away from the screen. Jotting down the kernel of an idea and getting on with other stuff lets the ideas percolate away in the back of your mind. When you sit down to actually write you'll find the words come more quickly.

Question 2: How can I squeeze every drop of value out of my content and my team?

Content efficiency is a big opportunity for small businesses with limited time and bigger businesses with limited budgets. Repurposing is your friend here. We've mentioned this before, in Chapter 8, but we back what Chris Butler of Newfangled has to say on the subject:

We're seeing a greater demand for a diversity of content experiences. Someone who doesn't have the time to read your 2,000-word article might have the time to listen to your 20-minute podcast or watch your 5-minute video. So spreading your content across platforms is going to be more critical.

I know that sounds like more, but the idea is diversity and spread, not necessarily volume. If you write a 2,000-word piece, could you turn that same piece into a video or podcast? Also, consider diversity in terms of the people creating content.

If you're managing a team of creators, a greater spread of formats means you can leverage their talents in a much more sensitive way. Maybe someone who isn't much of a writer would be a natural in front of the camera. This reduces pressure on the writing requirement that might not be a great fit for everyone trying to share their expertise. One person doesn't have to feel like he needs to be three.

Chris Butler, Creative Director of Newfangled, **www.newfangled.com**, @chrbutler

Question 3: How do I get over my fear of writing?

I find the biggest obstacle is myself! Being too scared to get things wrong and look unprofessional – I guess it's a lack of confidence.

This is a really common obstacle, so you're definitely not alone if fears about writing are holding you back. We hope the writing tips in Chapter 13 will have started to ease your worries.

However good you are at what you do, it is fear that can paralyse the most brilliant minds. Imposter Syndrome – or the terror of being found as a fraud – stops many new content creators in their tracks.

If I share my knowledge people will realize how little I really know.

Other people know way more than I do. I'm no expert.

My work persona is an act. I can't show the 'real me' or the world will realize I'm just playing at it.

I feel uncomfortable talking about my success. I know I don't deserve it.

It's easy to see how feelings like this can hold you back. Doubting yourself and your abilities makes the idea of putting yourself on the line by writing and publishing your own content very uncomfortable. Why on earth would you want to open yourself up to the world?

Understand that you're not alone. We both felt very unsure of our first blogging efforts. Very few people are so supremely confident in what they do that writing about it comes easy.

How to cure Imposter Syndrome

There is only one cure to Imposter Syndrome, as far as we know, and that's just to get stuck in to the writing. Feel the fear and do it anyway.

If you're worried about being uncovered as a fraud, try seeing your content differently. Instead of seeing the blog as a chilly window into your empty knowledge soul, view it as a chance to share the few slivers of really useful stuff that you do have. (Oh come on, you know *something!*). Remember, it's not about you; it's about helping your customers.

Valuable Tip

Hold one real customer in mind when you're writing and write just to them.

Turn your reticence about putting yourself forward into a strength. People with Imposter Syndrome aren't naturally disposed to write self-obsessed 'Me! Me! Me!' posts – they don't want the attention. But what *you* write will be customer-focused, and that's a good thing.

Once you begin and make blogging a habit, you'll find that the ideas start flowing. You will develop your own unique style. Applying your knowledge and experience to your customer's world is what's unique to you. This is the thing that will make your content fly. Your blog isn't the place you're going to get unmasked as an imposter, it's the place you're going to demonstrate how you can help, and that's way more valuable.

Having a writing buddy is useful. Someone you can throw ideas around with, and share early versions of content with is a great support. We're always throwing each other half-written blog posts to finish off, and trust each other's judgement enough to be thick skinned about any criticism. *I've cut that because it didn't work* feels helpful, not negative. We both want the best finished article, and co-creating is an efficient and rewarding way to make it happen.

If you struggle with confidence then working with someone else is a big benefit. You'll have already got over showing your work to someone else – a big hurdle – before the time comes to share it with the world. Editing collaboratively also makes your work feel less personal; these are words you've worked on with someone else, and not the workings of your inner soul committed to print. It lessens the fear of being judged, or of not being good enough.

Get used to writing and sharing what you've written with your peers. Ask for feedback and be open to making changes in response to the answers you get.

At the end of the day, it's really just a matter of practice. The majority of our clients start with us having never written a blog post before, and there hasn't been anyone yet who hasn't got into the swing of it after a few months.

Question 4: How do you keep it interesting over time?

This is the challenge facing people who've been playing the content marketing game for years.

How do you say the same thing again and again? And how do you make the most of what you've already created?

Do a stock check and reorganize

Often it's a question of restructuring the information on your website so that it serves up the right stuff to each user.

- Use analytics to measure what's working well on the site, and what's not getting read.
- Analyse your star performing content. What kind of content is it? Format? Tone? Length?
- Do a stock check – would reorganizing the content give important but unloved pieces of content a new lease of life, or have some of them passed their sell-by date?

With a fully stocked and well-designed resources cupboard and all the key content questions answered you're in the enviable position of being able to really pick and choose what you do next, so focus on content that's along the same lines of your winning work.

Check in with your customers

If your enthusiasm for the subject is starting to lag, maybe a conversation with a favourite customer or client would help. Ask them what's helped them most.

Feel the difference that you can make with valuable content, and it should motivate you to get back in the saddle.

You may feel you've said something again and again, but asking them will very likely get you to think about your subject in an entirely different way – over time you can make assumptions, but what do they really want to know?

Try new formats

Experiment with formats. If you're tired of blogging, try podcasts. Had it with video? Say it with an infographic. A SlideShare. Or fall in love with beautiful print.

Reawaken your creativity

Or maybe try a creative project on the side. Often the marketing that really flies starts life as something completely different. That's how it was for Bath-based design studio Mytton Williams. JazzTypes was a creative experiment for partner and Creative Director Bob Mytton that's taken them to surprising places and won them admirers and new clients along the way. As Bob explains:

> *Running a small studio, I get involved with every aspect of the business and sometimes creativity is not top of my mind. As creative director, I am constantly pushing other designers to develop the ideas, to make their ideas as good as they can be. But then comes everything else. New Business, Financials, IT, HR and so on. And after spending so much time on everything other than design and helping everyone else, I felt there was a danger of slipping into old solutions. Of being less creative.*

Bob decided on an experiment to challenge his creativity and imagination. The result? JazzTypes – designing 100 jazz posters in 100 consecutive days, each one representing a different musician. Each day, weekends included, he chose an artist at random with the aim of designing a poster in whatever time he had available, often only a few hours, sometimes longer, while documenting his thinking process and what he learnt about being creative along the way.

The project most certainly fired up Bob's creativity but the benefits to his business have been far greater than that. News of the experiment has gone far and wide. He has been asked to exhibit the posters in Bath and London. He's produced a book to accompany the JazzTypes work and design magazines have written about it.

Find out more at **www.myttonwilliams.co.uk**, @myttonwilliams

This very personal creative content project has brought Mytton Williams publicity, admirers and some great new clients too.

Take some time out to put your creativity to work too.

A final note: happy people create the best content

Does your frame of mind affect the content you create? We think so. And we're not alone in thinking that way. Our friend Doug Kessler says: '*Great content happens when the people making it are enjoying it.*'

It makes sense, doesn't it? If you're bored by what you're creating it's hard – if not impossible – to write anything that inspires. If nothing about it makes you smile, you're unlikely to make your readers feel good. When you're enjoying what you're doing it's easier to be creative, to write with warmth and wit, and to pull people into your world with the words and images you choose.

The greatest content comes from people who love what they do – and care about the people they are in business for.

So are we saying you can't create valuable content if you're miserable? Kind of, but not exactly. What we're saying is you can't create valuable content if you don't care about the people you're creating it for. Genuinely wanting to help your customers will make you feel good, and that feel-good feeling will shine through the content you create.

If everything you try to write makes your heart sink, maybe it's time to look for another job. Find something you love to do, something that makes your heart beat faster and then content marketing (and everything else in life!) will become much easier.

We believe the content creation process should be enjoyable and that helping people you care about is rewarding. Combine the two and you're on your way to creating some truly valuable content.

Take action

- If there's a challenge here we haven't dealt with join the Valuable Content Club and drop us an email.

- The question 'What's the biggest challenge you're facing?' is a really good one to put to your clients and customers too. It'll give you great ideas for your content.

CONCLUSION AND MANIFESTO FOR MARKETING PEOPLE LOVE

We will focus our marketing on creating really valuable content for our customers.

We hope this book inspires you to put valuable content at the heart of your marketing, because we see what it does for those that adopt this thoughtful, customer-centred joined-up approach. Yes it will take work and commitment – it's not all simple – you'll need to take some risks, and probably make a few mistakes along the way (we have!). Being valuable is not something you can pay lip service to, or tackle half-heartedly, but you have the tools and resources right here, and you can make it work. You have the most fantastic opportunity to build your business, starting right now. We hope you will seize it.

Since we wrote the first edition of *Valuable Content Marketing* in 2012, we've seen more and more businesses realizing that they need to change the way they promote their products and services. We're gratified that the conversation has moved on from 'what's content marketing?' to 'how do I really make content marketing work for me?' And we're delighted by the imaginative and creative ways that businesses are rising to the challenge of creating the really valuable stuff.

What makes us happiest of all is the way that marketing with valuable content is becoming the hallmark of a genuinely good business. Our belief that to succeed you need to shift from simply selling to *seeking to be of value to your customers* has become part of a mainstream movement to find a better way to do business, and that feels right.

Valuable content marketing stands for human business; business that delivers some value to the world, whether or not people buy from you; it's about connecting people to people – delivering the early promises of the web; helping, not selling; business with a wider purpose – and we are right behind all that. For in reality, it only works if you care.

So if you want to make content marketing work for your business? Prepare yourself for BIG CHANGE. This is not the latest marketing fad; it's the spearhead of a revolution in business practice. That's why we love it.

Are you with us?

We'll leave you with a manifesto for your marketing...

The Valuable Marketing Manifesto

WE WILL FOCUS OUR MARKETING ON CREATING
REALLY VALUABLE CONTENT
FOR OUR CUSTOMERS: * * * * * * *

- We will put our **customers'** needs **first**
- We will **help**, not sell
- We will **give** ideas away generously .... FOR FREE
- We will always **know why**
- We will **focus** on a niche
- We will tell a **bigger story**
- We will commit to **quality**
- We will **write from the heart**

...and a very important question to answer: **What content will your customers value?**

Be generous, get creative; we wish you the very best of luck.

VALUABLE RESOURCES

1. Get to know your customers questionnaire

Persona exercise

Hold a real person in mind when developing your customer personas – maybe someone you've really enjoyed working with and would like to work with again – and answer the following questions. Conduct research to help you complete this process.

Background information

- Who are they?
- What type of company?
- Sector and role?
- Their role in the buying process?
- Career to date?
- Education and qualifications?
- Location?

Why are they an ideal customer for you?

- What would they buy from you?
- What are the actions you want them to take?
- Why would they choose you over the competition?
- What value do you bring for them, in their words?
- How do they describe what you do?

Their business world (if you sell to businesses)

- What's going on in the world that affects their behaviour?
- What do they like or dislike about their job?
- What are they trying to achieve? Why is this so important to them?
- What drives them?
- What's going on in their sector that affects the way they do their job?
- How do they feel about these pressures?
- Favourite business book or influencers in their field?
- What's the challenge they want you to solve?
- What words do they typically use to describe that challenge?
- What are their concerns?

Close to their hearts

- What do they want to achieve with their lives; what's their real wish for the future?
- Do they want to get promoted or change the world?
- Short-term goals?
- Long-term goals?

Communications preferences

- Where do they like to hang out? Where are they searching for answers to their questions?
- How do they like to be communicated with? Are they digital natives or not?
- How would they typically find your company?
- What resources do they check when searching for a solution?

Enrich your personas and think wide (wider than role and subject knowledge)

- If you could have any job in the world, what would it be?
- Where would you most like to be in the world right now?
- Do you love your work?
- Live to work or work to live?
- What's harder, managing people or managing technology?
- What's your unfulfilled ambition?
- Favourite activity on day off?
- Favourite film?
- Hero?
- Favourite books?
- Best present you ever got?
- Extrovert or introvert?
- Team player or soloist?

Name your personas, photograph or draw them, and record all the information.

What information do they crave?

What content would they really appreciate at each step? Top five questions they are asking?

Remember: their questions = your content. So what can you create to add value at every step?

Your persona	Questions when researching	Questions when evaluating	Questions when starting work with you
Persona 1			
Persona 2			
Persona 3			
Persona 4			
Ideas for content you can provide at each step:			

2. Example measurement report

Business goals

- Our business aims and objective, eg grow the business by 50 per cent.
- Content marketing aims, eg improve the effectiveness of our website with valuable content marketing – drive long-term profitable sales results via the web.
- Measurable objectives for content marketing, eg inbound leads via web form.
- Target, eg five good inbound leads over next six months.

Lagging measures

Track your progress against your targets.

Leading metrics

Measuring movement through the buying cycle on the journey to a sale, eg:

- ranking for key search terms;
- number of shares on social media;
- number of unique site visitors each month;
- bounce rate (a good indicator of engagement);
- number of site visits longer than three minutes (a good indicator of engagement);
- number of new sign-ups to newsletter (a good indicator of interest);
- number of sign-ups to webinar (a good indicator of evaluation); and
- number of sign-ups to trial (a good indicator of evaluation).

Insights

Record insights from the month, eg most successful referral sites, most successful content (when it comes to your goals).

Questions and actions

eg how do we decrease our bounce rate?

3. Content planning questions

Use this thinking to help you plan and structure *every* piece of content you create. Answer these questions before you start to write.

- WORKING TITLE:
  Title and subtitle ideas.
- TARGET READER:
  Who is this piece of content designed for? Who'd be your ideal reader for it? Name a client or prospect this would be useful for and describe why they need it.

- YOUR GOAL:
  Why are you creating this content? What's the goal? At which stage of the buying process does it help you most? What do you want the reader to think and feel about your company as a result of reading this content?

- CALL TO ACTION:
  What do you want the reader to *do* having read it? What action would you like them to take?

- THE FOCUS:
  What's the main concept? What's the search phrase (keywords) you're targeting with this?

- QUESTIONS:
  What questions and challenges does this content answer for the reader?

- MAIN MESSAGES:
  Summarize the points you want to make in this piece of content. What will the reader learn?

- MAKING IT HAPPEN:
  What format will this content be created in? Who will research it, write it, edit it, design it, post it? Delivery date?

4. Guide for your website content

Through answering the questions within the structure laid out below, this should help you pull together a file of information to build the content for your website. It should also allow you to get to the heart of your proposition and make sure the content of your site reflects your message accurately.

About us

What? In a nutshell, describe what you do.

Who? List the different types of company and people that benefit from your services.

Where? Where are your clients based?

Why? Explain why they need you – what issues do you solve for them?

Keywords – What would your clients search for online to find your services?

Specialism – What are your particular skills and expertise?

Company history – How long have you worked in this industry? When did you set up your company?

Quick company facts – What's the company structure, number of employees, etc? Describe the team.

Awards – List any awards, accolades or relevant qualifications/ associations.

Ambition – Where would you like to see the business going?

Aims – What do you want from your communications and website?

Our approach

Motivation – What inspired you to set up in business? What was the idea behind it? What difference did you set out to achieve?

What does your company stand for? What do you believe in? What values are important to you?

Biggest frustration – What bugs you about your industry?

What do you most enjoy? What is the biggest kick you get out of work?

Approach – Describe your approach to your work.

Benefits – How does your approach make life easier for your customers?

Competitors – Who are your competitors?

Why choose you? What makes your approach different and better than all the other companies in your space?

Who/what inspires you?

Our services

Specialism – What are your particular skills, specialisms and expertise? What are you known for?

What do you do? – List and group your services.

Core services – Which are your most popular ones?

Useful structure for service copy – For each service, list the following:

- name of service;
- who this is relevant for;
- why they need it/what problem it solves;
- what your service involves;
- benefits;
- relevant image/photo/video;
- case studies;
- client testimonials, if any.

Our people

Staff details – list staff members, job titles and profiles for the team.

Photos – provide professional photos of all staff (consistent style).

LinkedIn – provide links to the staff's LinkedIn profiles.

Business personality – any other information that conveys the human side to your business.

Valuable resources

Deeper written content – eg guides, handbooks, support information.

Different formats – video or audio downloads?

Other useful information – what else would your clients find useful/interesting? For example: FAQs, Jargon Buster, Online Assessment?

Additional information

Contact Us page – contact details (and map).

Further features:

company blog;

sign up to mailing list or newsletter form;

download forms;

contact form;

search this site;

client login area;

press releases;

in the news;

downloadable documents;

jobs;

case studies;

social media – links to your active profiles,

contact forms.

5. Questions to help you write a good case study

Every important project deserves a well-written case study. Use these questions and template to create valuable case studies as success stories for your website.

A. Questions for you

1 Client and project information

Company name:

Website address:

Type of business:

Client names/positions:

Dates of project:

Name of project:

Type of project/service you delivered:

Your expertise that you are looking to highlight with this case study:

2 Describe the challenge (for your client, not for you)

What is your client's business and marketplace?

Why did the client hire you? Describe their situation – what were they looking to achieve? What problems did they want you to solve for them? What were the business issues?

What did they ask you to do?

What would have happened if they had done nothing?

What other approaches did they look at?

What was it about your company or approach that they particularly liked?

3 Describe your solution to their problem

What did you propose?

What did you deliver? What was the service?

What was unique or interesting about your approach? Describe any interesting methods/tools/technologies that you used.

How was the client involved? Who did you work with? How long did it take?

4 Describe the results for the client

How has the client benefited from your work? What were the immediate benefits? What are the longer-term benefits/what do you expect the longer-term benefits to be?

How did the client feel about your work and the results achieved? What did he/she say?

5 Highlight your expertise

What particular skills did you bring to bear on this project?

What do you want this case study to demonstrate?

What kind of client/company could benefit from this type of service?

At what point would they pick up the phone to you?

6 Client quotes

What has the client said about your work?

What would you like the client to say about your work? If they asked you to write the quote for them, what would you say?

7 Design

Do you have any images/pictures/design ideas to illustrate this example?

Layout and style ideas?

8 Target audience

Who is this case study written for? Who would you like to read it?

What style of writing suits this audience – eg formal, conversational, technical, straightforward?

9 Learning points

List things others customers or clients can learn from this experience.

What valuable tips can they take away from this case study?

Actions:

Complete this overview in as much detail as you can. Then ask someone unrelated to the project to interview your client contact(s) and record their feedback on your work. Combining the information from both sources makes for a compelling case study.

B. Questions for your clients

The best case studies tell the client's story, not your own. The best way to do this is to involve the client in the writing of the case study. Before you put pen to paper, interview your client contacts. Ask them about the challenge they faced and why your solution was so helpful, what results they achieved. There's nothing like hearing it played back in the client's words. Use these questions to get feedback from client contacts, to help create case studies for your website.

Hi. I'm conducting interviews for company X. You are a great success story. Can I ask you a few questions about the project?

- How did you initially come into contact with Company X?
- What challenge did you want their help with? What was your original objective?
- What other solutions did you consider to deliver this work?
- Why did you select Company X? What expertise did you hope they would bring?
- What solutions have they provided for you?
- What results have they delivered?
- What are the benefits to your company? What has this enabled you to do?
- How have you found dealing with Company X? Overall, have they done a good job?
- What advice can you offer them for similar projects in the future? What should they do more of, or less of, in your view?

- How do they compare with other suppliers you have worked with?
- Would you recommend Company X? For what types of project?
- If you had to describe Company X to a colleague what would you say?
- Is there anything else you want them to know?
- Thank you very much for your comments. Is there any other feedback you'd like to give?
- Anything else you'd like to say?

6. Checklist: Is this content valuable?

When coming up with initial ideas for content, check each one against these criteria. This will help you decide which content ideas to take forward, and which to park.

1 Does this content have a clear business goal? *Are we clear why we are creating it?*

2 Do our customers crave this content? *Does it answer a real question/ solve a real challenge for an ideal customer?*

3 Does this content fit with our story? *Is it in line with our purpose as a business?Does it further our cause?*

4 Is it unique? *Different enough from other content we have created? Not repetitive?*

If the answer is 'no' to any of these questions, then park the content idea. The content will not be valuable.

If the answer is 'yes' to all these questions then plan the piece of content in more detail and then check it against the following criteria:

1 Is the content surprisingly useful, human or entertaining? *Does it make the reader think, laugh or teach them something new?*

2 Is the tone right for us and our readers? *eg help, don't sell; talk, don't yell; show, don't tell?*

3 Is it the right format for the reader and for the subject matter?

4 Is it set at the right level for the reader? *Not too basic or too complex?*

5 Is it focused? *Not too specific; not too broad?*

6 Is it concise? *As concise as needed? And not too specific, and not too broad?*

7 Is it actionable? *Does it have a clear call to action – answering the question 'what next?'*

8 Is it shareable? *Clear social and share buttons?*

9 Is it tagged and labeled correctly so it gets found *on our website and in search?*

10 Does the image(s) that accompany it add value? *Not stock shots, interesting, relevant, high quality?*

11 Is the design and layout consistent? *In line with our guidelines, follows the rules of good typography?*

If you answer yes to the most of these questions then your content is on track.

If the answer is 'no' to any of these questions, then some rethinking and editing is required.

7. Recommended reading

On content marketing and content strategy

- Meerman, D (2013) *The New Rules of Marketing & PR: How to use news releases, blogs, podcasting, viral marketing & online media to reach buyers directly*, 4th edn, John Wiley

- Pulizzi, J (2013) *Epic Content Marketing*, McGraw Hill

- Rose, R and Pulizzi, J (2011) *Managing Content Marketing: The real-world guide for creating passionate subscribers to your brand*, CMI Books

- Halvorsen, K (2009) *Content Strategy for the Web*, New Riders

- Halligan, B and Shah, D (2010) *Inbound Marketing: Get found using Google, social media and blogs*, Wiley

- Pulizzi, J and Barrett, N (2009) *Get Content, Get Customers*, McGraw Hill

- Handley, A and Chapman, C C (2011) *Content Rules: How to create killer blogs, podcasts, videos, e-books, webinars (and more) that engage customers and ignite your business*, Wiley
- Follow Doug Kessler and the Velocity team's content at **www.velocitypartners.com**

On business development

- Jiwa, B (2014) *Marketing: A love story*, The Story of Telling Press
- Thomas, B (2013) *Watertight Marketing: Delivering long-term sales results*, Ecademy
- Meerman Scott, D (2014) *The New Rules of Sales and Service*, Wiley
- Green, C H (2006) *Trust-based Selling: Using customer focus and collaboration to build long-term relationships*, McGraw Hill
- Stratten, S (2010) *UnMarketing: Stop marketing, start engaging*, Wiley
- Brogan, C (2012) *The Impact Equation: Are you making things happen or just making noise?*, Portfolio
- Enns, B (2010) *The Win Without Pitching Manifesto*, Rockbench

On business

- Maisner, D and Green, C H (2002) *The Trusted Advisor*, Simon and Schuster
- Green, C H and Howe, A P (2012) *The Trusted Advisor Fieldbook: A comprehensive toolkit for leading with trust*, Wiley
- Frederiksen, L W and Taylor, A E (2010) *Spiraling Up: How to create a high growth, high value professional services firm*, Hinge Research Institute
- Burg, B and Mann, J D (2010) *The Go-Giver: A little story about a powerful business idea*, Penguin Books
- Kawasaki, G (2004) *The Art of The Start*, Portfolio
- The Get Real Project, **www.thegetrealproject.com** @projectgetreal
- Northcote, J (2008) *Making Change Happen: A practical guide to implementing business change*

- Stone, B (2014) *Things a Little Bird Told Me: Confessions of the creative mind*, Grand Central Publishing

- Nahai, N (2013) *Webs of Influence: The psychology of online persuasion*, FT Press

On websites

- O'Brien, M (2011) *A Website That Works: How marketing agencies can create business generating sites*, Rockbench Publishing

- Butler, C (2012) *The Strategic Web Designer: How to confidently navigate the web design process*, North Light Books

- Listen: The Future of Websites talk on **www.valuablecontent.co.uk**

- See how your website is performing now. Try Hubspot's Website Grader: **marketing.grader.com**

- Sign up for Newfangled's newsletters and content: **www.newfangled.com**

- Check out Noisy Little Monkey's excellent blogs and guides on SEO: **www.noisylittlemonkey.co.uk**

On email marketing

- *Email Persuasion: Captivate and engage your audience, build authority and generate more sales with email marketing*, Ian Brodie, Rainmaker Publishing, 2013.

On writing and blogging

- Duistermaat, H (2014) *Blog to Win Business: How to enchant readers and woo customers*, Enchanting Marketing Ltd

- King, S (2000) *On Writing: A memoir of the craft*, Scribner

- Handley, A (2014) *Everyone Writes: Your go-to guide to creating ridiculously good content*, Wiley

- Camp, L (2007) *Can I change your mind? The craft and art of persuasive writing*, A&C Black

- Maslen, M (2015) *Persuasive Copywriting: Using psychology to engage, influence and sell*, Kogan Page
- You will find content writing tips and inspiration on **www.copyblogger.com**, and on **www.enchantingmarketing.com**.

On finding your business purpose

- Hieatt, D (2014) *Do Purpose: Why brands with purpose do better and matter more*, Do Books
- Sinek, S (2011) *Start with the Why: How great leaders inspire everyone to take action*, Penguin
- Weylman, C R (2013) *The Power of Why: Breaking out in a competitive marketplace*, Amazon Publishing

ACKNOWLEDGEMENTS

This book wouldn't be here without the support of some very special people. Here's a list of those we want to thank.

- JJ and Bill and our gorgeous kids – Jacob, Ben, Evie, Joe and Rosa – for putting up with us again through the writing process and for keeping the home fires burning!
- Anna Wilson – for her unswerving support, detailed referencing and general positivity.
- Doug Kessler – for writing our foreword, and making it so positive. We couldn't be more delighted.
- Lizzie Everard for her lovely illustrations, friendship and many cups of tea.
- Chris Thurling – our chairman and business coach. For helping us carve out time, and backing us all the way. We couldn't do this without you, Chris.
- Bill Maryon for his clear-sighted edits at the 11th hour.
- Jon Gaunt, our accountant – we know, weird right! For keeping our business on track, and your enthusiasm and belief in us.
- Kogan Page – for your professional and insightful support.
- Matthew Smith – for instigating this 2nd edition.
- Jon Payne of Noisy Little Monkey – for help with the SEO chapter, and for making us laugh.
- Henneke Duistermaat – for helping us to write our profiles. Hope to work with you more in the future.
- The swimming pools and cafes of Bristol – Clifton Lido, David Lloyd Ashton and our home cafe at Spike Island – for making the writing experience fun this time round.
- Bella the dog – for staying calm in the midst of the chaos!

We'd like to say a big thank you to some of our special clients past and present, particularly – Geoff Mason, Glynis Ward, Ian Hellens and the fabulous team at Project One; Kevin Freedman and Carmen Camacho at Freedman International; Amy Grenham and Matt Morris at Desynit; Dave James and the team at Ascentor; the Web and International teams at Bristol University – exciting working with you at the start of your content strategy journey; Terri Lucas at Hymans Robertson; Paul Hajek; Jane Northcote; Andrea P Howe; Chris Williams and Sarah Jezard at Wealth Horizon; Heather Townsend, the 7 Secrets team; Mike Rapps at Gregg Latchams; Paul Hajek at Clutton Cox and Andrea P Howe of the Get Real Project.

Those who have inspired our thinking – Simon Sinek (how many times have we watched that TED talk!); Bryony Thomas for her *Watertight Marketing* framework and strategic guidance when working together for Desynit and Ascentor; Doug Kessler for reminding us to be brave; David Meerman Scott for introducing us to the world of blogging and content all those years ago; Mark O'Brien and Chris Butler at Newfangled – no one gets web better; Henneke Duistermaat; Lee Frederiksen and the team at Hinge Marketing; Robin Sloan, Alan Cahoon, Ian Sanders; John Beckley at Sands Beach Resort; James Perrott, Jane Northcole, Ian Brodie, Joe Pulizzi and the Content Marketing Institute; Blair Enns, David Hieatt, Mark Masters and his Talking Content series, Tim LeRoy, Charles H. Green and of course Chris Brogan.

Those who kindly provided stories for the book and reviewed our work – Neil J Fletcher, Brian Inkster, Peldi Guilizzoni at Balsamiq, Matthew Curry, Vaughan Merlyn, Mel Lester, Newfangled, Richard Fray at HSBC Expat, Mark Durnford, Rachel Goodchild, Rick Short at Indium, Jason Miliki at Rattleback, Mel Lester, David Gilroy, Jim O'Connor, Bob Mytton, Novatech, Mick Dickinson, Lee Duncan, Tim Tucker, Amanda Thomas, Ann-Marie McCormack, Chris Budd, David Nutley, Andy Maslen, Jay Bigford at Yoke, Trevor Lever, Sian Tucker at Fforest, Iain Claridge, Teresa Harris at Woolley and Co, Dan Waller at Wriggle and Jane Ni Dhulchaointigh and the Sugru team.

All those from the Valuable Content Club who answered our call for information on their content challenges – including Annette Peppis, Christian Tait, Gill Cooper, Glynis Ward, Ben Sherwood, Kathryn Catera, Kirsten Razzaq, Laura Hamlyn and Carla Harper. We're delighted to have you with us and wish you all the best with your content.

Phew. That's a list and a half! We're grateful to you all.

NOTES AND REFERENCES

Part One: Why valuable content?

1 Seth Godin via EBA (2014) Marketing is no longer about the stuff that you make, but about the stories that you tell. Seth Godin 03/04 [Online] www.twitter.com [last accessed 12 February 2015]

Chapter 1: Buying has changed. Has your marketing caught up?

1 Quotes to help you with change (2014) *For Impact* 30/06 [Online] http://forimpact.org/org-dev/quotes-to-help-you-with-change-2/ [last accessed 27 January 2015]

2 Article/Report (2015) www.hingemarketing.com/library/article/2015-professional-services-marketing-priorities [last accessed 27 January 2015]

3 Frederiksen, Lee W, McVey, Sean T, Montgomery, S and Taylor, A E (2012) Online marketing for professional services, *Hinge Research Institute*, Virginia [Online] www.hingemarketing.com/library/article/online_marketing_for_professional_services [last accessed 12 February 2015]

4 10 new rules of marketing professional services (2014) *Hinge Marketing* [Online] www.hingemarketing.com/blog/story/10-new-rules-of-marketing-professional-services [last accessed 27 January 2015]

5 CeB Marketing Leadership Council (2012) The Digital Evolution in B2B Marketing [Online] www.executiveboard.com/exbd-resources/content/digital-evolution/index.html [last accessed 27 January 2015]

6 Behind the scenes at the alpine content factory (2015) [Weblog] *Medium.com* 29/01 [Online] https://medium.com/@iansanders/behind-the-scenes-at-the-alpine-content-factory-fb5515ad3c04 [last accessed 13 February 2015]

7 Office for National Statistics (2014) Internet Access – Households and Individuals 2014 [Online] www.ons.gov.uk/ons/dcp171778_373584.pdf [last accessed 13 February 2015]

8 Kanye West (2011) *Don't ever try and sell me on anything. Just give me all the information and I'll make up my own mind.* @kanyewest 27/02 [Online] http://en.wikipedia.org/wiki/User:Ev3rything_I_Am [last accessed 28 January 2015]

9 Master, D, Green, C and Galford, R (2000) *The Trusted Advisor*, Simon & Schuster, London

10 Master, D, Green, C and Galford, R (2000) *The Trusted Advisor*, Simon & Schuster, London

11 Curry, Matthew (2011) *Uh oh, sales guy has just emailed with the words 'discount available if you sign up before the end of the month' – red rag to a bull. 23/06* [Online] @mattycurry, www.twittercom [last accessed 28 January 2015]

12 Curry, Matthew (2011) *Really annoyed now – tempted to stop the whole sales process. I hate people trying to use sales tactics on me. 23/06* [Online] @mattycurry

Chapter 2: What is valuable content and why does it win you business?

1 Meerman Scott, D (2011) *The New Rules of PR and Marketing*, 3rd Edition, John Wiley & Sons, Chichester

2 Master, D, Green, C and Galford, R (2000) *The Trusted Advisor*, Simon & Schuster, London

3 Sinek, Simon (2014) Trust begins to emerge when we have a sense that another person or organization is driven by things other than their own self gain 22/09 [Online] www.facebook.com/simonsinek/posts/10152740980966499 [last accessed 28 January 2015]

4 Sometimes content is not the answer – a content marketing fail (2013) [Webblog] www.velocitypartners.co.uk 08/04 [Online] www.velocitypartners.co.uk/our-blog/a-content-marketing-fail/ [last accessed 28 January 2015]

Chapter 3: Guiding principles for your marketing

1 Why we had to start another factory (2014) [Weblog] *medium.com* 31/07 [Online] https://medium.com/small-giants/why-we-had-to-start-another-factory-ec3815f225c9 [last accessed 29 January 2015]

2 Nobody cares about your products and services (except you) (2008) [Weblog] *WebInkNow* 18/08 [Online] www.webinknow.com/2008/08/nobody-cares-ab.html

3 Master, D, Green, C and Galford, R (2000) *The Trusted Advisor*, Simon & Schuster, London

4 Nahai, N (2012) *Webs of Influence*, Pearson, Cambridge

5 Why clicks aren't the whole story when it comes to e-mail engagement (2013) [Weblog] 28/03 [Online] www.marketingdonut.co.uk/blog/2013/03 [last accessed 29 January 2015]

6 Kawasaki, G (2008) *The Art of Start*, Portfolio, London

7 Rose, R and Pulizzi, J (2011) *Managing Content Marketing: The real-world guide for creating passionate subscribers to your brand*, CMI Books, London

8 Talking content marketing – with Joe Chernov (2014) [Weblog] *The ID Group* 03/03 [Online] http://theidgroup.co.uk/2014/03/talking-content-marketing-joe-chernov/ [last accessed 13 February 2015]

9 Gary Vaynerchuk (www.garyvaynerchuk.com) *Best Marketing Strategy Ever. Care.* Available from Facebook.com [last accessed 13 February 2015]

Part Two: What valuable content?

1 Why we had to start another factory (2014) [Weblog] *Medium.com* 31/07 [Online] https://medium.com/small-giants/why-we-had-to-start-another-factory-ec3815f225c9 [last accessed 29 January 2015]

Chapter 4: Blogging

1 Nothing more important in my life than blogging (2009) [Weblog] 01/09 [Online] http://elearningtech.blogspot.co.uk/2009/09/nothing-more-important-in-my-life-than.html [last accessed 29 January 2015]

2 Your content sucks – fix it! (2012) [Weblog] 14/08 [Online] www.ianbrodie.com/ your-content-sucks-fix-it/ [last accessed 29 January 2015]

3 Generate more leads with b2b social media (2012) [Weblog] 29/03 [Online] http://socialmediab2b.com/2012/03/b2b-social-media-leads-infographic/?utm_source= Webbiquity [last accessed 29 January 2015]

4 Strategist video series: how much content should you post to your website each month? (2015) [Weblog] *Newfangled.com* 15/01 [Online] www.newfangled.com/ how-much-web-content-you-should-write-each-month/ [last accessed 13 February 2015]

Chapter 5: Social media

1 Why content marketing and social media are a powerful match (2009) [Weblog] 15/05 [Online] www.copyblogger.com/content-social-media/

2 Townsend, H (2011) *The Financial Times Guide to Business Networking*, Pearson, Cambridge

3 Why copyblogger is killing its Facebook page (2014) [Weblog] 17/10 [Online] https:// plus.google.com/+MarkTraphagen/posts/VchLgMEzh3t [last accessed 29 January 2015]

4 Content Marketing Institute (2014) The Content Marketing Institute's 2014 B2B Content Marketing report [Online] http://contentmarketinginstitute.com/2013/10/2014-b2b-content-marketing-research/

5 Master, D, Green, C and Galford, R (2000) *The Trusted Advisor*, Simon & Schuster, London

Chapter 6: Email newsletters

1 Dumb things small businesses do #6: ingratitude (2008) [Weblog] Remarkable Communication 27/11 [Online] www.remarkable-communication.com/dumb-small-business-6/ [last accessed 02 February 2015]

2 A sample blog topics email (2011) [Weblog] 25.01 [Online] http://chrisbrogan.com/sampleemail/ [last accessed 2 February 2015]

3 Jantsch, J (2006) *Duct Tape Marketing: The world's most practical guide to implementing business change*, Thomas Nelson Publishers, Nashville

4 Duncan, L (2012) *Double Your Business*, Financial Times/Prentice Hall, London

Chapter 7: Search engine optimization

1 Lead generating high performance websites (2011) [Weblog] *Hinge Marketing* 28/01 [Online] www.hingemarketing.com/blog/story/lead_generating_high_performance_websites [last accessed 2 February 2015]

2 ComScore smartphone platform market share (2014) [Online] http://goo.gl/hKv14a [last accessed 19 March 2015]

3 Google's top 3 tech trends marketers should watch in 2015 (2015) [Online] http://goo.gl/DpBpGj [last accessed 19 March 2015]

Chapter 8: Deeper written content, e-books, white papers, SlideShares and published books

1 The great Twitter debate: she said, he said (2011) [Weblog] 28/07 [Online] www.socialmediatoday.com/content/great-twitter-debate-she-said-he-said [last accessed 2 February 2015]

2 Stock & flow (2010) [Weblog] 18/01 [Online] http://snarkmarket.com/2010/4890 [last accessed 2 February 2015]

3 How to think like a writer (2014) [Weblog] *The Huffington Post* 15/05 [Online] www.huffingtonpost.com/2014/05/15/how-the-worlds-best-write_n_5331610.html [last accessed 2 February 2015]

4 Content Marketing Institute (2015) 2015 B2B Content Marketing Benchmarks, Budgets and Trends – North America' [Online] http://contentmarketinginstitute.com/2014/10/2015-b2b-content-marketing-research/ [last accessed 12 February 2015]

5 2014: The Year Social Content Dominated B2B Technology Marketing (2015) [Weblog] *Radix Communications* 28/01 [Online] http://radix-communications.com/2014-year-social-content-dominated-b2b-technology-marketing/ [last accessed 13 February 2015]

6 New complimentary e-book – the new rules of PR: how to create a press release strategy for reaching buyers directly (2006) [Weblog] *Web Ink Now* 16/01 [Online] www.webinknow.com/2006/01/new_complimenta.html [last accessed 13 February 2015]

7 Master, D, Green, C and Galford, R (2000) *The Trusted Advisor*, Simon & Schuster, London

8 Krug, S (2014) *Don't Make Me Think – Revisited: A common sense approach to web usability*, Newriders, Oxford

Chapter 9: Video, audio, infographics and more

1 9 experts answer 'what makes an online video worth sharing?' (2011) [Weblog] *Modern Marketing Blog* 16/08. [Online] blog.eloqua.com/online-video-marketing-tips [last accessed 4 February 2015]

2 How to get your videos ranking in universal search results: a video SEO study (2011) [Weblog] *Aim Clear* 24/03 [Online] www.reelseo.com/videos-ranking-universal-search-results-video-seo-study/ [last accessed 4 February 2015]

3 Pennywise pound foolish – production value depends on what you pay for (2015) *Indie Films India 28/01* [Online] https://indiefilmsindia.wordpress.com/2015/01/28/penny-wise-pound-foolish-production-value-depends-on-what-you-pay-for/ [last accessed 4 February 2015]

Chapter 10: Widen your reach: PR, guest blogging, events and paid advertising

1 Pack your bags: how content marketing & PR combined can generate leads (2010) [Weblog] *HubSpot* 16/02 [Online] http://blog.hubspot.com/blog/tabid/6307/bid/5609/Pack-Your-Bags-How-Content-Marketing-PR-Combined-Can-Generate-Leads.aspx [last accessed 4 February 2015]

2 Good times with inbound links (2008) [Weblog] *Google Webmaster Central blogspot* 09/01 [Online] http://googlewebmastercentral.blogspot.co.uk/2008/10/good-times-with-inbound-links.html [last accessed 4 February 2015]

3 Do you recommend article marketing as an SEO strategy? (2011) [Videoblog] *Google Webmasters* 07/03 [Online] www.youtube.com/watch?v=x5xP-pTmlpY [last accessed 4 February 2015

4 Hinge Marketing beyond referrals: how today's buyers check you out (2014) [Online] www.hingemarketing.com/library/article/beyond-referrals-how-todays-buyers-check-you-out [last accessed 4 February 2015]

Part Three: How to supercharge your business with valuable content

Chapter 11: Pulling together a valuable content strategy

1 Andy Crestodina (2014) An ounce of strategy is worth a pound of tactics @crestodina 23/10 [Online] www.twitter.com [last accessed 12 February 2015]

2 Arjun Basu (2014) Without strategy, content is just stuff, and the world has enough stuff @Arjunbasu [Online] www.twitter.com [last accessed 12 February 2015]

3 Content Marketing Institute (2015) 2015 B2B Content Marketing Benchmarks, Budgets and Trends – North America' [Online] http://contentmarketinginstitute. com/2014/10/2015-b2b-content-marketing-research/ [last accessed 12 February 2015]

4 The single most effective change I made to my digital presence (2014) [Weblog] *chrisbrogan.com*, 10/04 [Online] http://chrisbrogan.com/the-single-most-effective-change-i-made-to-my-digital-presence/ [last accessed 12 February 2015]

5 7 simple steps to writing product descriptions that sell (2014) [Weblog] *Kissmetrics.com* 03/01 [Online] https://blog.kissmetrics.com/product-descriptions-that-sell/ [last accessed 12 February 2015]

6 Sinek, Simon (2010) How Great Leaders Inspire Action, *TED.com* [Online] www.ted.com/speakers/simon_sinek [last accessed 12 February 2015]

7 Sinek, Simon (2010) How Great Leaders Inspire Action, *TED.com* [Online] www.ted.com/speakers/simon_sinek [last accessed 12 February 2015]

8 Keroac, Jack (1971) *The Dharma Bums*, Penguin, London

9 Mason, Geoff (2014) *Project One.* [Online] www.projectone.com/about-us/what-we-believe [last accessed February 2015]

10 B2B content marketing: finding your sweet spot (2012) [Weblog] *Econsultancy* 13/03 [Online] https://econsultancy.com/blog/9279-b2b-content-marketing-finding-your-sweet-spot/ [last accessed 12 February 2015]

11 Content Marketing Spotlight Series: A Q&A With Joe Pulizzi (2014) [Weblog] *Open Topic* 29/09. [Online] http://opentopic.com/blog/content-curation/content-marketing-spotlight-series-qa-joe-pulizzi/ [last accessed 12 February 2015]

12 Meerman Scott, D (2011) *The New Rules of PR and Marketing*, 3rd Edition, John Wiley & Sons, Chichester

13 How to measure the success of content marketing (2012) [Weblog] *The Content Marketing Institute* 15/06 [Online] http://contentmarketinginstitute.com/2012/06/measure-success-content-marketing/ [last accessed 12 February 2015]

14 Q & A: Doug Kessler on avoiding 'crap' content marketing (2014) [Weblog] *Econsultancy* 29/10 [Online] https://econsultancy.com/blog/65681-q-a-doug-kessler-on-avoiding-crap-content-marketing/ [last accessed 12 February 2015]

15 Thomas, B (2013) *Watertight Marketing*, Anoma, St Albans, Herts

16 Mason, Geoff (2014) *Project One* [Online] www.projectone.com/about-us/what-we-believe [last accessed 12 February 2015]

Chapter 12: Making your website valuable

1 A 7-step plan for getting started with content marketing (2010) [Webblog] 10/03 [Online] http://savvyb2bmarketing.com/blog/entry/557551/a-7step-plan-for-getting-started-with-content-marketing [last accessed 9 February 2015]

2 Hinge Marketing (2014) Beyond referrals: how today's buyers check you out [Online] www.hingemarketing.com [last accessed 13 February 2015]

3 Lester, Mel, Home Page, *The Business Edge* [Online] www.bizedge.biz/ [last accessed 9 February 2015]

4 Thomas, B (2013) *Watertight Marketing*, Anoma, St Albans, Herts

5 Maya Angelou quotes, 15 of the best (2014) [Weblog] 29/04 [Online] www.theguardian.com/books/2014/may/28/maya-angelou-in-fifteen-quotes [last accessed 9 February 2015]

6 O'Brien, M (2011) *A Website that Works: How marketing agencies can create business generating sites*, Rockbench Publishing, Nashville

7 Writing for the web (2010) [slideshare] *Slideshare.net* 03/06 [Online] www.slideshare.net/nadiacferri/writing-for-the-web-presentation-4400579 [last accessed 9 February 2015]

8 What is important? (Or, a case against the grid homepage) (2014) [Weblog] *Newfangled* 20/06 [Online] www.newfangled.com/what-is-important-a-case-against-the-grid-homepage/ [last accessed 9 February 2015]

9 The risk of stripping down customer case studies (2014) [Weblog] *Stories That Sell* 17/12 [Online] www.storiesthatsellguide.com/blog/ [last accessed 9 February 2015]

Chapter 13: How to write valuable content

1 Zinsser, W (2006) *On Writing Well*, 30th Edition, Harper Collins, London

2 Here's how Sonia Simone writes (2013) [Weblog] *Copybloggers*, 07/06 [Online] www.copyblogger.com/how-sonia-simone-writes/ [last accessed 9 February 2015]

Chapter 14: How to sell with valuable content

1 Lumpy Mail: Lead Generation Q&A day 3 (2012) [Weblog-video] *Ian Brodie* 23/10 [Online] www.ianbrodie.com/?s=lumpy+mail [last accessed 9 February 2015]

2 Does your marketing support every step of a sale? (2014) [Webblog] *Watertight Marketing* 04/06 [Online] http://watertightmarketing.com/2014/06/04/does-your-marketing-support-every-step-of-a-sale/ [last accessed 13 February 2015]

3 State of the sales rep: brainshark survey shows 1 in 3 frequently can't find the sales materials they need to close more deals (2013) [Weblog] *Brainshark* 29/10 [Online] www.brainshark.com/company/in-the-news/press-releases/2013/october/10-29-pr.aspx [last accessed 9 February 2015]

Chapter 15: Winning the challenge of constant content generation

1 The secret sauce to content marketing: they ask, you answer (2014) *Casual Fridays* 22/05 [Online] http://casualfridays.com/secret-sauce-content-marketing-they-ask-you-answer/ [last accessed 9 February 2015]

Chapter 16: Troubleshooting Q&A: answers to the big content questions

1 Bucchianeri, E A (2011) *Brushstrokes of a Gadfly*, Batalha Publishers, Portugal

INDEX

Page numbers in *italic* indicate drawings, figures and tables.
'Take action' and 'Valuable tips' are indexed as such.